Graphic Politics in Eastern India

Bloomsbury Studies in Linguistic Anthropology

Series Editors:
Sabina Perrino, Paul Manning and Jim Wilce

Presenting and exploring new and current approaches to discourse and culture, **Bloomsbury Studies in Linguistic Anthropology** examines the most recent topics in this field. Publishing contemporary, cutting edge research, this series investigates social life through everyday discursive practices, making these practices visible and unveiling processes that would remain concealed without careful attention to discourse.

Titles focus on specific themes to advance the field both theoretically and methodologically, such as language contact dynamics, language revitalisation and reclamation, and language, migration and social justice. Positioning linguistic anthropology at the intersection with other fields, this series will cast light on various cultural settings across the globe by viewing important linguistic ethnographies through an anthropological lens. Standing at the frontier of this growing field, **Bloomsbury Studies in Linguistic Anthropology** offers a balanced view of the current state of the discipline, as well as promoting and advancing exciting new directions for research.

Titles in the Series:

Graphic Politics in Eastern India
Nishaant Choksi

Language and Revolutionary Magic in the Orinoco Delta
Juan Luis Rodríguez

Remaking Kichwa
Michael Wroblewski

Saying and Doing in Zapotec
Mark A. Sicoli

Graphic Politics in Eastern India

Script and the Quest for Autonomy

Nishaant Choksi

B L O O M S B U R Y
NEW DELHI • LONDON • OXFORD • NEW YORK • SYDNEY

BLOOMSBURY INDIA
Bloomsbury Publishing India Pvt. Ltd
Second Floor, Building No. 4
DDA Complex LSC, Pocket C – 6 & 7
Vasant Kunj, New Delhi 110070
www.bloomsbury.com

BLOOMSBURY, Bloomsbury Academic India and the Dianalogo
are trademarks of Bloomsbury Publishing Plc

First published in India 2021
First published in Great Britain 2021

Cover design: Ben AnslowCover image © NishaantChoksi

This edition published with permission from Bloomsbury Publishing Plc,
50 Bedford Square, London, WC1B3DP, UK

British Library Cataloguing-in-Publication Data
A catalogue record for this book is available from the British Library.

Library of Congress Cataloging-in-Publication Data
A catalog record for this book is available from the Library of Congress

ISBN: 978-93-90358-73-1

For sale in the Indian subcontinent only

Series: Bloomsbury Studies in Linguistic Anthropology Typeset
by Newgen Knowledge Works Pvt. Ltd., Chennai, India

Digitally Printed and bound in India by Replika Press Pvt. Ltd.

Contents

Figures

Tables

Acknowledgments

This book is the product of the generosity and labor of many people in many different places. To thank them all would take much more space than I have available, although I would like to mention a few names here.

First, my deepest gratitude goes to the people of Jhilimili, who have taken care of me as one of their own for several years now. They have been so kind to let me into their homes and lives, and have never become irritated with my naïve questions. Sarada Prasad Kisku and the members of the Kherwal Marsal Gaonta have been especially generous, facilitating my stay from the beginning. During my research period, the teachers and staff of the local high school gave me warm company on many a night. Sagun was the best research assistant one could ask for, and this study would not have been possible without his dedication and enthusiasm. In addition, many in the Santali writer and activist community took me under their wing and helped guide this research, including Mahadev Hansda, Nobin Besra, Dilip Hembrom, Parimal Hansda, Kolendranath Mandi, A. K. Soren, Dhuni Soren, and the teachers at the Ol Chiki Secet' Asra, Santaragachi.

This project grew from the dissertation I wrote while I was a graduate student at the University of Michigan. My supervisor, Barbra Meek, supported me from early on in my graduate career, and she has been an inspiring mentor and guide ever since. Matthew Hull was also an important interlocutor, and traces of my many conversations with him can be found throughout this book. Judith Irvine and Marlyse Baptista thoroughly read through the dissertation and offered several valuable insights.

It is certainly true that the relationships you make in graduate school will be very important the rest of your career. Many of the friends I made during my time as a graduate student read and discussed chapters of this book with me. This includes Haydar Darici, Christina Davis, Erika Hoffman-Dilloway, Chaise Ladousa, Durba Mitra, K. N. Sunandan, and Susan Thomas. Their comments and suggestions are deeply appreciated. My ongoing conversations with Christopher Berk, Carlos Carmona, Sonia Das, Joshua Friedman, Erica

Feldman, Anneeth Hundle, Rachel Lee, Lamia Mognieh, Neha Paliwal, and Gbenga Olumolade, have shaped (and continue to shape) the ideas presented here.

My three years in Japan as a postdoctoral fellow changed many of my ideas and allowed me the time, space, and intellectual freedom to transform a messy dissertation into a proper book. A special debt goes to Masato Kobayashi, Toshiki Osada, Madhu Purti, and Nathan Badenoch who facilitated my stay at Tokyo and Kyoto Universities. In Kyoto, Miles Kenny-Lazar read and discussed with me the entire draft of this book cover to cover over several rounds of coffee at the Kamo Café, offering a much-needed critical eye. Many other colleagues in Kyoto and Tokyo helped me grow intellectually, motivating me to complete this project, including Rika Yamashita, Takashi Sekine, Takamichi Serizawa, David Dippong, Kia-Meng Boon, and Ai Kawamura.

This book is ultimately a product of my engagement with a diverse range people and places in India. My time in Baroda during 2004–6 at the Bhasha Centre and the Adivasi Academy working under G. N. Devy introduced me to the wide vista of India's rich Adivasi cultures and traditions. I thank all my friends and colleagues in Baroda and Tejgadh for caring for me and showing me the way forward. In Kolkata, Animesh Pal, Surhid Kumar Bhowmick, and the late Dhirendranath Bhaske introduced me to Santali and made the initial connections for me. Throughout my field research, Bodhisattva Kar served as my local supervisor, and he and my colleagues at Centre for Studies in Social Sciences (Iman, Debarati, Subhashree, Swati) provided me the intellectual environment to reflect during the often disorienting experience of village-level fieldwork. In Delhi, Prathama Banerjee was always kind, generous, and helpful, inviting me to her home to discuss my work and agreeing to be on my dissertation committee even under difficult circumstances. Finally, I would like to thank my colleagues and students at my current home, IIT Gandhinagar, especially those in the Humanities and Social Sciences discipline who have created a vibrant professional atmosphere where I can advance my ideas, engagements, and collaborations.

As always, my family has stood by me through the many years of fieldwork, traveling, separation, and other hardship. My parents, grandparents, and other family members have always supported my endeavors even if they did not fully understand my goals or motivation. My partner Farah has kept me going throughout, lifting my spirits when things looked low and acting as my ethical and intellectual compass when I was lost. Our many conversations have gone into this book, both in content and in character.

Many thanks also to the team at Bloomsbury, including Andrew Wardell, Becky Holland, and series editors Paul Manning and Sabina Perrino for taking an interest in this work and seeing it through. The research has been funded with generous support from the University of Michigan, Fulbright-Hays/DDRA, America–Scandinavia Foundation, Japanese Society for the Promotion of Science (P16744), and Research Initiation Grant, IIT Gandhinagar.

A Note on Transcription Conventions

Transcribing Santali

As this book concerns the politics of script, how I have chosen to gloss the Santali language terms is an issue that deserves a few words. Some of my interlocutors requested that I use only Ol-Chiki script to transcribe the Santali. However, because this book is meant to be read by a wider, English-reading audience, I have instead chosen to use a modified Roman script to represent Santali words. As a disclaimer, in no way am I arguing that this script is more accurate than Ol-Chiki or Santali Roman or any other script in representing the sounds of Santali. In order to make my transcription choices more transparent, I have provided a table below showing the orthography I have chosen to employ in this book, and its IPA and Ol-Chiki equivalents.

Modified Roman (transcription)	**International Phonetic Alphabet**	**Ol-Chiki characters**
a	a	ᱟ
e	e, ɛ	ᱮ
i	i	ᱤ
o	ɔ, o	ᱚ ᱳ
u	u	ᱩ
t	t̪	ᱛ
k	k	ᱠ
s	s	ᱥ
c	c	ᱪ
p	p	ᱯ
ṭ	ʈ	ᱴ
g, k'	g, kˀ	ᱜ
j, c'	ʒ, ɟˀ	ᱡ
h	h	ᱦ
d, t'	ḍ̪, tˀ	ᱫ
ḍ	ḍ̪	ᱰ
b, p'	b, pˀ	ᱵ
ng	ŋ	ᱝ
m	m	ᱢ

Modified Roman (transcription)	**International Phonetic Alphabet**	**Ol-Chiki characters**
n’	ɲ	ᱧ
n	ɳ	ᱬ
n	n	ᱱ
ow	ow	ᱶ
l	l	ᱞ
w	w	ᱣ
r	r	ᱨ
y	j	ᱭ
ṛ	ɽ	ᱲ
h (cons+h, aspiration)	(consonant)ʰ	ᱷ
ạ	ə̃	ᱹ
	- ʔ (word final deglottal)	ᱽ
n (nasalizer)	n	ᱸ

1

Introduction

There was a festive atmosphere on the streets of Kolkata, the largest metropolis of eastern India. Rani Rashomoni Road, situated right in the center of the city, was lined with bookstalls, and green banners were fluttering in the light breeze. From the rear, trams slowly meandered past the towering visages of the likes of Clive, Marx, Lenin, and Subhas Chandra Bose. This was a regular scene on these streets: the site of political protests by everyone from hawkers to transit workers, industrial laborers, or any of the other subsection of the population who routinely gathered to demand rights or improvements in wages or regulations. However, this time the rally was about an issue that the bustling metropolis was for the most part unfamiliar—script. Under the aegis of the West Bengal Adivasi Socio-Educational Association (ASECA), hundreds of groups from villages across West Bengal, spanning the length of the borders with neighboring Jharkhand and Odisha as well as from the city's neighboring suburbs around the city filled with migrant worker families, came to demand that the West Bengal government properly implement the Ol-Chiki script for Santali-language education.

These protests were large, noisy, and a particularly visible expression of the politics around script in the Santali language, a language spoken mostly by members of Scheduled Tribe (or Adivasi) communities in the border regions of West Bengal, Jharkhand, Odisha, Bihar, and Assam. Yet the city itself teemed with Santali literary activity, mostly hidden from the majority Bengali-speaking population. For instance, not a hundred meters from the protest site, a famous Santali-language poet was preparing for a radio broadcast in the Santali language, in which performers, poets, and playwrights from all over eastern India had assembled. Scattered throughout the offices adjacent to the protest areas were office workers originally from Santali-speaking areas who gathered in the canteens and over tea to work on publishing Santali-language magazines and books in Ol-Chiki, Roman, and various other scripts.

Taking place in the heart of a Bengali-speaking metropolis, hundreds of miles away from the areas where most Santals lived, the noisy protests or quiet literary activities perhaps would confirm many scholars and activists' criticism of the politics of language and script as an elite-led movement organized under the framework of culture or identity. That these politics are happening in the capital city of the state of West Bengal, Kolkata, also suggests that the promotion of script is about making demands upon the state, a clear politics of recognition.

If my study had focused on the politics in and around Kolkata, perhaps my assessment of the Santals' push for script and language would have ended there. However, as I left the rally the day after and returned to my primary field site in the village of Jhilimili, a village located in a region of West Bengal colloquially known as the "Jungle Mahals," close to the border of Jharkhand and Odisha (see Figure 1.1), I encountered a much different situation. I had just entered the village one day before a three-day strike (*bandh*) called by the Maoist parties during which buses stopped plying the roads for fear of being torched, shops remained shuttered, and markets lay hauntingly deserted. The day after I arrived, the normally busy intersection where the road to Jhilimili intersects the highway that leads to the regional centers of Jhargram and Purulia was empty; only a green flag, hung on a stick, remained fluttering at the crossroads. Roaming the deserted streets were the central government's paramilitary forces (Central Reserve Police Force [CRPF]) with maximum power assault weapons on the lookout for left-wing insurgents. The Jharkhand Party office, which controlled the local panchayats in the area, looked deserted; its activists scattered for fear of being abducted by armed militias of the ruling Communist Party, Maoist party insurgents, or the paramilitary forces. Here in Jhilimili, politics consisted of a struggle over political and material resources, pitting the state against armed groups, and a political formation that continues the struggle of one of the oldest social movements for Adivasi autonomy in modern India.

Yet at the same time, one does not have to look far to see the presence of the Ol-Chiki script and written Santali sewn into the very fabric of life in Jhilimili. It is visible on signboards in the marketplaces, scrawled on the walls of the

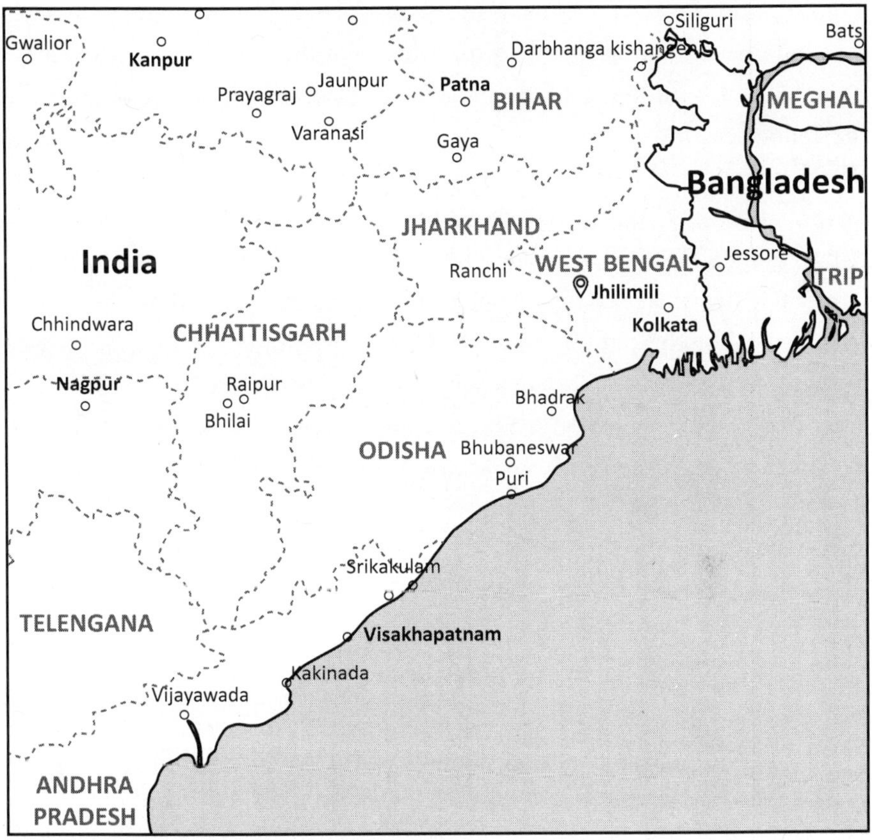

Figure 1.1 Map of Jhilimili within eastern India.

village school, and circulating from shop to shop and household to household in the form of printed media. The script is invoked in the form of song, ritual, and in visions of territorial autonomy that derive from, but are not tied to, the historical movement for a separate Jharkhand state. Script and language are much more than symbolic instruments employed for the recognition of an identity. Instead, this book suggests that script complicates the division between the symbolic and material, and argues for the centrality of the *graphic* dimension of language in the contemporary politics among Santali-speaking Adivasis in today's West Bengal. Taking a semiotic approach in which language and script, as much as the hallmark Adivasi issues of *jal* (water), *jangal* (forest), *jameen* (land) is embedded in a political economy,[1] this book ethnographically elucidates the linkages between the development and propagation of script, ongoing struggles over territory and resources, and the evolution of a politics of autonomy in the wake of the formation of Jharkhand state. One of the main premises of the book is that the movement for autonomy that characterized the Jharkhand movement, one in which region, territory, and community were reimagined against the backdrop of historical oppression by caste-Hindu "others," continues through a politics of script even if the Adivasis of West Bengal failed to join the separate Jharkhand state. Given the criticism of what Jharkhand state has become (or not become), among both scholars and those who find themselves in the situation where state-centric politics has proved unsuccessful, graphic politics reveal how autonomy may persist beyond state-centric or identity-based demands. The book therefore seeks a new path, one in which script, hitherto rarely discussed in studies of language politics in South Asia, and even less with respect to Adivasis, becomes a central vector for autonomy in a new political era.

A Graphic Politics of Autonomy

When I first arrived in Kolkata in 2007, I began studying Santali, an Austro-Asiatic language spoken by over three million people in eastern India, Nepal, and Bangladesh, and by a plurality of West Bengal's Adivasis. I initially began my lessons with a retired professor of linguistics who had learned the language through his students during his time teaching in the rural areas of the state bordering Jharkhand. At the very outset he told me that the study of Santali was vexed by the issue of "script." Santali was being written in Eastern Brahmi[2] script, the script used to write Bengali; Roman script, the script developed by the missionaries; Devanagari script (used for Hindi) in neighboring Jharkhand; and Utkal script (used for Oriya) in Odisha. In addition, many Santals were vehemently pushing for their own recently invented script, Ol-Chiki, to be used. My teacher dismissed Ol-Chiki as a romantic and impractical notion, simply an appeal to "sentiment." The issue of script, he said, was stunting the development of the "language."

Discourses such as these were common both among academics and many Santali-language activists. Language was seen in abstract, structural terms: a delineated, grammatical system underlying speech forms. Script, on the other hand, was considered a secondary representation of language, a distraction for literary production and linguistic development. Arguments such as these echoed long-running debates in the field of linguistics, anthropology, and philosophy vis-à-vis the status of writing. For many linguists of the structural tradition, such as Ferdinand de Saussure or Leonard Bloomfield, the "phonic substance" (Saussure [1916] 1959: 116) reigned supreme, best captured through abstract units such as "phoneme." Since written characters were simply visible representations of this substance and contained no inherent unifying logic; they proved outside the purview of linguistics. Even an anthropologically minded linguist like Edward Sapir considered linguistics "the study of speech" (Sapir 1921). With the structuralist turn in anthropology led by the French anthropologist Claude Levi-Strauss, this attitude toward writing also informed broader social scientific and ethnographic study.

The questioning of the distinction between writing and speech, and the systematic form of thought that this entailed, has in many ways marked the poststructuralist moment. In developing his critique of the metaphysics underlying linguistics and the social sciences more broadly, Jacques Derrida (1976) argues that writing, far from providing a secondary representation of speech, provides a framework for understanding social phenomena in general. Writing troubled linguists and anthropologists precisely because it evaded any reduction to "origin"; it presented features such as durability, iteration, and a potentiality to constantly transform the contexts of use (Derrida 1988). By displacing the analytical focus from language to writing, Derrida opens the structure of language to politics. In doing so, his arguments challenge a conception of a politics of language as rooted in debates over the representation of a structural reality, suggesting instead a *graphic* politics in which communicative practices and politics are inextricably linked and mutually co-constitutive.

Anthropologists, linguists, and students of politics have yet to grapple with the implications of Derrida's broad concept of writing (called *arche-writing*).[3] Drawing on a different tradition however, linguistic anthropologists have argued that the delineation of what is called language from communicative practices in general is in fact an inherently political enterprise, also suturing the study of linguistic structure to political ideology (and vice versa) in a transformative way. For instance, one of the essential premises for delineating ethno-linguistic groups is that they share the same language, forming a "speech community."[4] Yet this concept of a homogenously organized speech community is undermined by the fact that people living side by side interact frequently but still speak quite differently, while people may in fact be speaking the same and yet call it something quite different. For example, linguist John Gumperz described a service encounter between a South Asian origin British resident and his white counterpart where both were speaking what they considered English, yet they consistently misunderstood one another. This contrasted with his village studies in India where Hindi and Urdu speakers in North India, or Marathi and Kannada speakers in South India, claimed they were speaking different languages, but in fact were speaking very closely intelligible linguistic varieties (Gumperz 1964, 1982; Gumperz and Wilson 1971).

Hence, what is called language does not represent the facts of speech on the ground. Instead, as scholars such as Michael Silverstein (1998, 2000) have argued, the meta-delineation of language itself is an ideological construct: a specific variety that is either elevated through historically specific processes of standardization, or, for those without standard languages, a particular denotational description of a speech repertoire to which people claim allegiance.[5] Thus, from this point of view there can be no "language" without some kind of social or ideological component.[6] The difference between writing and script could be seen similarly. Like speech, writing too is a set of communicative practices, related to spoken language, but as Derrida noted, distinct from it. Written repertoires can also be plural, and, as even the most rigid historians of grammatology admit, have been for most of history. In this way, there is no substantive difference between spoken language and script; both are ideological effects of struggles over what and who defines a repertoire, a community, and a territory, and over what slice of the plethora of communicative practices serve as emblematic of an existing or desired social order. Sometimes language and script come together in the process of standardization, as when an emerging nation legislates away its multiscriptality in the process of reform, such as the case of Turkey (Trix 1999, Colak 2004) or Vietnam (Bianco 2013, Marcucci 2009) where they adopted the Roman scripts over the Arabic or Chinese characters respectively. In other cases, such as that of Japan, efforts to institute monoscriptality were explicitly rejected, and multiple script systems (Chinese characters, phonetic alphabets) were organized under the rubric of a single national language (Japanese).[7] In India, given its dense concentration of scripts and the decision to organize federal states along linguistic (and by implication, graphic) lines, together with the protean definition of what constitutes national language, the relation between script, language, territory, and identity remains for many unsettled and unsettling. The presence of multiple scripts, the association of script with claim-making on the state, and the wielding of graphic repertoires in the creation and transformation of what constitutes community make India a case where the *graphic* continues to be a salient modality for politics.[8]

Graphic Politics in India

As linguist Udaya Narayan Singh (2001) has noted, South Asia, for much of its history, has been suffused with multiscriptality. By the first century CE, the Indian subcontinent was home to several Brahmi-derived scripts, which varied by region and community. Sanskrit, which was the "perfected" language of the Vedas, and, during the classical period, the primary language of elite literary production in much of South and Southeast Asia, was written in multiple scripts, as the graphic medium was deemed irrelevant in a ritual and literary culture that valued recitation (Pollock 2006, Kelly 2006, Shulman 2016). After the establishment of the first Islamic kingdoms in the twelfth century, Persian became an important literary language, and the Persio-Arabic script became a critical component of scribal culture. Indeed, in addition to an emerging regional vernacular in northern and parts of southern India called "Urdu" (Hindustani), languages as diverse as Gujarati (Isaka 2002), Punjabi (Mir 2010, Murphy 2018), and Tamil (Tschacher 2018) were all routinely written in the Persio-Arabic script in addition to Brahmi characters. Persio-Arabic script was also used to translate and transcribe Sanskrit texts in the Mughal court, challenging contemporary notions of script and language as associated with religious identity (Truschke 2016).

Hence, script itself was not a salient modality of politics for much of the subcontinent's history, though there existed several scribal communities, who used multiple scripts and wielded writing to gain significant power, especially in the early modern period.[9] Yet, the arrival of the printing press in Bengal at the dawn of the nineteenth century, and the subsequent mass production of the written word, led to both a "standardization" and "homogenization" (Brandt and Sohoni 2018: 6) of linguistic production, such that in various parts of India, certain scripts were selected for mass printing (often times by a caste-Hindu elite), and these scripts became synonymous with "language." For instance, the eastern variety of Brahmi (Eastern Brahmi or Eastern Nagari), which is used to write several languages in eastern India, became known as the "Bengali" script, while a southern variant of Brahmi that was used for Marathi, Kannada, Konkani, Tulu, and even Portuguese, started to gain currency as the "Kannada" script (ibid: 7). In other cases, such as in Maharashtra, the Modi script, which still retained popularity among many groups, had to be actively legislated away, and significant effort had to be made to institute a standard regime in which Marathi would be written in Devanagari over scripts like Modi (Sohoni 2018).

The most famous case of what historian Christopher King (1999) called "one language, two scripts" was the Hindi movement in the nineteenth century, a movement that primarily took place in northern India that sought to cast Hindustani lingua franca as a national language for an independent India *only* in the Devanagari script (cf. Rai 1984, Ahmad 2008). This new script-language was called Hindi, and, except for newly derived vocabulary, was grammatically the same as what had been called colloquially as "Urdu," a link language that developed into a literary vernacular under the Mughal courts and later promoted by the British. Yet by demanding that the new language Hindi should be written only in Devanagari, Hindi proponents sought to marginalize the Persio-Arabic script and the competing elites, mainly Muslims, who lacked proficiency in Devanagari. Religious reformers among Muslims on the other hand started taking advantage of divides introduced by the Hindi movement to promote Urdu and the Persio-Arabic script as an Islamic language that would unite Muslims across South Asia.[10]

What were essentially graphic politics had repercussions across the subcontinent. As the British withdrew and the subcontinent barreled through Partition, the new states of India and Pakistan were formed at the expense of millions of lives and massive displacements. "Hindi" (in the Devanagari script) and "Urdu" (in the Persio-Arabic script) became the official languages of India and Pakistan, respectively. In India, the effort to institutionalize Hindi was resisted by elites in the various regions (especially in southern India), and in response, Prime Minister Nehru convened a commission in 1953 to reorganize states along linguistic lines (King 1997). States were constituted on the basis of language and script; many northern Indian states, such as Bihar and Uttar Pradesh (Central Provinces), adopted Hindi in the Devanagari script as an official language and Urdu in the Persio-Arabic script as a secondary language. In some places script and language were seen as separate; for instance, in the Bombay state, Marathi adopted as an official script, "Devanagari," the same script used for Hindi, Nepali, and a few other languages, while in other states, such as Assam, local elites fought to have what was essentially the same script used to write neighboring languages such as Bengali, considered a fully separate script as part of the Assamese language movement (Kar 2008, Sengupta 2012).[11]

Scripts, as much as language, ethnicity, or any other mark of difference, shaped how territory and community came to be imagined in India. Yet India is home to hundreds of linguistic varieties and distinct ethnic groupings, many spread over a vast territory. For many of India's Adivasi communities, like the Santals, the creation of linguistically organized states that centered on metropolitan areas transformed the "hinterlands" in which they resided into border zones. While the Santals were dispersed far and wide, even the substantial population clusters, such as areas in the erstwhile Santal Parganas or Chota Nagpur and the Jungle Mahals, were cut through by newly formed state borders, with communities having found themselves strewn across states like Odisha, West Bengal, and Bihar. This had material consequences for many with communities such as the over 2.2 million Santals in the state of West Bengal, having no recourse to land provisions in the Santal Pargana or Chota Nagpur Tenancy Acts. These provisions guaranteed the inalienability of land for Scheduled Tribe and legal autonomy for Adivasi-majority areas in the Fifth Schedule to the Indian Constitution.[12]

The reorganization of states along linguistic lines therefore not only linguistically marginalized indigenous and minority communities but also resulted in their politically and materially diminished position. Consequently, graphic politics among the Santals emerged at the same time as in the rest of India, though with very different consequences. A component of the movement for a separate state of "Jharkhand," these politics, embedded in a dispersed, minority language community where processes of standardization, homogenization, and graphic regimentation had not fully taken root, became bound up not with processes of nationalism or recognition in the strict sense, but in an ongoing struggle for autonomy. This is especially true for Santals in places like southwest West Bengal, who after years of demanding to be included in a future Jharkhand state, were left out of the eventual Jharkhand state, carved out from the southern districts of Bihar in 2000. The graphic politics eventually led to a movement for recognition, and in 2003 Santali was made an official language of India, but even this watershed moment both emerged from and was subsequently mobilized by a longer-standing politics of autonomy that marked Santals' relationship to language, territory, and community.

Graphic Politics of Autonomy

In a two-volume work titled *The Materiality of Politics*, the political theorist and historian Ranabir Sammadar described the situation in contemporary South Asia as one "first and foremost" characterized by the "urge to autonomy." He says that while autonomy may in "many ways reproduce the structure from which they want to be autonomous, in every such reproduction there is a difference being enacted." Moving "beyond governmental rationalities or of relations of freedom and domination," a politics of autonomy creates "new spaces in politics" that speak of "rights and their plank, justice" (Sammadar 2007: 140–1). Sammadar suggests that the theorization of autonomy is of utmost importance in studies of contemporary South Asian politics, characterizing a broad spectrum of social movements and relations between self, group, and government. Following Sammadar, I suggest that unlike sovereignty or other relations of power that seek to establish new forms of governmentality, autonomy lies in the liminal space between legal and socioeconomic orders and corporeal, aesthetic, and ritual practices. It is in many ways a reflective practice of engaging with power that, as Sammadar suggests, "propels" (ibid.) the emergence of alternative spaces within the governmental fabric of the state.

Graphic politics offers a semiotic field through which the material dimensions of autonomous practice, and the creation of autonomous spaces, can be traced and analyzed. Script is at once ideologically and materially tied to the governmental concept of language, which is a discursive terrain upon which communities have struggled for recognition, rights, and territory since Indian independence. Yet script also has a material dimension that transcends language; its visual construction, durability, and circulatory potential allow it to, as Hull writes in his analysis of bureaucratic practices in Pakistan, "mediate . . . relations between subjects and the world" in ways that significantly differ from oral channels (Hull 2012: 13).

These politics of autonomy may be present in major languages, such as Urdu, a script-language that once had imperial standing in India but is now relegated to a marginalized status (as opposed to Pakistan where it is a national language). Given that Urdu primarily manifests itself in the form of a script, not as a language, what many people mourn is the loss of the script; its visibility only present now in historical relics or in ghettoized, predominately Muslim, spaces in some parts of India. Yet studies of contemporary practices among Urdu speaking/writing communities present a different picture, for Urdu becomes a semiotic resource to express autonomy in the increasingly right-wing and religiously polarized environment of contemporary India, where Muslim minority communities are openly discriminated against and violently targeted.

For example, in Ahmad's study of younger Muslims in Delhi (Ahmad 2011), once the major center of Urdu literary production, he notes how the loss of proficiency in the Persio-Arabic script is leading to digraphic Urdu literary production in Persio-Arabic and Devanagari. Since Urdu and Hindi are grammatically similar, Ahmad says, certain diacritic marks not known to Hindi-educated speakers are being employed to transform the script into an Urdu Devanagari, in which, even in the face of loss of script, Delhi youth maintain linkages to a literary and religious tradition that connects them with a precolonial past and with other Muslims across the subcontinent. A similar situation could be seen in Parvez's analysis of Muslim politics in Hyderabad (Parvez 2017). While she does not discuss the role of language explicitly, her detailed ethnography shows how even if Urdu competency is declining, political parties and wealthy Muslim residents continue to patronize the Urdu press, and poor women in slums cultivate Urdu literacy in religious meetings. Urdu appears therefore be important to the "autonomy" that the Muslim minority in Hyderabad, an erstwhile Muslim kingdom never conquered by the British, can actively create in the face of repression. Parvez contrasts this with Muslim minorities in France, which lack such a sense of autonomy (of which graphic resources are a part), resulting in a religious form of "antipolitics."[13]

Urdu presents a case of the way in which graphic autonomy is expressed by a religious minority in India. However, the case of Santali, and other Adivasi languages in eastern India that are in the process of producing new scripts, is different. Urdu has an imperial past, a recognized and classical literature, and is even a hegemonic language of the neighboring nation-state. Santali has no such associations; its past and present are always created through a sense of struggle. In this way the graphic politics of Santali, especially the creation of new scripts, and the way in which these scripts are cultivated and deployed in everyday contexts resembles what is happening in many indigenous communities in other parts of the world.

Graphic Politics and Indigeneity

The notion of "indigenous" as a term marking the experience of different groups across the globe is a recent phenomenon, arising at the confluence of the establishment of an international human rights discourse and similar experiences vis-à-vis aggressive postcolonial or settler states such as forced assimilation and displacement (Niezen 2003). However, the term is still contested, and the politics of indigeneity differs depending on the location and sociohistorical conditions of colonization. For instance, Sturm notes that in Canada and the United States, indigenous politics centers around the notion of "sovereignty" while in Mexico and much of Latin America, the prevailing framework is that of "autonomy" (Sturm 2017: 341), entailing a different legal and political relationship to land and state authority. In India, many scholars question how applicable the term "indigenous" is to "Adivasis," arguing that there are significant continuities between the tribal communities and marginal Hindu castes (Beteille 2006, Guha 2013). Others argue that the embracing of transnational indigenous discourse has created class divides between elites and the majority of poor and rural Adivasis who understand their politics in different ways (Ghosh 2008, Shah 2010).

There are clear similarities, however, between Adivasis and other minority communities deemed indigenous around the world. Nationalist and developmentalist discourse has placed Adivasis in the category of the "primitive," a hierarchical relation to upper-caste Hindu society in which certain cultural practices are marked as temporally backward.[14] This marking of the Adivasi as "primitive" has created a legal and developmental regime within the Indian state that resembles what Povinelli, in the context of late-liberal settler colonial states, has called the "governance of the prior" (Povinelli 2011). Consequently, much of what has been written about Adivasis in the sociological literature in relation to the developmental state has discussed how they might be "mainstreamed" (a word resembling "assimilation") or "protected."[15]

The process of "assimilation" in settler colonial contexts has resulted in massive language loss and linguistic alienation, and therefore the reclamation of language has become one of the central pillars of indigenous politics. The struggle for "language" includes both the "preservation" of existing indigenous idioms and the struggle to navigate "contemporary life in the foreign tongues of the colonizers" (Weaver 2000: 229–30). While in postcolonial situations such as India, language loss has not been as high, there has been a discourse of "illiteracy" leveled against Adivasi communities to mark their primitive status, and their languages, like with Native peoples in the Americas or Australia, have been associated with this negatively valorized form of difference.

Consequently, both in settler societies and postcolonies, the creation of new scripts and the use of independent scripts have become a critical semiotic modality in which to create autonomous spaces in conditions of ongoing colonization. Many times, new scripts created visible continuities between the past and present or home and elsewhere for communities of speakers in times of displacement and migration.[16] Sequoyah's Cherokee script, which was created and circulated around the same time that many Cherokees were forced to migrate from their traditional lands in the southeastern United States to areas west of the Mississippi, became an important part of Cherokee Christian religious practice. Today, Cherokees use the script in spaces to index "authentically Cherokee spaces" (Bender 2008), showing how under certain conditions graphic signs come to index a politics of autonomy. Similarly, the Pahawh script, created in the mid-twentieth century for minority Hmong speakers in Southeast Asia, became popular during the time of the Vietnam War, and now serves to connect the Hmong diaspora across both nations and oceans (Smalley et al. 1990). Newly created scripts have also played an important role in visibly indexing the existence of indigenous language communities perceived by dominant communities to be already extinct, such as the Taino in Puerto Rico (Feliciano-Santos 2017).

Graphic politics among Santali speakers display many similarities to the cases mentioned above. Like with Hmong and Cherokee, the creation of new scripts is counterpoised to a widely used Roman orthography, devised by Christian missionaries in the late nineteenth century for writing Christian religious texts as well as transcribing Santali oral narratives.[17] Newly created scripts among Santals such as Ol-Chiki, as well as scripts for other Adivasi groups in eastern India such as Varang Kshiti (Ho), Sorang Sompeng (Sora), and Tolong Siki (Oraon), are often attributed to divine and revelatory origins and are deeply implicated in ritual practice and connections with the spirits (Choksi 2018). The connections between newly created scripts and ritual practice and the origin stories of scripts, as not invented but revealed, show close parallels with the descriptions of recently created scripts for indigenous and minority language communities around the world.[18] While many have called termed this practice as "messianic,"[19] I see these scripts as emerging at the confluence of multiple literacy traditions; ritual interactions with spirits that inform conceptions of migration, temporality, and political action; and encounters with multiple forms of institutional mediation, such as the state, Christian missionaries, and legal regimes. Hence, rather than use the word messianic or millenarian,[20] I posit the invention of new scripts as well as the resignification of already existing ones (such as Roman or the Indic scripts, which are also used to write Santali) as a graphic politics of autonomy.

On the one hand, these scripts in part reproduce the structure in that they pair graphic signs with linguistic ones and emblematize a denotational code that is a legible marker for community in the eyes of the liberal state. Yet on the other, they mark another kind of spatial and temporal logic that emerges from a history of migration and rebellion, and more recently, from a social movement for the creation of an autonomous legal-political arrangement for Adivasis and others in the hills known as "Jharkhand." Script-making emerged at the same time as the borders of new federal states split Adivasi communities, subjecting them to different governmental regimes and political economies. This resulted not only in communicative barriers but also loss of access to land and resources. A flowering of Santali-language literary activity in multiple scripts (Devanagari, Utkal, Eastern Brahmi, Roman) in the early to mid-twentieth centuries as well as the creation of a multiplicity of new scripts for the language coincided with this call for Jharkhand. Hence, as I argue in the following pages, among the Santali speakers of West Bengal, the overall basic ideology of autonomy that informed the Jharkhand movement persists as a graphic ideology. Even in the failure of a movement for the separate state, the continued use of Santali as a graphic emblem, deployed in multiple scripts and in interaction with languages such as English or Bengali, serves to maintain and develop this politics of autonomy in innovative and transformative ways.

Jharkhand as a Politics of Autonomy

When I arrived in Jhilimili in 2010, both the state of West Bengal and the districts of the region (Bankura, West Midnapur, Purulia) had been governed for decades by the iron-clad rule of the Communist Party of India (Marxist) (CPI-M). The party was highly centralized and ruled by an upper-caste Bengali metropolitan elite committed to Marxist ideals. Yet, as I heard more than a few times in the hills, the CPI-M's rule was also seen as a form of colonization by the "East," as many CPI-M leaders had their roots in refugee communities from East Bengal (what is now Bangladesh). Yet there was a local CPI-M Adivasi assembly representative and a loyal and disciplined cadre made up of Adivasis and non-Adivasis. At the local level, the panchayat, the elected village council, was dominated by the Jharkhand Anushilan Party, one of the several Jharkhand factions operating in the area. Led by a former Santali playwright and publisher, the party's scope of operations was limited to nearby villages. Throughout my stay in Jhilimili, my closest interlocutors and mediators were mostly affiliated to this political party, and their members spanned multiple generations, from senior members to college students. The party's discourse centered on what (in Bengali) they called *swashashon* (self-rule or autonomy).

By many accounts, the Jharkhand movement in West Bengal, and in fact the *idea* of Jharkhand even in the newly created Jharkhand state, has been a failure. As early as 1993, much before the establishment of Jharkhand state in 2000, analysts such as Arunabha Ghosh saw the situation of the Jharkhand movement in West Bengal as one of factional dispute, electoral failure, and what he called "ideological confusion." He writes that whatever the outcome of the Jharkhand movement, he seriously doubted any form of autonomy would be extended to the districts of West Bengal (Ghosh 1993: 127). In Jharkhand state, the failure of the Jharkhand-based political parties has been described by Basu (2012) as the result of embracing a politics of "recognition" over "redistribution." The elevation of a politics of development and identity over autonomy in electoral politics has allowed a space for the right-wing, Hindu nationalist Bharatiya Janata Party to hijack the statehood agenda, leaving, Basu suggests, the fight for redistribution for "extra-parliamentary means" (Basu 2012: 1219).

At the time of my fieldwork, the state of Jharkhand politics was opaque. In the Binpur constituency (south of Jhilimili), there was one elected member of the state assembly from a separate Jharkhand Party faction, and Jharkhand parties controlled local village councils in several villages in the area. However, they did not enjoy support across the board from those involved in Santali cultural or literary politics. Some saw their fight as one for a failed dream of a separate state, while others were simply affiliated for whatever reason to another party, usually the CPI-M. Yet, despite the limited electoral power of the official political parties or the fluctuations in support, the presence of the Jharkhand parties was important in maintaining autonomy as a viable politics through multiple generations. For instance, the head at that time of the Jhilimili village panchayat was a young man whose father was a loyal member of the CPI-M. However, he became frustrated with the top-down approach of the party, and after listening to a speech by Shibu Soren, a Santal leader from Jharkhand, he gravitated toward the local Jharkhand political faction and became active in its politics. Though there was no chance a separate state was ever going to be formed, Jharkhand, he said, was "ours" (*aboak'*), a critical component of an underlying politics of autonomy that has informed the movement since its inception.

In addition, the broader politics in the Jangal Mahals region of southwest West Bengal was in transition at that time. Following the failed attempts at seizing land for industries in the towns of Singur and Nandigram in West Bengal,[21] the 34-year-long reign of the Communist Party was coming to an end. In order to spur job growth in a so-called underdeveloped region, the CPI-M had also proposed a chemical plant near the town of Salboni in southwest West Bengal. When the chief minister of the state, Buddhadeb Bhattacharya, was on the way to inspect that site, in November 2008, a land mine exploded near the chief minister's convoy . The CPI-M suspected members of banned

Maoist insurgent groups of conspiring to attack the chief minister and started a program of severe police repression, including beatings and arbitrary detention in areas throughout southwest West Bengal. It also mobilized militias known locally as *harmad*, which violently enforce Communist Party diktats. As a response, in the village of Lalgarh, a group led by Chhatradar Mahato started the People's Committee against Police Atrocities (PCPA, *Jan-gan committee* in short). They, with suspected help from outside Maoist groups, began to retaliate against the CPI-M rule. The PCPA and Maoists articulated similar demands for autonomy as the Jharkhand party, but Jharkhand activists, being trapped between positions of state power and a politics of autonomy directed against CPI-M rule, were targeted from both sides.

During my research period in Jhilimili, the Communist Party offices were closed. The Jharkhand Anushilan party still operated the panchayats, although several senior members had gone into hiding. The major opposition party in the state, the Trinamool Congress, had very little backing. Hence there was an administrative vacuum in the area, and it was marked by extended periods of violence. Police surveillance was everywhere. This was the case through most of my fieldwork, until the end of my period in 2011, when elections were called, and the CPI-M lost in a landslide to the Trinamool Congress in a landmark result. By the time I returned to Jhilimili in 2013, the Trinamool Congress, adopting similar means to the CPI-M (although with no accompanying ideology except *poriborton*—change), had pushed its way into an area in which it had scant political support only two years ago.[22] By the next panchayat elections, the Jharkhand Party was run out and the Trinamool Congress captured the village councils.

Consequently, when I refer to a politics of autonomy as a "quest" for Jharkhand, I do not see the Jharkhand movement as culminating in a politics of statehood or electoral success. This understanding aligns with anthropologist Alpa Shah's skepticism after working with Munda villagers in the neighboring Jharkhand state, when, echoing their sentiments, she asks, "Who cares for the new state?" (Shah 2011). As Shah notes, statehood involves the *sarkar* (administration) and thus subsumes a politics of autonomy more fully within electoral politics and bureaucratic administration, which is the space of governmentality. Yet Shah, Basu, and other scholars[23] have noted aspects of the Jharkhand movement that are not subsumed by discourses of statehood, such as redistribution, the sustenance of autonomous governance, a regional political consciousness, and the assertion of cultural identity as a mode of politics combating caste and class orders. Regardless of political affiliation, these politics are actively cultivated in places like Jhilimili, where separate statehood no longer is on the horizon. Critical to this cultivation of a Jharkhand consciousness in southwest West Bengal has been the creation and deployment of scripts.

Graphic Politics and the Quest for Autonomy

For many throughout India, the independence of the country from the British in 1947 was simply one step in the unfinished business of decolonization. Like other regions that witnessed unrest such as Kashmir or Hyderabad, Mayurbhanj in Odisha was an independent kingdom ruled by a caste-Hindu monarch who patronized his Adivasi, plurality Santal, subjects, yet chose to join the state of Odisha at the time of Independence. Many revolted, hoping to join the southern regions of Bihar, in order to gain legal guarantees under the Chota Nagpur Tenancy Act, and eventually be part of what could be an independent Jharkhand. This never came to pass, and the revolt was put down by the Indian army. Ol-Chiki, the script created (or revealed to) Pandit Raghunath Murmu in Odisha, gained in popularity around that time, appealing to the displaced and dejected Santali speakers who aspired for something more.

The script spread to the nearby city of Jamshedpur, where Adivasi migrants from parts of Odisha, West Bengal, and Bihar gathered to work in the steel factories, themselves migrants from their own villages and attempting to build up a unified political community under the conditions of economic displacement.[24] Printing presses were created, and it spread to Calcutta, Howrah, and Hooghly in West Bengal, where migrants also gathered, and pedagogical and literary material in the script was then brought back to the villages of the southwest of the state, which was the site of an already vibrant Santali-language literary movement using the Eastern Brahmi script, and where newly created scripts had already been invented. Ol-Chiki then entered an already existing graphic field, where language, script, and a politics of autonomy had already been wedded together by people in villages, and where literature and oral performance, such as song and dance, were brought together so even the vast population who were not "literate" in the traditional sense participated jointly in its production.

As the newly created Jharkhand state excluded vast swaths of Adivasi plurality areas in places like southwest West Bengal, Ol-Chiki has taken on a new significance, especially among younger Santali speakers. The script has been the rallying point for the institution of Santali-language education in government schools that had otherwise resisted its institution; the creation of media networks that span across political boundaries; and the semiotic emplacement of a regionally defined territorial consciousness in caste- and class-delineated spaces such as the village market. The deployment of Ol-Chiki in concert with Eastern Brahmi and Roman, and Santali together with Bengali, provides a vision for Jharkhand that is not static, proposing autonomously delineated notions of "region" or "nation" in dynamic interaction with the diverse complexity of local settings. Indeed, even though Ol-Chiki is often equated to a strong ideology of "unity," and many of its proponents insist that it *should* be the only script for writing Santali, this book will detail how the articulation of this ideology draws heavily on the existing situation of multilingualism and multiscriptality present in the Santali-speaking areas. Script—present on signs in village markets, painted on the walls of the schoolhouse, or printed on magazines, posters, and newspapers—provides a way that ideas of autonomy may visibly circulate in Adivasi communities. The visible and material aspects of script, and their connection with oral performance practices such as song, dance, and drama, links a politics of autonomy with Santal-specific temporalities, ritual practice, and histories of migration, helping transform the caste and class-delineated public sphere in the localities where Santals live. However, this autonomy has limits as well. The conflation of Ol-Chiki with Santali has created a sense among many that, contrary to Raghunath Murmu's intentions, this is only a script for the Santali language and the Santali community. This coincides with power relations among Adivasi communities in which Santals, as a relatively more well-off and numerically dominant community, marginalize through a discourse of autonomy other tribes and local communities that live in and around southwest West Bengal.[25] Yet, while this may be the case, the continued presence of multiscriptality and multilingualism still robustly allows for the organization of multiple communities around the politics of autonomy, as

I will demonstrate through ethnographic accounts of graphic politics in spaces such as schools, bazaars, or in media.

Finally, much of the graphic practices that underlie the politics of autonomy are gendered, that is, ritual and literary spaces are dominated by men. Yet graphic politics is also cultivated in several spaces shared by both men and women such as the *akhdas*, or spaces of song and dance performance, village fairs, and schools and colleges. While women have long played an under-recognized role in the Jharkhand movement, the increased and more assertive engagement of women with graphic politics in these shared spaces has the potential to alter the male-dominated status quo. Consequently, while these limitations are present in the politics of autonomy ethnographically analyzed in this book, and their absence exacerbated by my own position as a caste-Hindu and male ethnographer, I suggest that the graphic politics that this book discusses generates possibilities for which these limitations may be surpassed, bringing with it new, relevant, and more inclusive conceptions of autonomy.

Sites and methods

This book is primarily set in the region of southwest West Bengal, in the small area at the meeting point between the districts of Bankura, West Midnapur,[26] and Purulia. The motivation for selecting this site was a combination of intention and fortune. I knew from my initial inquiries in Kolkata that the Santali-speaking regions of West Bengal were particularly known for their literary activity, producing a high number of magazines, books, and newspapers in the Eastern Brahmi and the Ol-Chiki scripts. Ol-Chiki was also popular in the southern regions of Jharkhand, around Jamshedpur, and northern Odisha, but West Bengal, perhaps due to the influence of the spread of Communism, the valorization of literary production among the upper-caste Bengali-speaking rural elite, and the enduring influence of the Jharkhand movement, had a particularly rich (and graphically diverse) literary culture in Santali.

However, my first interaction with residents of Jhilimili was in Dumka, Jharkhand, where members of a Jhilimili-based regional club went to perform at the winter harvest festival known as *Sohrae*. I found out that many in this club were affiliated with the Jharkhand Party although their political outlook differed from those living in Jharkhand proper, in which tribal communities were more starkly divided between an elite section closer to the state and non-elites who were alienated from it. Instead, as I traveled for several hours back with my interlocutors from Dumka to Jhilimili, crossing through the Chota Nagpur plateau into the forests of Singhbhum and Jungle Mahals, I found in my conversations that my companions from Jhilimili had a strong locally inflected version of autonomy in which their political vision for what they called Jharkhand differed from what they saw and experienced in the state proper. Many said explicitly that they had no desire to separate from Bengal and that the fight for Jharkhand was about another type of autonomy for their region and for Santali-speaking and Adivasi communities elsewhere.

These visions for autonomy beyond the demand for Jharkhand state intrigued me, and I became interested in investigating further how the culture of literary production related to such political ideologies. Jhilimili proved an ideal site, lying at the crossroads of the three major districts of the Jungle Mahal region, and as such, was relatively insulated from the war raging around it. While constant strikes, road closures, and police checkpoints hampered my mobility to move between the market space where I resided and outlying villages, there were many Santali-dominated villages in walking distance of Jhilimili, and places such as the market or the school witnessed constant circulation of people from throughout the region. Interestingly, as this book will show, they were also sites where the use of written Santali and the Ol-Chiki script was most visible, even more so than the Santal-dominated village hamlets. As a result, I began to understand that graphic politics and a politics of autonomy also emerged from relations with other castes and communities who also resided and stayed in Jhilimili market and as part of the larger pathways of circulation of people, goods, and ideas that characterized the region.

As I tried to apprehend the role of script in the politics and life of the people, I had to employ a mixed methodology. I lived in Jhilimili for substantial periods of my fieldwork, chatting with residents, both Santal and non-Santal, in the open spaces of the bazaar, on the grounds of the school, or in homes.

I also visited frequently Santali-speaking hamlets surrounding the area and spent nights and shared meals with residents, gaining a better sense of lived realities in the region. I recorded everyday interactions, rituals, song and dance performances, and various festivals that marked village life. I attended football matches, dramas, and village fairs.

While this form of participant observation formed the bulk of my research and provides most of the background knowledge that informs this book, much of my data was also material and textual. Throughout my time in the market, I could see how the built environment constantly transformed, even from day to day, and posters and graffiti would cover the walls projecting new kinds of political announcements, advertisements for traveling performances or film showings, and changing signboards on shop fronts. I recorded this by taking pictures, supplemented by conversations with residents about the changing nature of the landscape. Similarly, as my quarters adjoined the local high school, I was lucky enough to interact with students, who discussed with me their own changing attitudes to script, language, and politics and allowed me to take pictures of their living quarters. I was also fortunate enough to recruit one of these students as my research assistant, who continued to work with me through his time at university and provided friendship and collaboration at most stages through this research.

Finally, in addition to being involved in the life of Jhilimili, I also traveled throughout West Bengal, Jharkhand, and Odisha, following sites of textual production. I attended literary events such as poetry gatherings or cultural meetings in order to meet authors, editors, reporters, script-makers, and others involved in textual production, and frequently followed up with them, visiting them in their villages and places of work and residence for more formal-style interviews. I saw how the Santali language brought people together from various regions of eastern India, and how the use of multiple scripts, through often contentious, created a rich and flourishing literary culture even in the absence of state support. All of this were part of how autonomy became cemented; thus my methods and sites mirrored in the graphic politics themselves, rooted in the social relations and specific spaces where Santals reside, yet also highly dispersed, creating connections across the vast range of eastern India.

Organization of the Book

The following chapters will elucidate for the reader how Santali speakers deploy graphic and linguistic registers in visible ways across both space and time in order to assert a politics of autonomy. The book argues that in spite of the exclusion from the Jharkhand state, the spread of graphic politics has allowed Santali speakers (and to an extent other Adivasi communities as well) to assert autonomy from the state of West Bengal and for their region by semiotically transforming history, community relations, and territory in correspondence with the historical aims of the Jharkhand movement. Through the materiality, visibility, and durability of script, Adivasis of southwest West Bengal both maintain relations and distance themselves from the state, creating autonomous domains from within and without the governmental apparatus.

Chapter 2 provides a historical overview of the role of writing and the creation of new scripts in Santali-speaking and other Adivasi communities of eastern India. Instead of seeing Santali history as essentially one of "orality," the chapter will argue that writing (called *ol* in Santali and other Austro-Asiatic languages) provides an important ritual interface for Santals between them and their spirits (*bonga*) and also features in their narratives about important events such as the Santal *Hul*. Hence, according to Santali accounts of their own history, as well as contemporary ritual practice, writing is associated with much more than language or ethnic politics, such as Santali-specific ritual practices, histories of migration, and political insurrection. It will then show how this autonomous conception of *ol* historically interacted with the arrival of Christian missionaries, the rise of the anti-Christian Kherwar movement, the independence of India, and the Jharkhand movement. The chapter suggests that the flourishing of script-making in the area arises from these diverse historical strands, in which graphic repertoires emerge as both signs of autonomous forms of writing and of an independently delineated language legible to the state and its institutions.

Chapter 3 takes the reader to the heart of Jhilimili market to see how scripts are visibly deployed in the linguistic landscape. I employ linguistic anthropological discussions of scale to show how the use of multiple scripts on the landscape allow residents to evaluate Santali as both a national and regional language in order to combat the caste-Hindu perception that it is a local and caste-delimited variety. The chapter examines the deployment of Santali in Ol-Chiki, Eastern Brahmi, and Roman script in political graffiti, shop signs, posters for Santali-language media such as films or dramas, and on places like the offices of the *pargana*, which form a part of the autonomous system of governance among Santali communities. I suggest that multiple scripts provide a way for Santals to transform the bazaar into a trans-regional space of Jharkhand: grounded in the concrete experiences of life in southwest West Bengal, while also scaling this region as part of a larger territory connected to Santali diasporas throughout eastern South Asia. The chapter will also look at how Santali has been taken up by caste Hindus, engendering competing scalar evaluations of Santali and its scripts that contrast with its use by Santali-speaking residents in the market.

Chapter 4 broaches the topic of caste, tribe, and community, especially with respect to the recent institution of Santali-language education at the local village high school. It argues that script has been a critical semiotic vehicle in which the Santals have attempted to refigure a subordinate caste-like status, which has been based on the exclusion of their spoken language, into an equally legitimate "linguistic community." Important to this process has been the ways in which Santals have used script as a rallying cry to demand that the local village high school institute Santali-language education. While their demand was begrudgingly accepted by the school, the chapter will show how high school students have in fact embraced Ol-Chiki in a different manner than simply demanding recognition for it as a medium of class-room instruction. Examining the painted exteriors and interiors of student hostels, oral sung performance, and students' attitude toward script, the chapter will argue that the use of Ol-Chiki and even other scripts like Eastern Brahmi for writing Santali have allowed students to create autonomous spaces within institutions such as the school. These spaces at once sustain the legitimacy of Santali through the Ol-Chiki script through generations of students, but at the same time, create a new axis of differentiation through which an ideology of literacy takes root in the Santali-speaking community which subordinates spoken language and various other scripts used to write Santali.

Chapter 5 discusses Santali-language print media and the "Jharkhand imagination." Starting by discussing criticisms of Benedict Anderson's work from scholars in South Asian Studies and linguistic anthropology, this chapter attempts to highlight how different scripts and languages have been used in media locally produced and read in southwest West Bengal to create an autonomous domain of Jharkhand. This domain, I suggest, is based on the assertion of difference, yet also through the use of multiple scripts and codes, attempts to craft a vision for a trans-ethnic polity that scales the regional through discourses of supranational citizenship. The use of language moves beyond discussions of the "vernacular" popular in discussions of South Asian media demonstrating how even varieties assumed to be locally and regionally based such as Santali can in fact function as a part of a cosmopolitan discourse of Jharkhand identity through the use of multiple scripts in and in conjunction with different languages. The chapter ends with discussions about new possible directions for locally produced media among the younger generations, including a brief reflection on the use of electronically mediated communication.

Finally the book will conclude by discussing the relation between graphic politics, autonomy, and insurgency in eastern India, and the possible futures for the Jharkhand movement in West Bengal after the fall of Communism and the increased political polarization of the state and India, more broadly. The conclusion comments on how the study of graphic politics in southwest West Bengal provides a framework for subsequent interdisciplinary studies on ongoing struggles by minority and indigenous communities in liberal settler and postcolonial societies in other parts of the world.

2

Ol as an Autonomous Practice

Setak' ayup' baba tala n'idạ
seṛay mey sey bạbu olok'-birdạ
Olok' birdạ khonak' chet' ho marang bạnuk',
Uihạr achur kin mey Sidhu Kanhu,
ehop' leda kin ol akhor geyan,
aṛgo lena kin disom susaṛ.

—Santali song, sung by a college student at Kapgari College (West Midnapur), West Bengal

[Morning, evening, in the middle of the night,
learn how to write,
there is nothing greater than writing-knowledge.
Recall those two, Sidhu and Kanhu,
the ones who created the knowledge of writing and script,
the ones who descended to spread good over our country.]

When traveling through Jharkhand or surrounding Adivasi-majority regions, it is hard not to see memorials to Sidhu and Kanhu Murmu, the two brothers who led the various tribal groups of the erstwhile Santal Parganas in the 1855 Hul, a large-scale and bloody revolt against the British administration and the caste-Hindu elite. Their names are etched on roads, parks, government buildings, and universities; their likenesses tower over the main square in Jharkhand's northern capital Dumka and can be found in villages throughout the state. These are the official memorials of the Hul, the historical moment of insurgency that has become incorporated as one of the founding narratives for the modern Jharkhand state. Sidhu and Kanhu fought so that the Santals could have a land of their own, one that, in theory, belonged to the purported original inhabitants or Adivasis, and that land is now Jharkhand.

The state project of commemorating the Hul stems from accounts by nationalist, upper-caste historians in the early twentieth century that subsumed the Hul under the history of what was becoming the Bengal nation. They characterized the Hul as a proto-political event, an ephemeral moment in historical time that later was to transform into a more legitimate state-based politics. However, as historian Prathama Bannerjee (2006) notes, these accounts contrasted with the way that many Santals themselves recounted the Hul—as an event that blurred the lines between ritual and everyday practice to assert an alternative and autonomous political order that interrupted the colonial and nationalist tropes of historical time and cartographic space.

In a small corner of West Bengal, just a few kilometers from the border with Jharkhand, students at a small, rural college depict a different Sidhu and Kanhu. These students hailed from villages that fought for, but were eventually excluded, from the new Jharkhand state. Nevertheless, the sentiments that underlie the idea of "Jharkhand," a polity that united the dispersed Adivasi communities and allowed them to live free from the yoke of caste-Hindu controlled administration, an idea which, for them, was the true patrimony of the Hul, continued to shape their everyday practice. For them, unlike nationalist historians, the brothers Sidhu and Kanhu were not historical personages or messianic warriors, who fought and lost for their freedom. Instead, as the song suggests, Sidhu and Kanhu, who were illiterate as per the colonial historical accounts, were the originators of an alternative literacy tradition that the students embraced even as they moved through the traditional, Bengali-language education system. The knowledge (*geyan*) of writing (*ol*) and letters (*akhor*) were the weapons that Sidhu and Kanhu offered subsequent generations who now wield them to carve out spaces of autonomy within the caste-Hindu-dominated institutions that subordinate Adivasi languages, aspirations, and history. At the peripheries of both the states of West Bengal and Jharkhand, the students, who have excelled at the rigors of a stringent and rigid academic system, exhort one another to "learn" the knowledge of an alternative conception of writing and to therefore embody Sidhu and Kanhu in their daily lives.

Despite many Santals embracing writing, scholars and state institutions have typically identified the Santals, and other Scheduled Tribe (Adivasi) communities, with orality. Stories collected in Adivasi languages usually come under the term folklore, and many of the ethnological institutions tasked with the study of Adivasi communities conflate "tribal" with "folklore." Even India's premier literary body, the Sahitya Akademi calls their division focusing on Adivasi expressive culture as the division of "tribal and *oral* literature."[1] The idea of the Adivasi entrenched in an oral culture, along with the image of the bow-and-arrow wielding Sidhu and Kanhu and the image of Adivasi protest that focuses on *jal, jangal, jameen* (water, forests, and land), serves to exclude writing from any discussion of Adivasi histories, politics, or cultural life. When it is discussed, it is often seen as *external* to Adivasi histories and practice. This externality is often attributed to the influence of the supernatural, the encounter with Christian missionaries, or as a result of the more recent acquisition of literacy in the dominant Indo-Aryan languages. While all of these elements have shaped Santali practices of writing, none of these elements alone explain how writing, or what in Santali (and other Munda languages) is called *ol*, has become a salient marker of autonomy.

By expanding the concept of writing beyond the representation of speech, this chapter offers history of *ol* as a long-standing practice that binds Santals to the land, kin, and their spirits. It follows a path through the moments of insurgency, missionization, and the Jharkhand movement, tracing how *ol* comes to constellate a conception of autonomy for the Santals on the peripheries of Jharkhand. By autonomy, I do not mean here legal political autonomy vis-à-vis the state, of the sort that comes from the "scheduling" of areas according to the Indian constitution in which Adivasi customary law has legal force,[2] or the rights of Santals and other Adivasis to inalienable land encoded in the colonial-era Santal Pargana and Chota Nagpur Tenancy Acts.[3] The fight to maintain these rights, to forest, land, and water, and to practice customary law within the Indian nation-state free from government interference certainly formed one of the pillars of the Jharkhand struggle. However, another dimension of autonomy informed the Jharkhand movement, one that was not bound to the state and to the law in the same way. It was the struggle to reassert ideological control over territory and history, through which the past, which was considered a time free from the domination of caste-Hindu rule, and the sacred, where spirits and humans are connected, are enacted in the space–time of the everyday, opposed to, but also in interaction with, dominant institutional and legal orders.[4] This chapter suggests that one of the major ways this ideological autonomy, which, in their *longue durée* view of history,[5] has accompanied the Santals through periods of disruption and dispersal, becomes materialized[6] in everyday life is through the production of script. Script, and its semiotic associations with kin, spirits, geography, and language, affords a potentiality for autonomy that persists even for those Santals who were left out of the Jharkhand state, and hence from the legal guarantees of autonomy that inclusion in Jharkhand would have provided. From the point of view of legal autonomy of the type guaranteed by the tenancy acts or constitutional schedules, the struggle for Jharkhand by the Santals of West Bengal was a failure. However, as we will see, the failure resulted in an embracing of graphic politics in which a conception of autonomy not tied to legal or statist frameworks endured, leading to alternative forms of struggle against caste-Hindu domination and new political imaginations. The chapter will describe this new form of autonomy by charting a history of the production and circulation of script among the Santals. Weaving its way through the colonial and early postcolonial periods, it will end where it started, in the villages of contemporary southwest West Bengal at the periphery of Jharkhand.

The Semantic Field of *Ol*

In 2009, I was attending the winter harvest festival known as *sohrae* in a village in Dumka district, northern Jharkhand. When I entered in a house to sit down, one of my hosts stopped me and pointed out a freshly chalked diagram on the threshold of the entrance. Knowing that I was interested in script and writing, he said to me, "Look at that, it's *ol*." I looked again, "Is it *ol-chiki* [name of the Santali script]?" "No, no." he said, "it's not any kind of *chiki* [symbol] it is just *ol* [writing]."

The diagram was a type of *ol* called *khonḍ ol* (see Figure 2.1), which during the winter harvest festivals, mark houses as belonging to specific migratory specific subclans, mapping a history of migration and dispersal while at the same time connecting the subclan members who are scattered among various

Figure 2.1 *Khonḍ ol* in the entrances of houses during the *sohrae* festival, Tilaboni village, West Bengal 2010 (photo by author).

villages in the region. During the subsequent winter harvest, in 2010, during my fieldwork in southwest West Bengal, I was to see this form of *ol* appear in houses of every Santal village I went to, suggesting the practice is widespread. The fact that the Santals call this *ol* is not surprising. As the anthropologist Marine Carrin suggests in her study of Santal diagrams, the semantic domain of *ol* covers both writing in the sense of scripted language as well as the language of ritual diagrams,[7] "formal systems of interpretation," which contain straight, circular, or hexagonal figures within which coded points are added (Carrin 1978:108). These diagrams delineate ritual spaces, connect collectivities (such as the subclan), and mediate interactions between human beings and spirits (*bongas*). They are drawn to prepare spaces for ritual sacrifice, cure physical sickness, ensure good harvests, demarcate clan and subclan membership, and ward off lurking malevolent spirits, forming a critical component of communicative practice in Santal homes and villages.

One could see the diagrammatic elements of *ol* as simply a form of "proto"-writing or a not quite modern confusion between pictures and orthography stereotypical of so-called semiliterate people. This particular view draws on influential histories of writing (or what is called grammatology) by mid-twentieth century scholars such as Gelb (1952) or Diringer (1962), who view alphabetic writing, or writing that *represents* speech as the most advanced, and authentic, form of writing. This view has also more or less been standard in linguistics, originating in the French linguist's Ferdinand de Saussure's notion of writing as "parasitic" on speech (Saussure 1959),[8] or in certain anthropological approaches to literacy, which view alphabetic writing as an "autonomous"[9] domain of practice, separate from oral communication or pictographic/diagrammatic marks.

Yet the very fact that the Santals and many other communities around the world consider the graphic representation of language and the diagramming of marks within the same semantic field has prompted scholars to question the primacy of alphabetic writing in the study of graphic systems. Scholars of pre-Columbian and contact-era South America have attempted to broaden the definition of writing to the "communication of relatively specific ideas in a conventional manner by means of permanent, visible marks" (Boone 1994:15) including systems like Mixtec ideography and Andean Quipu knots within their scope of study.[10] They have also sought to locate the distinctions between writing and drawing as one not rooted in the experience of European colonization, which encouraged the eradication of native ritual practice and sought to "create a conflict of consciousness" (Mignolo 1994: 298) about native graphic systems, resulting in self-perceptions of illiteracy.

The idea prevalent now among scholars of literacy that "writing does not suddenly occur against the background of pure speech" (Collins and Blot 2003: 164) allows us to see *ol* not as a premodern relic, existing as an aberration of the here and now, but rather as constitutive to a Santal conception of writing as an autonomous practice. Here, writing (*ol*) is more than a transparent and arbitrary form of linguistic representation but enacts a sense of community not tied to institutions, states, or progressive histories. For instance, writing calls the spirits, known as *bongas* in Santali, who are ancestral, and often antagonistic, forces that inhabit the landscape to commune with humans (*hoṛ*) to jointly pursue action for the well-being of the community. *Ol* also marks out the histories of kin relations, migration, and territory in relation to the present, forming what anthropologist Richard Parmentier (1985) calls diagrams *in* and *of* history.[11] A conception of writing that supersedes linguistic representation allows us to see how autonomy becomes materialized through the practice of *ol* in moments of insurgency, colonial encounters, and, more recently, the creation of new scripts.

Ol and Autonomy in the Colonial Encounter

Though official commemorations of the Hul, as well as classic histories of the event fail to mention "writing" at all, a small report in the 1856 *Calcutta Review* describing the brothers' encounter with writing plays an important role in contemporary South Asian historiography. The report described the brothers, Sidhu and Kanhu, recounting in court how they received orders from their supreme deity, "Thakur," on "bits of paper" upon which "words were written" and in a "white book." The account said that Sidhu and Kanhu were illiterate, so despite their claim to have interpreted the words themselves, the report asserts that some unknown "literate Santals" must have read out the words to them. The report forms one of the bases for Ranajit Guha's important study on insurgency in colonial India, where he suggests that colonial and nationalist historical discourse consistently subordinates peasant "religiosity" to its secular dictates, denying the Santals political consciousness in a moment of insurgency such as the Hul (Guha 1988: 80).

While Guha's analysis challenged the protocols of history writing at the time, in criticizing the subordination of "religiosity," Guha subsumes writing within the larger realm of religion. In doing so, he inadvertently reinforces a view of writing as *external* to the quotidian, characterizing it as a particular consciousness-raising encounter that leads to the spectacular events of the Hul.[12] "Writing," as it appears in in the English language colonial archive, is read as something extraordinary that precipitates the insurgency event. Yet, as Peter Anderson suggests, even as early as the 1890s, Santal recollections of the Hul viewed the two brothers Sidhu and Kanhu as literate, even with some narratives recounting that they actually went to school (Anderson 2008). Though Anderson casts doubt on the fact that the brothers were ever conventionally literate, the point is that, according to the Santal accounts, the practice, like ritual diagramming, was a skill sought out by the brothers to transform their relationships with both the spirits and other human beings; it was learned as much as it was revealed.

One such account is that of Durga Tudu, a resident of Santal Parganas who lived through the ravages of the Hul, and, in the 1890s, narrated his story to Sagram Murmu, an assistant of the Norwegian missionary P. O. Bodding. He says that Sidhu and Kanhu's father, a rich village headman, Bhogon Majhi, decided to send his two sons to the village school (*paṭsal*) so they could learn how to "write" (*ol*) from a learned Brahmin. However, on the way, they had to pass a *baru* tree. One day they saw a mendicant under the tree who "had no arms, no legs, but had heads on both ends" (Anderson et al. 1983: 175) Each time they went to school they saw the mendicant again, but each time his body shape had transformed, as he sometimes had legs on both ends. Finally, one day they saw him like a man, and he called them over to give them a "blessing" (*bhori*) so they could write a letter to the British Raj about excessive rents laid upon the people. As part of this blessing, he said, he would teach them how to read and write (*ol-paṛhao*) (177).

Sidhu and Kanhu therefore stopped going to school. They did not learn how to read and write according to the dictates of the Brahmin or his "school." Tudu goes on to say that, after skipping school and training with the mendicant, "somehow they wrote a letter (*chiṭhi ol-ket'a*), and by seizing it with pincers made of twigs they sent it to its destination, having passed it on from village to village" (179). This "letter" (*chiṭhi*) resembled a traditional form of Santal announcements where thread is wound around forked twigs and circulated from village to village, coding messages within the patterns (Anderson 2008: 186). As they wrote (*ol ket'a*) this letter, and circulated it, they became silent (*konkaena*), conducted ritual sacrifices, and called themselves *Suba*

Ṭhakur, embodying a spirit whose power they would draw on to transform the landscape and gather people around them to continue the insurrection (Anderson et al. 2011: 179).[13]

While the account is fantastic, it is not extraordinary, considering that even up to the present, ritual diagramming, sacrifice, and spirit possessions are very common in Santali-speaking communities. According to contemporary songs, many Santals believe that Murmu priests (to which clan Sidhu and Kanhu had belonged) were in fact "writing" as far back as when they lived in Chai-Champa, the land where the Santals resided in autonomy, before being forced to migrate due to war and internal treachery.[14] Contrary then to the idea that the encounter with writing created a "statement about a new epoch" (Banerjee 1999: 219), writing enacted a certain temporality of *autonomy* that was always there as a potentiality, embedded in the everyday practice of *ol*, and during certain moments, served to transform communities and spaces over large distances, creating the conditions for insurgency on the scale of the Hul.

In addition to describing writing as something less than extraordinary, a practice both acquired and revealed, Durga Tudu's account of Sidhu and Kanhu's encounter with the mendicant also reveals a certain binary split within the semantic field of *ol*. By the 1850s, or at least by the 1890s when Tudu was recounting this story, "writing" had already come to be associated with schooling and Brahminical learning, such that a Santal peasant in Jharkhand could imagine that a "rich" village headman like Bhogon Majhi would have even suggested to his sons that they should attend school and learn writing from the local Brahmin. Yet at the same time, *ol* also remained the provenance of ritual specialists, or others involved in matters of the *bongas*, such as the mendicant. In the case of Tudu's narrative, one sees how one facet of *ol*, associated with ritual practice and transformation, is leveraged against another facet, associated with institutional learning. It was decided that the former was the more powerful semiotic medium to petition the British Raj against the excessive rents laid on the people, perceiving the British as allies that would be receptive to ritually encoded information.

The British, however, viewed Sidhu and Kanhu's appeals as a law-and-order disturbance, and the subsequent struggle resulted in massive death and devastation in the Santal Pargana area, creating what missionaries thought to be the ideal conditions for evangelization in the late nineteenth and early twentieth centuries. While the events of the Hul brought to light the divisions between the Santals (and their allied Adivasi and lower-caste groups) and caste-Hindu landowners, there was still significant overlap between the communities of the Santal Parganas in terms of religious practice. Missionaries believed that by emphasizing linguistic difference, and materializing that difference in the form of a unique script, they could further delineate an autonomous Santali identity, which would alienate Santals further from caste-Hindus and move them into the Christian fold (Carrin-Bouez 1986).

This was particularly true in the case of the Norwegian mission, the largest and most influential mission in the Santal Parganas. The leader, L. O. Skrefsrud, decided to reject the Eastern Brahmi script adapted from Bengali and used by the earlier American missionary Jeremiah Phillips to write his collection of Santal folk songs in 1845 (the first known printed work in Santali). Instead, he opted for the Roman script, deciding to modify the German linguist Karl Lepsius's "universal" Roman phonetic alphabet (Lepsius [1863] 2014). The choice of Roman was decided after initial linguistic studies of Santali outlined a phonology (including vowels and glottalized consonants) that differed significantly from neighboring Indo-European languages. Skrefsrud, and his successor at the mission, Paul Olaf Bodding, argued that the Roman script, lending itself easily to diacritic marks, was superior to the Devanagari or Eastern Brahmi scripts, which were too tied to the Indo-Aryan sound structure (Bodding 1922).[15]

Following the establishment of a Roman script, Santali-language printing press at Benagaria mission in 1868, Skrefsrud embarked on an ambitious program of publication in Santali language. However, the script was not used to publish only Christian material, such as hymnals or translations of European church material, but also traditional stories as well. One of the most significant volumes published from the Benagaria mission was the 1868 tract *Hoṛ ko ren mare hapṛam ko reyak' katha* (The stories of the ancestors of the Santals), the Santal creation story told during the monsoon festival of *karam* or the ritual of *jom-sim*, and which Skrefsrud had meticulously recorded from a ritual expert, Kolean Guru. The press also published a variety of tracts on Santal folktales, studies on indigenous medical practices, song-books, and others in the Santali Roman script (Bodding 1924, 1925, 1983). In doing so, the missionaries intertwined the Roman script both with an independent, autonomously delineated Santali religious and cultural sphere as well as with the project of Christian conversion.[16]

The Christian missionaries' attempts to wed Santal autonomy with Roman script and evangelization also sparked opposition. For instance, in 1871, village leader Bhagirath Majhi started a new religious order called the "Kherwar" (or Kherwal) through which he promoted a unique and distinct religious practice, in which Santals cut themselves off from the village religion, dedicating themselves to particular spirits (*bongas*), dressing in all white, maintaining dietary restrictions, and incorporating hymn-like songs as part of their ritual practice. The Kherwar sect, as the Norwegian missionary P. O. Bodding noted, articulated a conception of autonomy that was syncretic,[17] adopting elements from caste Hinduism and Christianity but employing them in novel ways "to strike out new lines of their own" (Bodding 1922: 231). This is evident from the movement's embrace of writing as a medium on which to posit a separate religion (*dhorom*). For instance, Ramdas Tudu "Raska" 's *Kherwar Bongsho Dhorom Puthi* (The religious book of the Kherwar descendents), published in 1897, outlined distinct ritual practices and described the various relationships with Santal spirits, or *bongas,* which for the first time linked Santali ritual practice to the written word outside the mission context. The book was published not in Roman script but in Eastern Brahmi, the script used to write Bengali, and the one associated with schooled literacy.

This composite form of autonomy, in which Santals' specific histories and conceptions of freedom were articulated through caste-Hindu or Christian frameworks, was to become a primary frame for subsequent revolts throughout the Jharkhand area in the colonial period (Chandra 2016, Dasgupta 2016). These revolts served to cement a regional consciousness among the Santals and different Adivasi communities and introduced conceptions of autonomy that would serve as the foundation for later demands for an independent state of Jharkhand (Sammadar 1998). Yet less noticed by historians of this period but equally important is the way that these movements also shaped and were shaped by writing. Christian missionaries introduced the idea that "script," an orthographic system tied to a linguistic code, could be emblematic of autonomy, and while the Kherwars opposed Christianity, many, such as Ramdas Tudu and his followers, embraced the idea that written Santali would perpetuate their political, religious, and territorial claims. This conception of *ol* was to be carried through the turbulent period of Indian state formation, when the Jharkhand area would witness a surge in the creation of independent scripts.

Script-Making and the Movement for Jharkhand

A few kilometers outside the provincial town of Rairangpur, in Mayurbhanj district, Odisha, lies the small village of Dahardi. I arrived at the village on the day of *Guru Purnima* (or in Santali *Guru Kunạmi*), when I found it teeming with people from all over eastern India. One could hear Santali interspersed with Bengali, Hindi, and Oriya, and I saw parked motorcycles, trucks, and three-wheelers bearing the nameplates from all neighboring states. They had arrived to celebrate the birthday of their *Guru gomke* (teacher) Pandit Raghunath Murmu, the creator of Ol-Chiki script, and who was born and had lived and died in this small corner of Odisha.

After witnessing the rituals where Guru Gomke's spirit was invoked and hearing a beautiful song relating the circumstances by which Ol-Chiki was revealed to Murmu (sung by a famous blind singer from southwest West Bengal), I went to Murmu's family home to interview his descendants. His grandson, a young man around my age, invited my companions and me inside, and offered us a meal and a room to sleep in for the night. Showing us around the house, he pointed out the place where his grandfather, after having invented (or discovered) Ol-Chiki script, stored his original printing blocks, which he painstakingly had made in order to start creating primers. The script was to become popular, especially as Independence dawned and the Santals viewed the possibility that Jaipal Singh's dream of an Adivasi-majority Jharkhand state[18] would soon become a reality. Originally conceived by Murmu to be a script for all Adivasis, the Ol-Chiki script was to be part of that new reality.

Yet the erstwhile king of Mayurbhanj where Dahardi was located refused his subjects' demands to accede to Bihar and join the other Adivasi-majority districts to the north, the areas that were eventually to become the Jharkhand state. Instead, the kingdom acceded to its southern neighbor

Odisha, sparking an uprising. This uprising, led by Santal leader Sonaram Soren in 1948, was crushed by the Indian army.[19] As Murmu's grandson told us, during that period, the army and other state-sponsored vigilantes were terrorizing supporters of Jharkhand, taking them and locking them in prison, and were also trying to suppress any Jharkhand or anti-Odisha related material. This included Ol-Chiki. According to his grandson, Murmu had to hide the printing blocks in a secret room in the house so that they would be saved from the violence. Dahardi never joined the Jharkhand state, yet the Ol-Chiki script survived, and on that day of *Guru Purnima*, one could see how the script drew the Santals from different regions and across borders to the village, and how they continued to keep alive, indeed advance, the dream of political and territorial unity even after the formation of the official Jharkhand state.

While stories about Ol-Chiki have assumed a mythical status among many Santali speakers, during the period when Ol-Chiki was created and the call for an independent Jharkhand state echoed throughout the Santali-speaking areas, people in villages stretching from the Santal Parganas and Dinajpur in the north to Odisha in the south started creating distinct scripts for the Santali language. While some estimate as many as fourteen independent scripts of Santali were created (Hansdak' 2009), there are likely far more; for instance, I even came across one that was previously undocumented in the village where I conducted fieldwork (Choksi 2018). These scripts have several commonalities. For instance, most followed the phonetic structure of the Roman script; unlike Indian scripts, they were alphabetic (representing each vowel and consonant separately), and they placed special graphic emphasis on the glottalized consonant series (p', t', k', c') and the mid-central vowels. Thus, they integrated the Roman script within their framework while also incorporating elements of Indic graphic ideology (Choksi 2018). Yet, the script-makers also integrated diagrammatic elements into the graphic construction that were not present in either the Roman or Indic scripts. The graphemes, independent of their phonetic value, were endowed with a temporality that instantiated primordial history within the present, creating a new temporality through graphic practice. Moreover, the script linked the practice of writing a language with ritual, creating connections with the Santali spirits (*bongas*) through the graphic structure.[20]

Monj Dander Ank

One of the earliest Santali script-makers was Sadhu Ramchand Murmu, a renowned Santali-language poet and singer, who created the script Monj Dander Ank (Drawings of the Bliss Cave) in 1922. Like Pandit Raghunath Murmu, he also was an active participant in the movement for an independent Jharkhand. He was most famous for his lilting voice and rousing poetic sensibility, rallying different Scheduled Tribe communities around the political identity of Adivasi in the fight for Jharkhand with his famous song, *Debon tengon Adibasi bir* (Let us stand up, we the Adivasi heroes). The song was to later become an informal anthem for the Jharkhand movement in the southern Santali-speaking areas, and many older people even today recall how his songs enthralled audiences at rallies throughout eastern India.

While Ramchand Murmu was best known for his song performances and his literary poetic style, he also felt it necessary to devise a script that connected language and voice with spirits, rituals, and Santali graphic practice. Monj Dander Ank (Figure 2.2) not only challenged notions of writing as representation by focusing on the visual aspects of language (hence the term *ank*, drawing), but also expanded the traditional concept of *ol* by linking diagrams and etchings to a systematic structure of uttered sounds. Introducing his script, he explicitly writes, "By understanding the system of that language (*roṛ*) by which the god-sound (*ishrong*) emerges from the vocal chords as human sound (*aṛang*), this script (*ol*) was created" (Murmu 1997: 1). Thus the script created a rapprochement between the conception of writing brought by the missionaries and promoted by the colonial and postcolonial state, which viewed writing as a representation of language with the conception of ritual marking in which script allows humans to commune, and, indeed, embody spirits. In fact, the first and only full book Murmu wrote in the script was a book outlining a new philosophy on the relation between language and ritual practice, *Ishroṛ* (god-language).

In addition to connecting the script with ritual practice and Santali spirits, Murmu also incorporated the script into a larger history of graphic markings. He thus traced an alternative temporality of writing, one that started not with the missionary creation of Santali, but which brought in an old practice of marking into the new. For instance, he called his version of the script the "*nawa*

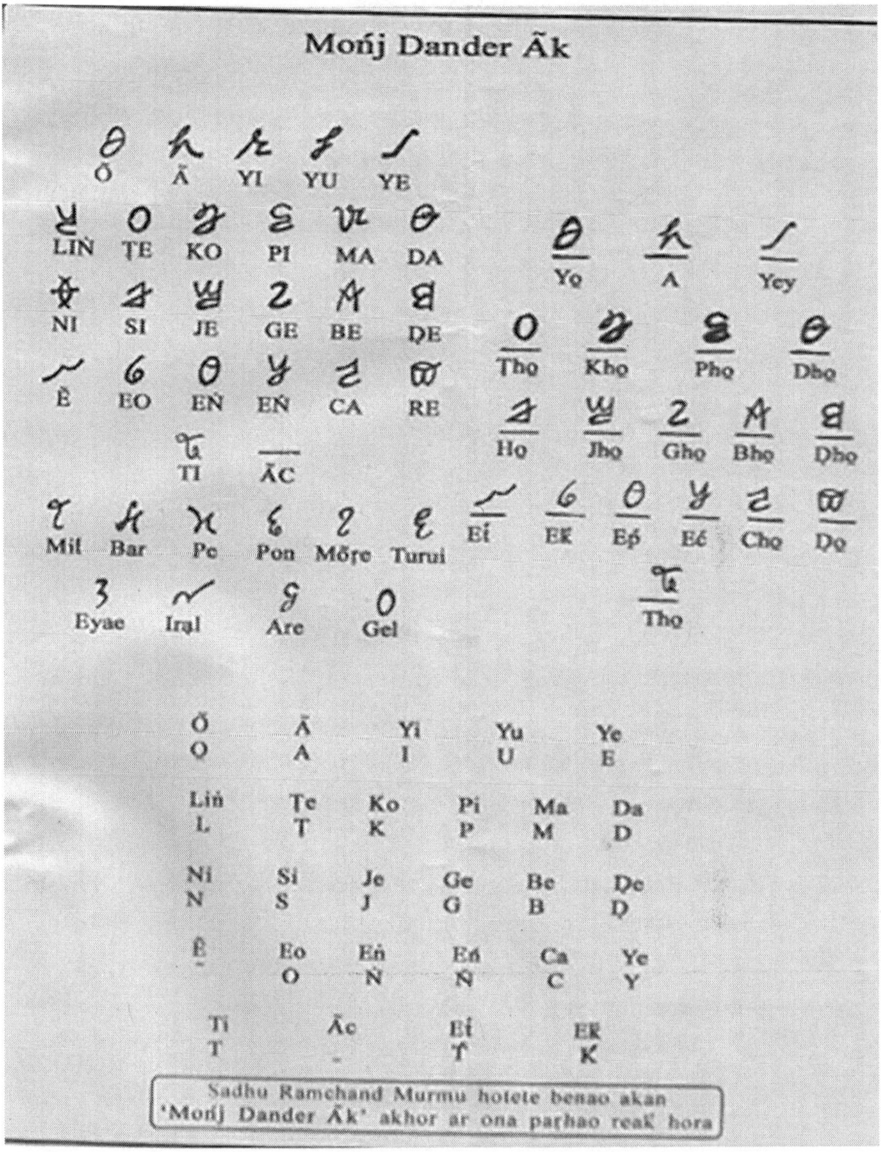

Figure 2.2 Monj Dander Ank from *Jugsirjol* magazine (Dilip Hembrom, editor, Kolkata), May 2010.

horop" (new script), viewing it as a continuation of primordial Santal marking practices, what he termed in general the *mare horop*(old script). In his book, *Ishroṛ*, he first presents these two scripts side by side, showing how the latter draws inspiration from the former and provides continuity for an alternative and autonomous literacy practice. In his later years, Murmu became especially interested in the script system discovered at Mohenjo Daro, which confirmed his belief that independent forms of writing existed outside and apart from either Indic or European writing traditions.

Unlike Ol-Chiki, the Monj Dander Ank script was never formally printed, nor was it extensively circulated. Yet for the followers of Ramchand Murmu, especially in southwest West Bengal, but also in other parts of the Santali-speaking areas, the script signifies a monumental and mystical achievement. It is still printed along with editions of his poetry collections and is thoroughly intertwined with Murmu's achievements as a master stylist of Santali as well as a tireless advocate for Jharkhand and Adivasi autonomy.

Ol-Chiki

The Ol-Chiki script, developed by Raghunath Murmu, is currently the most popular script used to write Santali and has served as the primary emblem for Santal movements of autonomy, especially in the southern areas, since Indian Independence. It was said to have been revealed to Raghunath Murmu in a dream by the *bongas* as early as 1925, but it was in the 1930s when Murmu, under the patronage of the royal family of Mayurbhanj (Odisha), developed printing blocks and a hand press for the script, which he displayed in the 1939 Mayurbhanj state exhibition (Lotz 2007: 246–7). In his Santali grammar (*Ronoṛ*), which he wrote in Ol-Chiki, Murmu argued that the new script could better account for Santal phonology, especially the glottalized consonants (*taput' aṛang*) and reduced vowels, than either the missionary-derived Roman script or existing Brahmi scripts such as Devanagari or Eastern Brahmi. Unlike existing Indic scripts (and like the Roman script) Ol-Chiki was alphabetic, with vowels and consonants represented independently. The script was also in part pictographic: each letter also had a word and image associated it with it. For instance, the Ol-Chiki letter for "a" is called *lo* "fire, flame" and iconizes a flame; the letter for "l" l is *ol* "writing" and iconizes a hand holding a pen (see Figure 2.3).

Despite the protests of the erstwhile kingdom's tribal majority, Mayurbhanj state eventually joined the Indian state of Odisha. The Santals in the region

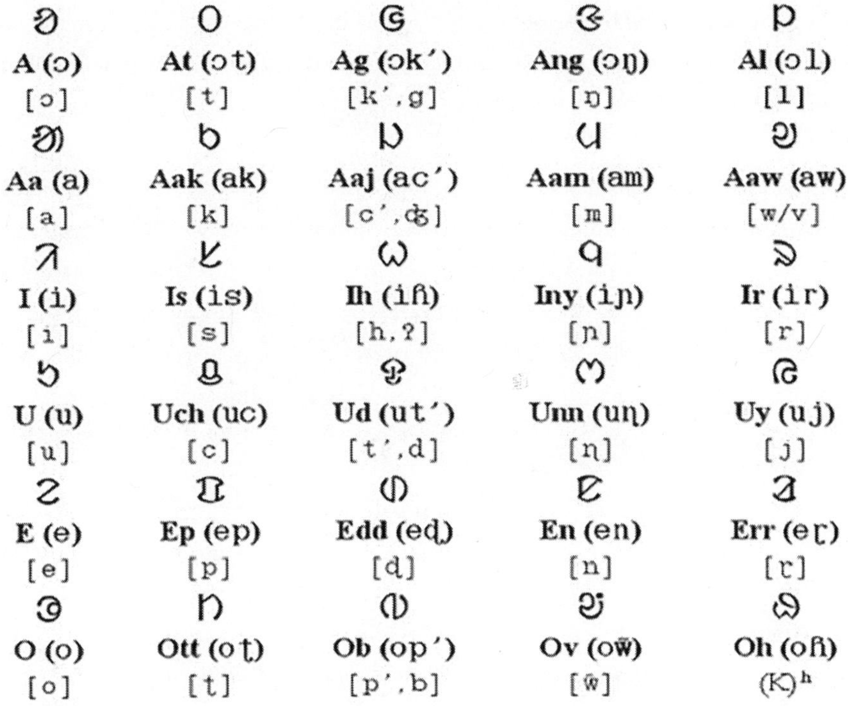

Figure 2.3 Ol-Chiki letters, from http://wesanthals.tripod.com/id45.html.

experienced an acute sense of defeat, but that defeat also created an aspiration among the region's Santals to connect with others across borders. Murmu and his script played a vital role in this movement, for, besides linguistic suitability, one of the main arguments for Ol-Chiki was that it could unite the dispersed Santali-speaking community, which, spread across different linguistic states, used different scripts to write in Santali. Murmu called scripts such as Devanagari, Eastern Brahmi, Utkal, or Roman (the dominant scripts used to write Santali) as *ol urum* or "dusty scripts" (Zide 1999) while Ol-Chiki, he argued, would instantiate a new territorial consciousness that sees the entire Santali-speaking area as graphically, and thus politically, united (Choksi 2014a). This notion forms an essential ideological element of the Ol-Chiki script, expressed in popular songs penned by Murmu where he asks his fellow Santals, "we are dispersed from Assam, down to Bihar, Bengal, and Odisha, our melodies and language are one, but why are not one, brothers, in our reading and writing?" (Murmu, n.d.).

Murmu expressly insisted on the "scientific" nature of his script and its suitability to represent not just Santali but all Austro-Asiatic languages (Lotz 2007). Yet, at the same time Murmu decided to make his script pictographic, arguing that the diagrammatic aspect of the script stemmed from Santals' experiences with nature, everyday communication, and history of marking (cf Mohapatra 1986). In fact, many of the proponents of Ol-Chiki argue that, unlike the Roman script, which makes scientific claims based on arbitrariness, Ol-Chiki is "scientific" precisely because it has an iconic relation to the ecologies Santals inhabit. For instance in an interview, the senior Ol-Chiki activist NB, who was also a friend of Raghunath Murmu's, said:

Interview with NB, June 24, 2011, Susuniya, West Bengal

Bhobhisho te mit'ṭen mit'ṭen roman do bang tahena, ona do bang tahena ona do bang tahena. Jehetu Santali bhasha renak' nijosho bhasha renak' nijosho lipi jehetu hui ena nonde ge hijuk' len. Ebong, Santali lipi jahan' hui ena noa do etak' kono lipi mit'tang jhaḍ do banuk'a . . . natural mit'tang prakriti ak' leka te. mit'tang ut', mushroom..mushroom mit'tang oka chitro kana chobi kana unka ge ona akhoṙ tet' kana ol chiki re.

[In the future, Roman will not be there. It will not be there. Since now the Santali language has its own script. And the Santali script, which now exists, no other script has its features. It is *natural*, it is like nature. For instance, [the letter] ut' (ᱩ) *mushroom. Mushroom*, it is a diagram, it is a picture, and at the same time it is also a letter in Ol-Chiki (emphasis added)].

Thus, while Ol-Chiki advocates extoll its suitability to represent the spoken Santali language, the script's scientific qualities, according to long-time propagators such as NB, do not lie in its graphemes' arbitrary relations with Santali phonemes. Rather, Ol-Chiki integrates communication with "nature" (*prakriti*), bridging the divide between diagram (*chitra*), picture (*chabi*), and phonetic unit (*akśar*). In addition, NB makes a point to discuss how the script creatively combines what he calls scientific and ritual worldviews, drawing on the diagrammatic qualities of the letter "ot" (ᱚ):

Interview with NB, June 24, 2011, Susuniya, West Bengal

NB: er pore ot soil tahole 'ot' renak' akriti chet' kana? Scientistko ko lại eda dembakriti mane sim bili leka apel bili leka nanarokom ko menkeda Pondit

> *Raghunath Murmu lại keda gol ge...mit'tang shishu gidrạ olok' paṛao lipi sonkrate jodi bujhao huyuk' khan earth renak' somporke tahole gota prithbi asen huyuk' a...ona do sombob bang kana...mit'tang gidrạ apel ho ạgu bang hui lena. mit'tang gidrạ sim bili ho ạgu bang hui lena. Nonḍe khon ge [...] keday prithob do burakar. biganik ko jahay ko lại keda. ac' do aroso 'ot' te lại keda, sohoj te...ar mit'tang huyuk'kana oka circle kana to?...santal ak' bonga buru huyuk' na bonga ko ak' jokhen khonḍ benao holong gol akaar—*
>
> [There there is "ot" ((O) soil [earth], then what is the form of this "ot"? Scientists say it is spherical, many say it is like a chicken's egg or an apple, Pandit Raghunath Murmu said that it is round . . . For instance, children, when they are learning to read and write a script, if they want to learn about the earth, then they have to describe the whole earth . . . that is not possible . . . [with Ol-Chiki] A child, one does not have to bring an apple or a chicken egg. From here, they know the form of the earth. What the scientists say, they know easily from this "ot" . . . and one thing is, it is a circle right? . . . Santals' rituals for the *bongas*, during the time when [one draws] the bongas' *khonḍ* it is a circle form.]

In this excerpt, NB describes a hypothetical example of children learning the scientific definition of the earth as a spherical object in school. Whereas, he suggests, by teaching in other scripts, one would have to describe the earth using a referential language, but with the use of Ol-Chiki, which has an iconic relation with nature, one can understand the scientific elements of the natural world without the mediation of spoken metalanguage. He then compares the knowledge of the scientist to the knowledge of the ritual expert, who diagrams the earth on the ground as a way encompassing nature and communing with the *bongas*. The script therefore offers a vision of Santal autonomy that is simultaneously grounded in the rationalist narratives of modernity ("science"), while also maintaining the connections with the landscape ("nature"), kin (*khonḍ*) and the spirits (*bongas*), which have long informed Santali practices of writing.

In addition to the iconic qualities of Ol-Chiki, which chart out a forward-looking path that combines nature, ritual, and scientific knowledge, Murmu also was keen to endow the script with an autonomous history as well. The story around the discovery of the Ol-Chiki script, in which Murmu received it as a gift from the *bongas* at the top of a hill nearby his native village of

Dahardi, exists alongside the narrative that the Ol-Chiki script, like Ramchand Murmu's Monj Dander Ank or other Santali scripts, derives from more ancient forms of writing. In fact, Murmu wrote a popular musical play called *Bidhu-Chandan*, which told the story of a hoary past in which two lovers find themselves on opposite sides in a war between two kingdoms and, cut off from all communication, use a secret code, Ol-Chiki, to send messages to one another. Indeed, the script could not be deciphered by anyone but the two lovers, and even then, it was not an ordinary language but combined Ol-Chiki like characters with ritual diagrams in order to, as Barbra Lotz notes, "read each other's feelings" (Lotz 2007: 254). In a series of thrilling scenes, the lovers are united, but then are separated again, both eventually dying and ascending into the heavens, taking the knowledge of the script with them (255).

The *bongas* Bidhu and Chandan are routinely invoked with the use of Ol-Chiki script in order to remind Santals that while this script was revealed as a product of divine agency, it also forms a link within a resolutely human historical practice. *Ol* is something that is both human and divine. It belongs to the past and present, recalling a history of war, displacement, and dispersal, and the striving for unity in the midst of hardships. For Murmu and other Santals throughout the Santali-speaking area, the immediate postindependence period was one such moment, in which the striving for unity and autonomy ("Jharkhand") amidst separation catalyzed Santals to rediscover *ol* as an autonomous practice.

Script-Making in Greater Jharkhand

Monj Dander Ank' and Ol-Chiki were only two of many scripts that emerged as the Jharkhand movement swept across eastern India. The flourishing of scripts suggests that despite the dominant projection of the goals of the movement as one for state power or legal rights to land and resources, in local villages throughout greater Jharkhand, among the Santals and other tribes such as the Ho, Sora, or Oraon, the ritual, temporal, and communicative dimensions of autonomy, materialized through script, had an equal importance for those communities involved in the struggle. Far and wide, those who were active or in some way influenced by the Jharkhand movement created new scripts, attempting to fuse their own conceptions of history, territory, and ritual with the larger goals of the movement (such as "unity"). What arose was neither a unitary vision of autonomy nor a unitary materialization of that vision but a multiplicity of locally produced scripts, which, when viewed together, created a mosaic of what Jharkhand meant for individuals and communities.

In the village where I conducted fieldwork (Jhilimili), I came across an elderly gentleman, Raghunath Hembrom, who created a script called *Hoṛ Ol* (Santal script). Hembrom was involved in the Jharkhand movement in his younger days and penned songs expressing his desire for autonomy. He recounted that when he was a young man in the village, never even in "his dreams" did he believe Santali would become a written language. However, after joining the Jharkhand struggle he, like Raghunath and Ramchand Murmu, also started to believe that Santali needed its own script. Like the others, he used an alphabetic system and endowed the script with temporality, saying that the script approximated the "mother sounds" (*ayu aṛang*) spoken at the times of the primordial ancestors of the Santals, Pilchu Haṛam and Pilchu Buṛi.

I came across another script created by an elderly man in Dumka, Jharkhand, called *Tonol Ol* (unity script), which again echoed the themes of unity among different and dispersed Santals. A third script I collected from Durgapur, West Bengal, was the *Hapṛam Hoṛ Ol Gentec'* (the script of the Santal ancestors). In terms of structure, each of these scripts were alphabetic (following the overall Roman model) but made special arrangements for the glottalized consonants and reduced vowels, preserving the linguistic distinction of Santali documented by the missionaries while also incorporating ritual and diagrammatic elements.[21] Though these scripts were hardly (if at all) circulated, their appearance and their similar structures and rationales displayed a growing consciousness among highly dispersed people that stressed linguistic and territorial autonomy and the assertion of an alternative history of literacy. In fact, it is in and through these politics of autonomy that the various practices of *ol* came together, recontextualized in different manifestations as "script."

While the Santals displayed an unusual propensity for script-making, and the Ol-Chiki script has become the most popular newly created script in eastern India, other Adivasi groups in Jharkhand created new scripts as well. Among the Ho, an Austro-Asiatic speaking group living mostly in Chotanagpur, a prophet named Lako Bodra invented the Varang Kshiti script. Like the Santali scripts, the individual letters in Varang Kshiti signify much more than spoken language; each letter has an iconic connection with a body part that is used to produce language. In addition, the script was initially devised for use in the ritualistic register of "Hieartic" Ho (*hayam*) as opposed to spoken Ho (*kaji*), and the primers made explicit connections between the letters and Ho spirits (*bonga*) (Zide 1999). Now, in independent Jharkhand, the Ho community is rallying around this script for its own demands of autonomy and, though at a smaller scale than Santali, education has now been instituted in Varang Kshiti.

Around the same time, the Austro-Asiatic-speaking Sora and the Dravidian-speaking Oraon also created their own scripts (*Sorang Sompeng* and *Tolong Siki*, respectively), both used to varying extents in Odisha and Jharkhand, respectively. In addition, new scripts among different Adivasi groups are still being created and disseminated. In Odisha for example, where the influence of Ol-Chiki looms large, Mundari-speaking groups have created a new script *Bana Hisir*, which according to one scholar, draws from Varang Kshiti and Ol-Chiki forms in its creation (Krylova 2016). Indeed other Adivasi groups outside Jharkhand, such as the Gond groups in Chhattisgarh and Adivasi communities in Telengana, are also creating their own scripts, showing that the phenomenon, though historically rooted in the Jharkhand movement, has now quickly spread to surrounding tribal regions.[22] The persistence of script-making in the region shows how script continues to mediate drives for autonomy for different sections within India and around the world.[23]

The Performance of *Ol* at the Jharkhand Periphery

Having first encountered Santali in the city of Kolkata, far away from the Santali-speaking rural areas of southwest West Bengal, I was led to believe that Ol-Chiki was a small phenomenon, embraced by a few committed activists. However, as I entered rural southwest West Bengal, I saw that it was embraced openly, and though proficiency in the script remained low, it was immensely popular, particularly among the younger generations. The southwest region of West Bengal, which had a long history of Jharkhand-related activism, also boasted of a burgeoning Santali literary scene. Magazines, newspapers, and

Santali-language material proliferated in villages, though the language was not taught in schools at the time. However, most of this material was written in the Eastern Brahmi script, the same script used to write Bengali. For the older generation, this script was the most practical, as one went to school learning Bengali; it was also easy to print, making Santali-language material widely accessible to the reading public.

The Santali literary movement was linked to Jharkhand-related activism, and although all writers did not politically support the various Jharkhand parties (which are still active in West Bengal), many of them shared deeply held beliefs in autonomy. At that time, Santali literary activity, and the ideas of autonomy that underlie it, was, as many older generation Santali-language editors told me time and again, about the "language" and not about the "script." However, in 1992, Salkhan Murmu of the Jharkhand Disom Party (Odisha) inaugurated the "Bhasha Morcha" (language movement) in West Bengal, which vocally and explicitly wedded Jharkhandi demands of autonomy with the Ol-Chiki script. Following the creation of Jharkhand state in 2000, and the subsequent exclusion of the Santali-majority districts in West Bengal, a new wave of Ol-Chiki activism affected not only the younger generation of West Bengal but also the battle-worn Jharkhand activists.

During my field research, I met a senior Santali writer GPS in a nearby village who was nearing 70 years of age. Throughout his life, he had fought tirelessly for Jharkhand. Even now, long after the Jharkhand state was created and the desire for the state has all but dissipated among the Adivasis of southwest West Bengal, he continues to attend Jharkhand rallies. He is also a very influential writer, having published several Santali-language books (in the Eastern Brahmi script) and writing regular columns in the regional newspapers. When I met him, we discussed how he believed that the teaching of Ol-Chiki script could lead to the creation of autonomous institutions and lead to greater success for Santali students within West Bengal:

Interview with GPS, Bandowan Purulia

GPS: yeah and regarding literacy. When will the government want to do anything? When will it start primary schools? It won't start primary schools. We will start primary schools. We will teach the children.

N (Nishaant, the author): On one's own?

GPS: On one's own . . . We will teach them Santali in Ol-Chiki. We will put them in competition in the government or whichever competition, our [children] will succeed . . . yeah they will pass their exams . . . they will get jobs . . . we will do it like that . . .I am not saying we should fight with weapons . . . but this is a fight too.

One of the major aims of the Jharkhand movement was to transform the systems of governance so Adivasis could shape state policy in order to guarantee their autonomy. Yet in the wake of the movement's failure in West Bengal, GPS still believes that this transformation is possible, in part through the creation of autonomous institutions that teach in Santali through the Ol-Chiki script. GPS, who himself was a primary schoolteacher who taught students Bengali, argues that Santali, not Bengali or English, and more specifically Santali taught in Ol-Chiki script, will ensure "success" for Santal youth. This is because GPS does not measure success in terms of practicality, since it is obvious that knowledge of English or, at the minimum, Bengali is necessary for employment and financial advancement in the current situation. Rather, GPS conceives "success" on a metric of autonomy, in which the Santali language and Ol-Chiki are compared to "weapons" that will create autonomous institutions and ideas of success within the existing territory of West Bengal, fulfilling the aims of the Jharkhand movement.

In present-day West Bengal, the explicit demands for a separate Jharkhand state, despite the persistence of people like GPS, have subsided. While there are several Jharkhand parties active in West Bengal, they have largely shied away from secessionist demands, instead emphasizing on "*swashashon*" (autonomy). Even though the movement, insofar as it sought to guarantee a separate state, was a failure, supporters and the younger generation now envision autonomy, in part through the circulation and institutionalization of Ol-Chiki script. This is noted by both supporters of Ol-Chiki, such as GPS, as well as by those who have not embraced the script in equal measure. For instance, one of my close mentors, a well-known Santali writer also from the same region, has always maintained an ambivalent stance toward Ol-Chiki. He writes Santali-language short stories and plays in the Eastern Brahmi script and has kept a distance from ASECA and Ol-Chiki activism, preferring to promote "Santali literature" against what he feels are the divisive politics of script. However, he acknowledged the recent decision of the West Bengal government to implement Ol-Chiki in schools and colleges and feels that the enthusiasm that this has generated among Santali-speaking youth contains the seeds for a new vision of political and cultural autonomy. If Santals are allowed to learn primarily in Ol-Chiki as part of their first language education, he told me, and become less competent in the Eastern Brahmi script and written Bengali, then they will start to demand administrative positions use Santali and Ol-Chiki. In this way, he portends the state will either have to offer Santals greater administrative and political autonomy within the borders of West Bengal (by creating Ol-Chiki-specific administrative roles), or agitations for a separate state will take hold again as the younger, educated Santali speakers start to see the state as intentionally curtailing the functional elaboration of Santali and Ol-Chiki.

Every year on June 30, the states of West Bengal and Jharkhand celebrate *Hul maha* (Hul day) marking the anniversary of the 1855 Santal rebellion. During my first year of field research, I was invited by an organization to attend a *padayatra* (walking journey) in the Santal Parganas in Jharkhand, sponsored by Jharkhand-based cultural activist groups, missionary organizations, and also promoted by the Jharkhand government. There we would start at the huge statue of Sidhu and Kanhu at the main square in Dumka city, the former capital of the Santal Parganas, and wind our way through the scattered villages, forests, and mountains until we reached Bognadih, the small village where Sidhu and Kanhu lived and where the Hul began. There the Jharkhand government had commissioned a large gold-plated statue of the bow-and-arrow-wielding Sidhu and Kanhu, celebrating their leadership and their historical role in the founding of the Jharkhand state.

As I went to officially celebrate the Hul in Jharkhand, I requested that my research assistant record some local celebrations near his home village in southwest West Bengal. He attended a small celebration in a nearby village in which people gathered to commemorate the Hul through songs and dances and recorded it. Later as I heard the recordings, some of which were recounting the story of Sidhu and Kanhu, while others were popular songs in the local repertoire, the last one on the tape caught my attention. It was a song about Raghunath Murmu and the discovery of Ol-Chiki script, one that I had heard also sung during my time in Murmu's village in Odisha:

> *Bidu-Chandan, onol bonga, jiwi janwar bir bonga, seba seba-tem konka len seba seba-tem konka len bir-buru-rem tahëy kan. kul bana ora-rem tahëy kan. ut', putkạ aṛak', jom-tem tahëy kaan. ut', putkạ aṛak', jom-tem tahëy kan. abowak' ol boyha abowak', roṛ. abowak', ol boyha abowak' roṛ. buru ḍhiri uḍuk' rem ṇ'am keda. buru ḍhiri uḍuk' rem n'am keda...pạrsi baha teley baha hisit' mey. enec' sereń teley lasarhet' [me], enec'-sereń teley lasarhet'. disom hoṛ teley atang mey. [p]arsi baha teley baha hisit mey. enec'-sereń teley lasarhed mey. enec'-sereń teley lasarhet' mey.[p]arsi khatir ja gomkey.*
>
> [Bidhu-Chandan, the prose-form bonga, the animal, and the forest bongas, you remained silent, you stayed in the forest, in the homes of wolves and bears, you stayed only eating mushrooms and leafy vegetables. Our writing (ol), my brothers, our speech/language (roḍ), our writing (ol) my brothers, our speech/language (roṛ). You received it from on a mountain rock. You received it, from on a mountain rock . . . we salute you with language-flowers, we welcome you with song-dance [enec'-sereṅ], receive our [salutations], the people of this country's, for the sake of language, [our] teacher].

The song discusses Murmu's self-exile in the forest, his communing with the various *bongas*, and his penance and sacrifice that eventually led to the revelation of Ol-Chiki script on a stone tucked away on the Kapi hill just outside his village. The script brought together language (*roṛ*) and writing (*ol*), and it was "sharpened" through oral and embodied performance (*sereń-enec,*' "song-dance"), inspiring the people of the country (*disom hoṛ*). At the end of the performance, as the performers themselves "received" Raghunath Murmu and the Ol-Chiki script into their small village on the margins of Jharkhand state, they were possessed by spirits and the recording went into *rum* (trance) speech.

I at first thought it peculiar that as I was away attending the official celebration of the Hul marking the struggle for Jharkhand, the place where I lived, the place that never realized its aspirations to join the Jharkhand state yet continues the fight for autonomy, celebrating the Hul by invoking Raghunath Murmu and the Ol-Chiki script. However, as I have suggested here, script carries a potentiality for autonomy that is important for both the historical imagination of insurrection as well as for contemporary struggles at the margins of Jharkhand state. Consequently, it should be no surprise that just as much as the image of the bow-and-arrow-wielding warrior, in this village, the script was also embraced as a "weapon" to continue the work of Sidhu and Kanhu as well as Raghunath Murmu. Carrying meanings beyond its modality as a representation of the Santali language, the script asserted new forms of temporality, projecting both an autonomous future and past in the unfolding present, while also carving out domains for autonomous practice within the spaces of the everyday, such as the marketplace at the center of villages, educational institutions, and in print and digital media. It is now to these spaces that we will turn in the following chapters.

3

Scaling Multiscriptality in a Village Market

Nestled in the forests between two rivers, surrounded by hills, Jhilimili is a small, picturesque village located at the spot where Bankura, Purulia, and West Midnapur, the three main districts of the Adivasi-dominated Jungle Mahals region of West Bengal, meet, around thirty kilometers from the Jharkhand border. Unlike the surrounding hamlets, which are inhabited predominately by tight-knit Adivasi communities and organized around subsistence agriculture, Jhilimili is a market village, or bazaar, littered with shops, food stands, and administrative offices, with a constant inflow and outflow of people. It bustles in the morning, when people arrive from their distant hamlets to buy their vegetables, eat breakfast, and go to the bank, local clinic, panchayat (village council) office, or catch the morning long-distance buses. A steady stream of schoolchildren in red-and-white uniforms flow through the market streets on their way to the local high school. By afternoon, Jhilimili is silent, as the hot sun pounds down on the streets and the shop doors are shuttered; only the occasional dog could be seen lying lazily on the road. Around sunset, however, the steel gates of the shops fling open, and the crowds start pouring in again, the streets fill with people, the sounds of Bengali, Santali, and sometimes Hindi carry through the air, as people chat, eat steaming hot samosas, and drink tea.

Through my contacts in Calcutta, three hundred kilometers away, I arrived in Jhilimili in 2009, eventually settling there to conduct my field research. Located in a region with a long history of involvement in the Jharkhand struggle, the surrounding hamlets are home to a dense network of cultural and political activists and Santali-language writers. Jhilimili is also the base of the Jharkhand Anushilan Party, one of the region's active Jharkhand political parties, and the dominant party in the local village council for the past decade. This has led to a political environment in which struggles around cultural and regional autonomy have flourished even under the otherwise highly regimented and centralizing political structure of West Bengal state, which had been ruled by the Communist Party for over thirty years. In addition, by the time I arrived, Jhilimili was also at the center of an ongoing Maoist insurgency, located next to a large tract of forest that formed a base for insurgent operations. The CRPF, the paramilitary security force of the Indian state, had set up a huge camp between the upper and lower markets of Jhilimili, manned twenty-four hours by armed police with shoot at sight orders. Every month Maoists would call for a strike in which the whole market shut down, sometimes for two or three days at a time, choking the village off from transportation and halting all commerce.

As historian Anand Yang has noted, village markets like Jhilimili have traditionally acted as a "container and crucible of solidarities as well as of antagonisms and contradictions of a particular locality" (Yang 1998:16). Unlike in caste-segregated residential hamlets, markets are spaces where different caste groups mingle, trade goods and services, and also actively contest for control over local resources. In Jhilimili though caste Hindus are a minority compared to the Santals, many Santals view the bazaar as a caste Hindu-dominated space. Yet, as Yang contends, bazaars are dynamic places, where life and politics, though taking place on the streets and on the walls of a particular place, acquire scalar dimensions, the place where "extracommunity and supracommunity connections and institutions" are most visible (Yang 1998: 16). For Santals, who have historically felt marginalized from the bazaar space, and whose language is subordinated in the market's daily commercial and administrative transactions, one of the primary ways to create spaces of autonomy within the bazaar is through the manipulation of different scripts. The presence of Ol-Chiki on the bazaar's surfaces, in combination with the Roman and Eastern Brahmi scripts, allows the Santali speakers to enact a multiscalar project of autonomy that engages with the region of southwest West Bengal, the greater Jharkhand area, and India as a whole. In employing these graphic repertoires, Santali cultural associations, Jharkhand political parties, and Santali-language media networks project Jhilimili not as a marginal location within the state of West Bengal but as part of a spatial network that stretches across eastern India, yet simultaneously remaining grounded in the village-based life of its denizens. Through this, as well as caste Hindus and the state's incorporation of Santali into their own respective scalar projects, the bazaar's surfaces become a dialogic space where different notions of autonomy, caste hierarchy, and territoriality are contested and graphic politics proliferates.

Disjuncture and the Scalar Project of Autonomy

While Yang rightly points to the importance of village markets in challenging the colonial stereotypes of the "self-sustaining" village unit, the Santals themselves have traditionally viewed their village hamlets (*ato*) as autonomous, self-governing spaces, while the markets (*bajar*) are the stronghold of upper castes and sources of exploitation and expropriation. The opposition between the hamlet and the market has informed the ways the Santals recount their own history as a once self-dependent people who were thrown into debt and poverty as the result of their entry into market relations. Around 1920, Sagram Murmu, a member of the Santal mission and collaborator of the Norwegian missionary P. O. Bodding wrote:

> In the ancient times, there was no deko caste, only we Hoŗ people lived here and all the work we did together on our own [kicric'] oil turmeric spices all of these [we produced] by farming or from the trees . . . then these deko entered our Hoŗ lands doing the salt trade and what did they do they did bad things amongst our Hoŗ people . . . like that they made Hoŗ people weak and they went to buy much salt and oil and they [Deko] would give it on credit . . . then they began stores that were selling salt and oil and they began to exert great power [jor harberko] . . . the Deko began ruling this country.[1]

Murmu's account, which begins with the autonomy (*kicric'* "our own") of Santals within their own village communities, charts a trajectory familiar to many Santals I interacted with in Jhilimili nearly a century later: the era of upper-caste (*deko*) exploitation and Santal debt bondage began with the market and establishments of bazaars in Santali-speaking areas.

According to accounts from resident Santals, the area around Jhilimili was all forest, in which mainly the Santals cultivated. They lived in scattered hamlets. Upper castes, such as Utkal Brahmins, who trace their origins to Odisha, and families of Vaishnav mendicants (known as "Das"), subsequently moved in and were given land grants by the local landowners. After acquiring these large tracts of land, they set up shops in what was to become the Jhilimili market. Basic commodities such as salt and oil started to be sold there, and Adivasis, barred from negotiating forest rights by colonial-era property laws, entered into a dependent relationship with the market to purchase basic goods.

In fact, despite many Santals living and working in the bazaar and many upper castes living in the surrounding hamlets, I often heard Santals refer to themselves as *ato-ren hoṛ* (village people, Santals) and to the upper castes such as Brahmins or Vaishnavs as *bajar-ren jạti* (market castes). This distinction indexed the perceived caste character of the market. For instance, in the market, behavioral norms and expectations differed from that of within Santal hamlets. In the market, men and women (especially those who were unmarried) rarely interacted except in the context of service encounters, while in the Santal villages or village fairs, interaction, even of the romantic sort, was visible and permitted. In addition, Santal spirits such as *pạurạ* (mahua-flower wine) or *hạnḍi* (rice beer) were not openly available in the market, nor were beef or pork, foods prohibited by upper castes but consumed by Santals. Foods sanctioned by upper castes such as English liquor, chicken, and fish, however, were freely available.

The caste character of the bazaar and the subordination of Santali within the bazaar space also inflected debates around language and script. On the one hand, Santals in Jhilimili understood their language had attained state, national, and international-level recognition, having been included in the list of official languages (Eighth Schedule) to Indian Constitution in 2003. Yet on the other hand, the local upper castes of Jhilimili, and throughout the Santali-speaking areas of West Bengal, Odisha and Jharkhand, refused to consider it even a language, often referring to Santali as *ṭhar*, or a type of sign language or grunt language attributed to deaf, mute, or other speakers with articulatory disabilities.[2] The younger generation of upper castes referred to the language simply as "Adivasi," considering it as a caste-based dialect. In Kolkata, or other metropolitan centers, I was surprised to find people routinely referring to Santali as a rural "dialect" of Bengali, enforced by media representations of Santals speaking in the rustic Bengali variety of the Jangal Mahals, known as "Jharkhandi" Bangla.[3]

The evaluation of Santali as both a subordinate, caste-delimited dialect and as a national language of India enact two distinct what anthropologists E. Summerson Carr and Michael Lempert have recently called "scalar projects" (Carr and Lempert 2016: 10). "Scalar project" implies an idea of "scale" not as a part of a set of already given social-cartographic coordinates (such as a presumed "local," "regional," or "national" scale), but rather a social practice of "scale-making," the result of how "contextual boundaries are discursively drawn by social actors who differentiate one place, time, social position, or experience from another" (Carr and Lempert 2016) This conception of "scale" as a pragmatic category developed out of previous sociolinguistic studies of linguistic differentiation in highly diverse and mobile multilingual and multigraphic contexts, in which social actors' evaluations of linguistic varieties are shaped by conceptions of translocal community, globalized space, and histories of migration,[4] as well as politically engaged social geography that shifted the focus to the "production of scale" as a form of situated "socio-spatial" organization (McCarthy 2005: 733–8).

In minority and indigenous language communities, where linguistic recognition and resources for language maintenance and revitalization are an issue, the various scalar projects enacted by the government and differently positioned members of the community can lead to what Barbra Meek has called, in her study of language revitalization in northwestern Canada, "sociolinguistic disjuncture" (Meek 2010). In this framework, competing perceptions of language result in "awareness" effects especially among the minority language users, of the misalignments between practice and ideology (Meek 2016, Choksi and Meek 2016). This awareness anchors scalar projects not only in the distribution of linguistic or graphic varieties but also within the interactive contexts in which these varieties are deployed and the social position of the participants involved. This was evident in Jhilimili, where Santals were keenly aware of both the status of their language, which was recognized by the state, and the subordination of that same language within spaces such as the bazaar, where local caste relations ensure the erasure of Santali within institutions and in the everyday practices of market exchange.

This awareness sometimes manifests itself in a dramatic form, such as during the celebrations of the Santal Hul in 2011, when a Santali-language play written by a Jhilimili-area playwright, was staged in one of the drama competitions.[5] In the play, Santal schoolchildren fall asleep as they read an article about Santali language being used internationally.[6] In their dreams, there appears a married couple, "Constitution" (*sombidhan*) and the "Santali language" (*pạrsi*). The marriage is happy until the character "*prashasan*" ('administration' i.e. the Diku governmental administration) barges into their house in order to harass them. In order to protect their household, they hire a guard, "the Law" (*ain*), but the guard eventually fails in its duty and the *prashasan* eventually burns their house to the ground. The characters manage to escape into the forest and see their village burning, standing on a hillside. Eventually a group of Santal fighters join them with their bows and arrows, and they return to recapture the village by fighting and subdue *prashasan* and its Diku entourage.

When I asked the playwright about this play, he told me it was inspired by the fact that even though Santali was being discussed "internationally" (i.e., the subject of study in foreign universities), and it had achieved "national" recognition, why was it not taught in primary schools, or spoken in banks or government offices in the village market? It was, of course, as the play suggested, due to the Diku administration, the apparatus of governance and the upper-caste controlled institutions, which prevented the fruitful union between the "Constitution" and the "Santal language" by ignoring the Santali language's legal status. The play thus presents two competing scalar projects: one in which Santali is recognized according to its status as an official language both at the state and national level and another in which Santali is relegated as a subordinate dialect, suppressed by the state administration. The awareness of the disjuncture between these projects opens up the space where control over language and territory, a politics of autonomy, can be asserted, epitomized by the play's finale, when like Sidhu and Kanhu, the bow-and-arrow-wielding Santals enter the village to drive out the Diku administration and restore the Santali language to its rightful place guaranteed by the law and the constitution.

The same disjuncture arose regarding the failure to adequately implement Ol-Chiki script in any government institution. For instance, a Jhilimili-area resident (who worked in Calcutta) wrote a Bengali-language pamphlet called *Paschimbongo sorkar olchiki-ke aini svikriti dey ni* (West Bengal government has not given legal recognition to Ol-Chiki), which outlined how, in 1976, the state of West Bengal recognized Santali language officially with Ol-Chiki script as its official script. However, due to dereliction of duty from the Diku administration as well as village politics, the state continued to promote the use of different scripts (such as the Eastern Brahmi script) to write Santali and did not sufficiently direct resources for the promotion of the Ol-Chiki script. The pamphlet directed village residents to organize and fight for the implementation of the script, and the writer enrolled village youth to distribute the pamphlet out in the market. Again the aim was to bring the scalar projection of the "law" in which Santali is considered an "official" language of the state and nation into line with the reality of the "local" everyday life, in which the exclusion of Santali in the institutions of the bazaar paralleled Santals' own perceived alienation from the market space more broadly.

Landscaping Autonomy in the Jhilimili Market

The combination of graphic and spatial politics renders what sociolinguists have called the "linguistic landscape" (Gorter 2006, Shohamy and Gorter 2008, Jaworksi and Thurlow 2010) of Jhilimili market one of the prime sites for the enactment of the scalar project of autonomy. As Jan Blommaert has written in his study of the city of Antwerp, the linguistically inscribed graphic surfaces on which linguistic codes and scripts were mixed and ordered in a diverse array form a "complex and multiscalar order" that serves as an ethnographic "diagnostic of social, cultural, and political structures" (Blommaert 2014: 112–13). In Jhilimili, where only two major languages, Bengali and Santali, are spoken, four scripts (Eastern Brahmi, Ol-Chiki, Roman, and Devanagari) are present (see Table 3.1). These scripts, along with the participant structure, provide a semiotic scaffolding for a wide range of multiscalar orderings.

Each of the scripts are stereotypically aligned with certain languages, for instance English with Roman, Eastern Brahmi with Bengali, Devanagari with Hindi, and Ol-Chiki with Santali, respectively. However, in practice scripts often variably align with several languages, and in the Jhilimili bazaar, one finds each language (Bengali, English, Santali) written in multiple scripts, with code-mixing frequently occurring. In Figure 3.1, for example, at the top right corner is a sign in Eastern Brahmi script for *Ipil* (Santali, "star") *Electronics*,

Table 3.1 Codes and scripts within Jhilimili (in variable alignment with one another)

English	Roman
Bengali	বাংলা (Eastern Brahmi)
Hindi	देवनागरी (Devanagari)
Santali	ᱚᱞ ᱪᱤᱠᱤ (Ol-Chiki)

Figure 3.1 Entering Jhilimili bazaar from the south road, with signs mixed in English, Santali, and Bengali in Eastern Brahmi script and Roman script. Photo by author.

with no Bengali at all in the sign name. Due to the frequency of this type of code-mixing in Jhilimili and India more generally, *script,* the relatively more regimented graphic dimension of language rather than *code,* or the referential dimension of language, comes to be seen as iconic[7] of language as a whole, and thus subject to scalar evaluations by social actors. For instance, in Chaise Ladousa's study of school advertisements in the central Indian town of Varanasi, Devanagari advertisements, even when using English words, were seen by Varanasi residents to be associated with spatial associations of a rural "periphery" while Roman script advertisements, though often employing Hindi words, came to be associated with the metropolitan "center" (Ladousa 2002). In Jhilimili, the Jharkhand movement, and the introduction of Ol-Chiki, have rendered scripts' associations with different scalar ideologies politically charged, particularly since Santali was written in Eastern Brahmi, Roman, and Ol-Chiki scripts sometimes simultaneously.

Scaling the Nation in the Jhilimili Bazaar

One of the major themes of the play cited above was the institutional neglect of Santali despite its constitutional recognition. As Part XVII of the Indian Constitution says, "The official language of the Union should be Hindi in the Devanagari script," with a provision made for the use of English "for all official purposes of the Union."[8] Every state, however, has the right to enact its own official language(s), and these languages are recognized under the Constitution's Eighth Schedule provision, so they are also considered "national" languages, and national institutions are constitutionally directed to recognize these languages in their operation at the regional level. Both Santali and Bengali are listed under the Eighth Schedule to the Constitution, and both are also official languages of the state of West Bengal.

As such, the "official" institutions of the union, such as the nationalized bank and post office, in most parts of India adhere to a "three-language formula," in which business must be transacted in either English, Hindi, or the regional language, which in the case of West Bengal, is Bengali.[9] This state of affairs is most visibly rendered through graphic variation. The Punjab National Bank (Figure 3.2), Jhilimili's only bank, has its English name rendered in three different scripts: Eastern Brahmi, Devanagari, and Roman. In this way, the board projects itself as a "national" institution, not through linguistic variation, nor through the language of its operation (which is Bengali) but in the graphic variation on its signboard, in which Hindi and English, official languages of the "Union" exist alongside Bengali, the language of the state of West Bengal. The same goes for the "Post Office" (Figure 3.3) which the Hindi and Bengali versions (*dākghar/dākghɔr*) are written in the Devanagari and Eastern Brahmi scripts respectively.

The signboards' projection of the "national," comprised of two scripts, Devanagari and Roman, and the "regional" script of Eastern Brahmi, does not display any reference to Santali, or Ol-Chiki script, despite Santali's constitutional recognition.[10] Consequently, for the denizens of the bazaar, both caste Hindus and the Santals, the erasure of Santali from government

Figure 3.2 A sign board in which "Punjab National Bank" is written in, from left to right, Eastern Brahmi, Devanagari, and Roman scripts. Photo by author.

Figure 3.3 A sign board in which "Post Office" is written in Devanagari, Eastern Brahmi, and Roman scripts. Photo by author.

Table 3.2 Interscalar assemblages in Jhilimili bazaar

Script	Associated code (Iconic)	Spatial associations (scalar)
A. "Three-language formula" in Jhilimili bazaar (bank, post office, etc.)		
Devanagari (देवनागरी)	Hindi	Indian Union (de jure official)
Roman	English	Indian Union/International (de facto official)
Eastern Brahmi (বাংলা)	Bengali	State of West Bengal, India (de jure official)
[Ol-Chiki] (ᱚᱞ ᱪᱤᱠᱤ)	[Santali]	["Local," de jure official, unrecognized]
B. Santali scalar project		
Ol-Chiki	Santali	Trans-regional autonomy, Santali-speaking areas across eastern India
Roman	Santali/English	Indian Union/International
Eastern Brahmi	Santali/Bengali	Regional autonomy, village Jharkhand politics

signs such as those of the bank and post office perpetuates an everyday status quo (see Table 3.2). For caste Hindus, it reinforces a scalar hierarchy in which the language they identify with, Bengali, is the official regional variety of both the state and the administration, and Hindi and English are recognized as official nonregional varieties ("national" languages). For Santals, on the other hand, who scale both their language and the Ol-Chiki script as both regional (officially "recognized" by the state of West Bengal) and national (constitutional recognition), the erasure reinforces the perception of the bazaar as a Diku space, and constitutes a scalar disjuncture between the "local" (everyday) and the "national" (Constitution, law). Yet, it is the awareness of this disjuncture that creates possibilities for carving out alternative spaces of autonomy through the deployment of multiscriptal repertoires.

In addition to being to the home of the "official" state bodies, such as the bank, post office, school, and the panchayat (village council), Jhilimili bazaar was also the central node for what Santals called their "social administration." Unlike in Jharkhand state, which incorporates these customary governing structures into law through the colonial-era Santal Pargana and Chota Nagpur Tenancy Acts,[11] this administration is not officially recognized by the government of West Bengal. Yet Santals in Jhilimili still maintain this administration, in which five-man village councils headed by a *majhi* (headman) are organized in geographical units called *disom* ("countries"), with each *disom* having an elected head, or *pargana*, who is responsible for convening meetings and discussions with the various village headmen and five-man councils. The mapping of this social geography extends across administrative boundaries, spanning the different regions of eastern South Asia where Santals reside, and formed the basis for the imagination of the territory of Jharkhand before the creation of the Jharkhand state. Within this geography, Jhilimili serves as the administrative center for the Marang Tung *disom* (Big Tung Country), and shortly after my initial fieldwork period, the *majhi mạḍwa*, or headman council, set up an office where the *pargana* would organize monthly meetings (Figure 3.3). Consequently, even though the bazaar itself was conceived of as a Diku space, the central location and administrative importance in the lives of Santals living in nearby villages rendered the market as a node in the larger network of Santal-specific village governance as well as a contested administrative location.

The sign on surface (Figure 3.4) also displays three separate scripts (Ol-Chiki, Roman, and Eastern Brahmi), although the name of the office is rendered all in Santali language. This contrasts with the three-language formula on the

Figure 3.4 The Marang Tung Country Pargana office, Jhilimili. (from top to bottom, Ol-Chiki, Roman, and Eastern Brahmi scripts). Photo by author.

signs of institutions such as the bank or post office, where script distinction iconizes linguistic distinction, that is, the Roman, Devanagari, and Eastern Brahmi script iconize the English, Hindi, and Bengali languages respectively, all of which are used to organize the scalar differentiation of administrative business within these organizations. Yet in Figure 3.4, three scripts (Ol-Chiki, Roman, and Eastern Brahmi) are united in iconizing a single code, Santali, which becomes associated within the sociopolitical territory of the Santali *disom* that both lies within but also transcends the boundaries of the West Bengal state.

In mirroring the "three-language formula," the signboard constitutes what Carr and Lempert have called an "interscalar assemblage" or a "configuration of scalar effects that exceeds any one scalar distinction within it" (Carr and Lempert 2016:14).[12] Drawing on the discourse of nation/region to represent a specific Santali political geography, the sign projects an alternative scalar order, constituting a differentiated territory that is autonomous from the caste-Hindu (*diku*) administration. In this presentation, the larger scale projection is created through the combination of Ol-Chiki and Roman, where Ol-Chiki functions, like the Devanagari script on banks and post offices, as a trans-regional script that unites the Santali-speaking population across borders, hearkening back to its origins as part of the Jharkhand movement. Roman, being a script that is "national" yet belongs to no state or ethnicity, reinforces this scalar projection, while Eastern Brahmi, which is the most commonly used script to write Santali in West Bengal, and is the script in which the *pargana* office conducts its business, speaks to the specific location of the office within Jhilimili bazaar, as well as to projects of autonomy at a regional level, such as Jharkhand party politics, which will be discussed later.

Table 3.2 outlines the interscalar assemblages present in Figures 3.2, 3.3, and 3.4, and which also serve as what Carr and Lempert (2016) have called a "scaffolding" (13) upon which linkages are made between the landscape and scalar projects. Part A of the table outlines the "three-language formula" present on institutions such as banks and post offices, and the scalar associations with the scripts that are salient for Jhilimili residents as well as part of institutional practice and legal decree. The omission of Santali from this particular assemblage coincides with the caste-Hindu scaling of Santali as a local, or subregional, caste-delimited dialect. The Santali scalar project, on the other hand, present in signs such as the one adorning the *pargana* office, complicate the administrative mappings between script, language, and territory in part A. In this assemblage, Santali operates at a trans-regional (Ol-Chiki), national/international (Roman), and regional scale (Eastern Brahmi). The graphic assemblage of the signboard enacts an alternative political geography, which casts the Jhilimili bazaar space as both politically autonomous from the state administration as well as asserts Santal claims over space that are not simply restricted to the scale of the local.

The association of Ol-Chiki/Roman with a trans-regional Santali consciousness can be seen in other signs, banners, and posters in Jhilimili bazaar. For instance, certain Santal-specific institutions that claim to be "All-India" but have branches or singular offices in Jhilimili often use the Ol-Chiki/English combination, such as the advertisement for a private Santali-language school in Figure 3.5 in which the header reads in English, but in Ol-Chiki (phonetically spelling out the English) and Roman, "All-India Santali Education Council." The rest of the relevant information outlining information about the school and admission procedures is in Bengali/Eastern Brahmi script. Thus even though the poster does not contain any actual Santali language, the use of the Ol-Chiki/Roman combination is enough to project the "All-India" scale of the institution through which the local private school connects to a broad, trans-regional movement that goes beyond the borders of West Bengal, or even eastern India. This same format is also followed by local branches of "All-India" organizations when they held programs in or around Jhilimili bazaar. For instance, the Bharat Jakat Santarh Pạṭuạ Gaonta (The All India Santal Students Organization), which had been quite active in the Jharkhand movement, and now focused on the fight for Santali-language instruction in schools and colleges in Odisha, West Bengal, and Jharkhand, had a local branch, which held functions in the bazaar from time to time. Their banners were in Ol-Chiki and Roman script (Figure 3.6), once again projecting an alternative scalar projection that connected Santali-language activism within Jhilimili and the surrounding areas with national ("All-India") politics.

In addition to posters and banners for All-India Santali organizations, the scalar project constituted by Ol-Chiki also was disseminated through the sphere of Santali popular culture. For instance, Santali-language films, which

Figure 3.5 "All India Santali Education Council," a private Santali language school in a village located near Jhilimili market, header in Ol-Chiki/Roman, information in Bengali/English. Photo by author.

Figure 3.6 A banner from a program in a village bordering the bazaar. This is from a local branch of the "All India Santal Student Organization." The script combination (from top to bottom) Ol-Chiki and Roman is the same as in the school advertisement on Figure 3.5. Photo by author.

arrived in Jhilimili market in the form of cheap video compact disks (VCDs), were advertised in Ol-Chiki and Roman, and appeared alongside Bengali- and Hindi-language film posters on the market's walls (Figure 3.7). According to residents, most films came from Jamshedpur, the urban center in nearby Jharkhand, although some came from West Bengal itself. The use of Ol-Chiki to advertise films was intentional on the part of the directors and producers within the Santali-language film industry, which, according to conversations I had with Jamshedpur-based filmmakers, saw itself as promoting and disseminating Raghunath Murmu's vision of uniting Santals across borders.[13] Jhilimili residents were aware of the networks in which Santali-language media circulated, and local groups sought to also emulate the graphic standards of the Santali-language film industry. For instance, a Jhilimili-based traveling musical orchestra also advertised primarily in Ol-Chiki/Roman combination within the bazaar (Figure 3.8), thereby, like the Santali-language film posters,

Figure 3.7 Film posters from Santali language film *Punḍ Ayang* (*White Cobra*) in Ol-Chiki and Roman alongside Bengali-language film poster *Shotter Bijoy* (*Victory of Truth*) in Eastern Brahmi. Photo by author.

Figure 3.8 Advertisement for the Jhilimili-based Rusika Ramjham Orchestra in Ol-Chiki/Roman. Photo by author.

graphically projecting a media network that circulated across the entire Santali-speaking area, transcending the orchestra's base of operation in Jhilimili or the state of West Bengal.

Localizing Autonomy

Yet autonomy was not simply about scaling Santali as "trans-regional" through appeals to the nation or participation in a widely circulating mediascape and commodity market, it was also about strengthening a local and regional spatial network through the use of the dominant script of the area, Eastern Brahmi. As was previously mentioned, at this time most Santals learned to read and write in Eastern Brahmi, since schooling was in the Bengali language, and even in Santali-language classes I observed at the local high school, students preferred writing Santali in the Eastern Brahmi script despite their stated support for Ol-Chiki. Most of the Santali-language magazines were in Eastern Brahmi, and local newspapers were often bilingual in Santali and Bengali, with many

Figure 3.9 Jharkhand Party's response to the Maoist insurgency: "We do not want murders, we do not want terrorism, we want food to nourish our hunger! We do not want exploitation, We do not want repression, We want autonomy (*swashashon*)! Compliments: Jharkhand Anushilan Party" (in Bengali/Eastern Brahmi script). Photo by author.

preferring Eastern Brahmi as the preferred script. Eastern Brahmi was, as many people told me, simply easier to read for all the Santals, most of whom were not proficient in Ol-Chiki, but also the use of Bengali/Santali combinations and Eastern Brahmi script scaled autonomy as salient at a regional level as well, where Eastern Brahmi was the dominant graphic modality (see Table 3.2). This was most evident in political graffiti of different Jharkhand Party factions, which would contest village and state level elections in West Bengal. They conveyed their messages demanding autonomy (*svashashon* "self-rule") primarily in the Bengali language (Figure 3.9), and also exhorted the denizens of Jhilimili bazaar to vote for their preferred candidates through either Bengali or Santali in the Eastern Brahmi script (Figures 3.10 and 3.11). As is standard for political messaging in West Bengal and other parts of India, the messages were inscribed directly on the surface of the bazaar and were whitewashed and then redrawn during subsequent election cycles. Hence, while Ol-Chiki linked the politics of autonomy with a scalar project that saw Santali as operating outside state or

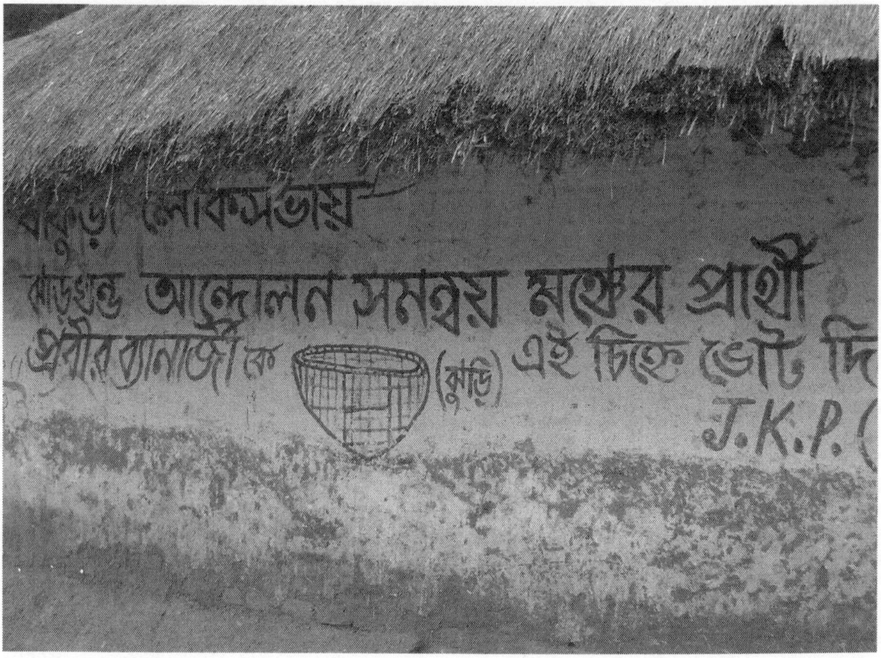

Figure 3.10 Graffito by the Jharkhand Anushilan Party in the Bengali language/ Eastern Brahmi script, saying please vote for the "Jharkhand Movement Group's Candidate Probir Banerjee, vote for this symbol." Photo by author.

Figure 3.11 Graffito by the Jharkhand Anushilan Party faction in the Santali language/ Eastern Brahmi script, saying *Noa chin-re vote em-pe alom* ("Do not vote for this symbol") (of the other Jharkhand faction). Photo by author.

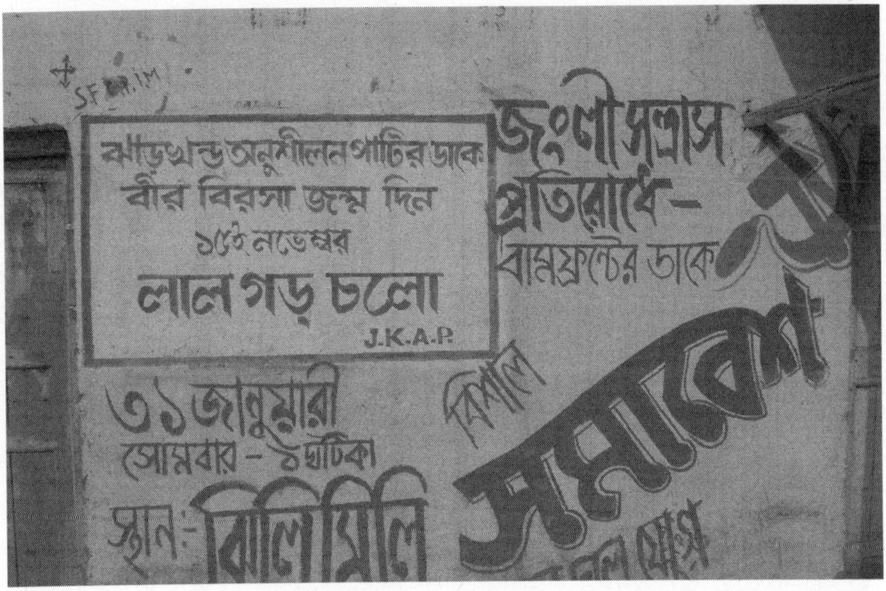

Figure 3.12 In square (top left): *Bengali/Eastern Brahmi*: "On the call of the The Jharkhand Anushilan Party on the birthday of Bir Birsa, let us go to Lalgarh!" Text outside the square: *Bengali/Eastern Brahmi*. Photo by author.

region, Jharkhand Party political graffiti, using traditional Santali instruments such as a drum or hatchet, projected autonomy as part of a project that aimed to create an autonomous "Jharkhand" region in southwest West Bengal, and within the Jhilimili bazaar itself, through the continued presence of the party and its territorial claims in the local political scene. This presence manifested primarily through multilingual messaging in the Eastern Brahmi script.

Though the Jharkhand Party supported the use of Ol-Chiki script, they did not employ it in their own political messaging. However, one could see complementary messages in different scripts and languages, each which projected autonomy at a different scale within the bazaar space. For instance, unlike the statewide political parties such as the Communist Party of India (Marxist) or the Trinamool Congress, the Jharkhand Party never held political rallies in metropolitan cities like Kolkata. Instead they focused their attention on shoring up support in neighboring towns and villages of southwest West Bengal, attempting to capture local village councils, support the rights of Adivasis, and continue the work of the Jharkhand movement by advocating for regional self-rule. Figure 3.12 presents Jharkhand Party graffiti that is advertising a political rally in a nearby village of Lalgarh, one of the centers of the Maoist insurrection in the area, in Bengali language/Eastern Brahmi script in order to celebrate the birthday of "Bir Birsa" Birsa Munda, an Adivasi leader of a famous colonial-era revolt in what is now Jharkhand state. Curiously the sign is painted over a sign for the ruling Communist Party, which was calling for a rally in Jhilimili to fight *jangali sontrash* (forest terrorism), a reference to both the Maoist insurgency and Adivasi autonomy movements. The Jharkhand Party signage, which connects the struggle for autonomy in Jhilimili bazaar with that of other villages (such as Lalgarh) and cities in the region, contrasts with the Ol-Chiki graffiti elsewhere on the bazaar's walls (Figure 3.13), which was put up by the Adivasi Socio-Educational Cultural Association (ASECA), the organization created by Raghunath Murmu and active throughout eastern India. The sign advertised a rally in Kolkata, the capital of West Bengal state, to advocate for the Santali language at the state level. Interestingly, though the script is Ol-Chiki, the sign incorporates both Santali and Bengali in the messaging, mimicking the standard structure

Figure 3.13 In Santali/Ol-Chiki—"On the call of ASECA, on 26 September (Bengali/Ol-Chiki) let us go to Kolkata!"

Table 3.3 Political messaging in Jhilimili bazaar

Party/organization	Script/language	Territory projected
1. Communist Party (CPI-M)	Eastern Brahmi/Bengali	West Bengal state (ruling party)
2. Jharkhand Anushilan Eastern Party	Brahmi/Bengali/Santali[14]	Southwest West Bengal (autonomous Jharkhand)
3. ASECA	Ol-Chiki/Santali	Santali-speaking area, eastern India

of political messaging though in a different script. Thus, contrary to the dominant framework, in which Bengali language and Eastern Brahmi script are the representative language of the state, in Jhilimili bazaar, Bengali in the Eastern Brahmi script projects an alternative regional formation (Jharkhand) that does not map on to West Bengal state, while Ol-Chiki messages advocate for linguistic and cultural rights in the metropolitan centers and state capitals (see Table 3.3).

Like with Jharkhand Party graffiti, the Eastern Brahmi script also mediates a notion of the local and regional within the realm of Santali-language media. While Santali-language film advertisements were steadily increasing, most of the Santali-language tokens in the bazaar are a special genre of advertisement for the hugely popular Santali drama or *gayan*. During the period between late winter and early monsoon (before the first sowing), traveling theaters from different parts of the Santali-speaking area, including Jharkhand and Odisha, perform elaborate musical dramas that combine song, dance, politics, and romantic entanglements. These dramas usually last one whole night, starting around 10 p.m. and lasting until 4 or 5 a.m. the next morning. The dramas take place in the nearby villages, and they are sponsored by village "committees": voluntary groups of community members who raise money to bring the drama troupes to their village. Because hosting a drama requires considerable time and money, the committees rarely garner a profit, but they aim to attract large local audiences, and in doing so, raise the prestige of their village.

Unlike, however, posters for Santali-language films that are centrally distributed and scale a trans-regional commodity market, drama posters, though the performers are indeed from different parts of the Santali-speaking area, are tied by both performers and residents to the local village who patronizes these performances. In an interview, one Jhilimili resident who used to run his own drama touring company, described his travels to various parts of the Santali-speaking area as a performing artist, scaling the "drama" itself as a trans-regional project. Indeed it was through drama that ideas about the Jharkhand movement, histories of the Hul, and Ol-Chiki script circulated across the administrative borders and to the far-flung villages in the Santali-speaking region. Yet even though the drama circulates across borders, the publicity, including the making and manufacturing of posters, is, in the words of the company director, the responsibility of the "local" (he used the English word) village committee. To use the participant framework proposed by Erving Goffman, while the "animator" of the posters are the drama company itself, which is a migratory entity, the "principal," or the one responsible for its circulation is scaled as "local" (Goffman 1981).

This meant that as you travel through the Santali-speaking area, different local committees, depending on where they were located, would relate posters for the same play in different scripts. For instance, take the play *Chemek' Chemek' taṛam tam okoe koṛa jawai tam* [Hey girl, the way you shake your hips when you walk, which boy will marry you?], which was a play performed by the Jharkhand-based "Soren Opera" company. In Jhilimili bazaar, the poster for the same play would be in Santali in the Eastern Brahmi script (Figure 3.14), while at one of the nearby railway stations located in the neighboring state of Jharkhand, the play, performed at a different village, would be advertised in Santali in the Devanagari script, which is the script of Hindi, the official language of Jharkhand (Figure 3.15). Thus, even though residents recognized the "Soren Opera" as being a Jharkhand-based touring group, the norms of publicity were such that the plays were associated with the patrons, a network of Santali organizations and groups that sought to increase their prestige locally, and thus they advertised their plays in the relevant script of their region.

Though the posters employed Eastern Brahmi or Devanagari scripts, their format considerably differed from either film advertisements or advertisements for Bengali-language plays. This was in part due to the way they employed Santali language as well as the themes and ornate language they brought into the space of the bazaar. As discussed above, the bazaar was

Figure 3.14 Poster for the Santali-language play *Chemek' Chemek' Taṛam Tam Okoy Koḍa Janwai Tam* (Hey girl, with that hip-shaking walk, which boy will marry you?) to be performed in a village near Jhilimili, in Santali/Eastern Brahmi script.

Figure 3.15 Poster for the same play in Santali/Devanagari script, to be performed in a village across the border in Jharkhand.

primarily an upper-caste space; Santali song and dance programs, weddings, fairs, and other Santal-specific festivals, performances, or celebrations would all take place in the nearby villages. This was in part why many Santals, though working and staying there, discursively disassociated themselves from the bazaar, viewing the village as the primary place where Santals exercise their political and cultural autonomy. On the other hand, as Jhilimili bazaar was flooded with drama posters in the Eastern Brahmi script, the life of the Santali-speaking village was visually and materially made visible on the very walls of the bazaar itself. For example, the text in the poster in Figure 3.16 reads:

> [In small letters] Berel hoṛmo amak' n'elte lob ena/idi mea-ṅ dalan oṛak' in'ren kukmu rinic' kunạmi [Big letters, title] Nenḍa tahe-ena Fagun Kunạmi
>
> [In small letters] Your unripe, turmeric-colored body, seeing it I became greedy, let's go, I will take you to my house, my dream-wife, [like a] full-moon, [in Big letters] Our appointed meeting time was the full-moon day of the month of Fagun [late Feb-early March].

Figure 3.16 Santali drama poster of the play *Nenḍa tahe ena fagun kunami* (Our appointed meeting was at the full moon of the Fagun month) alongside Bengali (Eastern Brahmi) and Hindi (Roman script) film posters.

The text, creating poetic correspondences between the "unripe turmeric-colored" body of the female lover and a full moon (*kunạmi*), sets up the dramatic introduction to the play, a story of why two lovers could not meet on the appointed day of the Fagun full moon (*kunạmi*). The poetic language draws attention to the Santali language rather than the script, and a particular form of language, such as the reference to non-conjugal sexual relations, which is appropriate in the Santal village, but which is considered taboo in the upper-caste space of the bazaar. These posters then bring in the everyday life of the Santal village into the bazaar, but by using Santali, they delimited their comprehension to Santals. In fact, most Bengali speakers, aware that these posters were in Santali, often ignored them entirely. Thus, despite their trans-regional connotations (this play was in fact produced by a famous Odisha-based group), they also connected the bazaar with the village space (*ato*). Autonomy therefore was not only about linking the bazaar with a dispersed Santali-speaking population across India, or to a regional grouping as Jharkhand, but also by placing the bazaar firmly within the network of villages where Santals resided, and where they exercised a degree of autonomy from upper-caste moral hegemony.

Santali in the *Diku* Bazaar

Even as Santals struggled to construct spaces of autonomy in Jhilimili market, the fact remains that most businesses in the bazaar are owned and operated by non-Santals and continue to employ Eastern Brahmi script on their surfaces (see Figure 3.1). The use of Eastern Brahmi script is consistent with the general attitude that this script is the most widely available to readers of all castes, as well as the equation of Eastern Brahmi with the standardized regional language, Bengali, and the use of Eastern Brahmi as the script mediating the general commodity market. Yet, although most caste-Hindu Bengali speakers do not consider Santali as an established regional language, and relegate it to the status of a local dialect, this does not mean that some have not responded to the increased activism by local Santals around the question of language and script. As Ol-Chiki has gained increasing visibility in the bazaar space, in addition to having been recently introduced in the local school system, some caste-Hindu shopkeepers have attempted to integrate a Santali "code" on to their signboards. Yet despite their efforts at appealing to the Santal audience, many Santals remain critical of these efforts, as they display combinations of script and code that lie outside the Santali scalar project of autonomy, and continue to reinforce Bengali-language hegemony and Santali language as subordinate within the bazaar space.

For example, when I first arrived in Jhilimili in early 2010, the medicine shop (Figure 3.17) on the road going from the upper bazaar to the lower bazaar was the only shop that visibly projected an explicitly delineated Santali code. The painted sign, which says, *kuchra oshud dokan* (spare medicine shop) in Bengali at the top, has, written in Santali, also in the Eastern Brahmi script, *ran dokan* (medicine shop) in Santali below. The only lexical alternation between the two parts of the sign is the translation of the Bengali word *oshudh* (medicine) with the Santali word *ran* (medicine). Consequently, in *translating* Bengali into Santali using the same script rather than *transcribing* Santali in

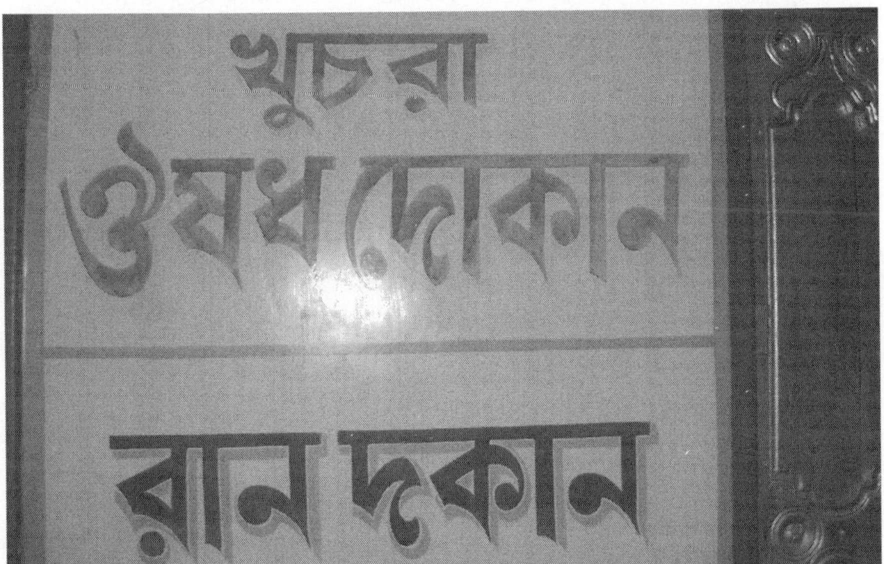

Figure 3.17 *Khucra oshudh dokan/ran dokan* (medicine shop) in Bengali/Santali, Eastern Brahmi script. Photo by author.

different scripts, the sign does not align with the multiscriptal assemblages characteristic of the Santali project of autonomy (Table 3.2). In fact, though shops employed different script combinations routinely (such as the Roman and Eastern Brahmi transcriptions in Figure 3.1), nowhere else in the bazaar did I see a token that employed translation. The shop owner, who as a Bengali-speaking caste Hindu was particularly excited to show me his sign when he found out I was studying Santali, saying he was the first owner to write Santali on his signboard. When asked why he decided on writing it in Santali, even though the Bengali was sufficient, he replied in Bengali, "*dekhe oder bhalo lage, oder ananda hocche*" (when they see it they feel good, they become happy). The "they" was unspecified, but he clearly meant the Santal customer, or caste-other of the bazaar. His evaluation of Santali therefore did not align with the scalar project of Santali autonomy, but rather he saw it as a practical way of pleasing a subsection of his local customer base. The excitement and pride with which he viewed his use of Santali also had the simultaneous effect of reinforcing the hegemony of Bengali and the scaling of Santali as a subordinate or local regional dialect.

During my stay in Jhilimili, I also witnessed two shops (Figures 3.18 and 3.19) newly place Ol-Chiki script on their signboards in addition to the Eastern Brahmi and Roman scripts. One of these shops (Figure 3.18) was the village bookstore, popular among school kids, and run by a local family of Utkal Brahmins. While the store mainly stocked Bengali and English books, there were plenty of Santali books and magazines as well, both in Eastern Brahmi and Ol-Chiki, as well as Santali-language textbooks for school. The Ol-Chiki along with the Roman and the larger Eastern Brahmi signage indicating the name of the store coincided, notably, with a rise in Santali language distribution, and increasing student interest in Santali since the language was instituted as a second language from class 9 at the local high school. The store in Figure 3.19 is a homeopathic dispensary run by the local primary school teacher, who commissioned what he termed a "multilingual" signboard, writing the same word, *Homeo Seba Sadan* (homeopathic clinic) in Eastern Brahmi, Roman, Devanagari, and Ol-Chiki.

When asked about their choice to use Ol-Chiki script on their signs, the owners of both the bookstore and the homeopathic clinic referred to the fact that they live in a "tribal" area so they should also use the tribal "language,"

Figure 3.18 Mahamaya book stall written in (from top to bottom) Ol-Chiki, Roman, and Eastern Brahmi scripts. Photo by author.

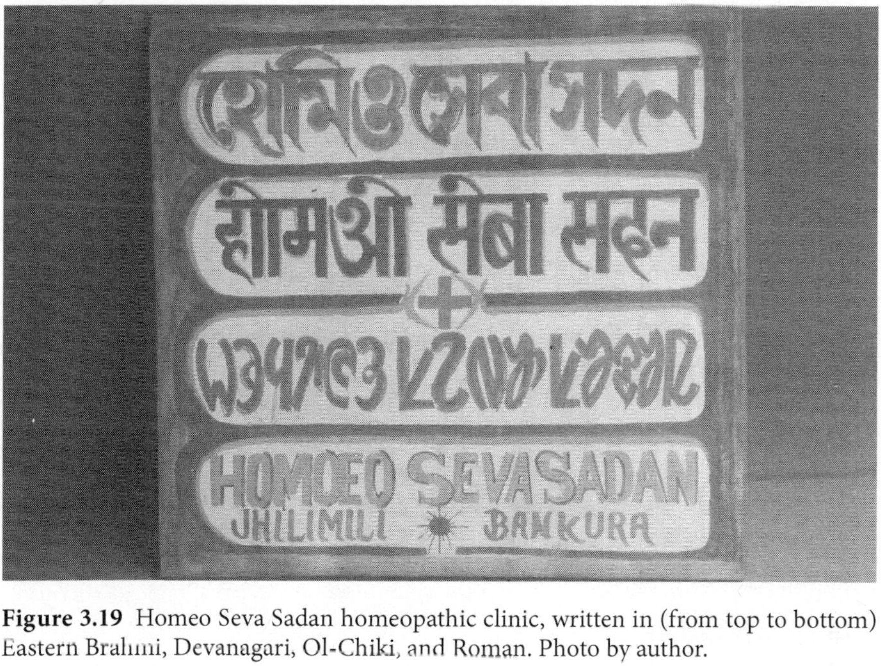

Figure 3.19 Homeo Seva Sadan homeopathic clinic, written in (from top to bottom) Eastern Brahmi, Devanagari, Ol-Chiki, and Roman. Photo by author.

which referred not to a distinction in code, but a graphic distinction, that is, the use of Ol-Chiki transcription on their sign. Referencing the "tribal area" as the motivation for placing Ol-Chiki script on the signboard suggests that there is a recognition, at least among the younger shop owners of the dominant bazaar castes (Brahmins and Vaishnavs) of a politics in which the Ol-Chiki script is employed to make a competing claim on territory. However, the scale at which Ol-Chiki operates in tokens such as the ones authored by Santali speakers referenced in the previous sections, in which Ol-Chiki functions to transcend delimited notions of region or territory. In fact the script is most often used to iconize networks of organization, flows of commodities, or other institutions that scale Santali as beyond the notion of territory implied by the shop owners' comments. Indeed the use of Ol-Chiki on each of these surfaces reinforce these scalar distinctions; in Figure 3.18, the Ol-Chiki/Roman combination is significantly smaller than the Eastern Brahmi one, something which I did not see on Santal-produced Ol-Chiki tokens, and in Figure 3.19, the Ol-Chiki follows the Eastern Brahmi, also a position I did not see on other Ol-Chiki tokens within the bazaar. In reframing the trans-regional scale as a local one through the use of Ol-Chiki, caste Hindus subordinate Santali within an established linguistic and graphic hierarchy.

The disjuncture between the Santali and caste-Hindu scalings of language and script surfaced in my conversation about these signs with the local sign painter. The painter is a Santal, who resides in a nearby hamlet, and while he is not the only sign painter in the bazaar, he is one of the most established. He has been responsible for painting many signs, including the one in Figure 3.17. I asked him why Santali storeowners and operators did not use Santali in their signboards, and he replied that the Santals preferred Ol-Chiki, but since most Santals did not know Ol-Chiki, the Santal shopkeepers were not going to use Santali. Whether this truly is the reason for the lack of Santali signs is debatable. However, the painter's reference to Ol-Chiki suggests an alliance with the scalar project in which Santali is linked with a larger territory beyond the locality of Jhilimili bazaar. It is this scaling, the painter suggests, that should be a critical component of any display of "Santali" on signs.

When I asked him in particular about the sign in Figure 3.17, which he himself painted, and why he used Eastern Brahmi to write Santali, he said that the reason was because the shopowner was a "Diku," and did not understand that Santali should be written in Ol-Chiki. The script combination displayed in that sign therefore, according to the painter, resulted not from his role as the "animator" of the sign, but was attributed to the sign's "principal," the Diku shopowner (Goffman 1981). Commenting on Figure 3.18, which did display Ol-Chiki, the painter voiced similar skepticism, saying that the Ol-Chiki was not "nice" (*napay*) because the painter of that particular sign was a Diku and he, as a Santal, could have done a better job. Thus, even if Ol-Chiki was used, both the "animator" and the "principal" were non-Santals, entailing a negative evaluation of a script that, if deployed in different circumstances, would be highly valued. The painter compared this inadequate use of Ol-Chiki to a recent painting of a private residence he did, where he painted a Santal family's clan name on their home entirely in Ol-Chiki script (Figure 3.20), citing a positively valuated instance of Ol-Chiki in which principal, animator, and script diagrammatically aligned.

When I asked other Santali students and teachers about the use of Ol-Chiki on the book stall, they remained ambivalent as well, mentioning immediately that those who ran the store were "Diku," seemingly negating the significance of the script's usage. The ambivalence about the signboards

Figure 3.20 "*Hansda bakol,*" the Hansda family home (Ol-Chiki). Photo by author.

expressed by Santals indicated that the signs, even though responding in part to Santali political movements, did not display, as the sign painter suggests, appropriate configurations of script and code, nor the appropriate alignments between principal and script. While it was not necessary that those involved in Santali literary production necessarily be Santal (there were non-Santals involved in magazine production for instance), the way one deployed scripts such as Ol-Chiki or Eastern Brahmi had to align with appropriate participant frameworks that did not subordinate Santali speakers and hearers to caste Hindu and Bengali language hegemony in order for the configuration to be understood as politically significant by Jhilimili's Santali speakers. Failing to order Santali according to the scalar project of political struggle, such as the Jharkhand movement, the use of Santali in the *diku* bazaar reinforced the scalar disjunctures that precipitated and perpetuated political organizing around language and script.

The ambivalence expressed by many Santals at the use of Ol-Chiki or Santali (Eastern Brahmi) by non-Santals suggests that the bazaar space is differentially scaled depending on participant evaluations of script-code constellations on the surface and the participant networks that are indexically associated with those constellations. For the Santal viewer having been exposed to Jharkhand and Ol-Chiki politics, as most have in Jhilimili, Ol-Chiki/Roman constellations (or through variable use of Ol-Chiki), evident in posters and on commodities, the performance circuits of Santali drama that connect the bazaar space and translocal circulation spheres to local village or Jharkhand Party scales all point to a locally understood politics of autonomy as one of the significations. The Santali of the shop signboards, however, formulated and commissioned by caste Hindus, is missing this index, incorporating visual icons of the Santal language within the larger hegemonic scalar framework of the bazaar, in which Santali is seen as a preeminently local and subordinate language, only to be expressed in a tokenistic form.[15] The fact that Santals repeatedly raised to me that the principals of these signboards were Dikus who do not participate in these politicized networks through which these other graphic material objects circulate, and therefore scale Santali script-code constellations in ways not consistent with those involved in these networks, created new disjunctures and spaces for political contestation within the linguistic landscape of the bazaar.

Graphic Politics of Counterinsurgency

While Santali is absent from institutions linked to the state such as the bank, post office, or other government offices, the one instance where Santali—both in Eastern Brahmi and Ol-Chiki scripts—was visibly deployed by the state government (both central and state), was in material related to counterinsurgency operations against the armed struggle by supposed Maoist insurgents. While indeed the Maoist leadership in the state is made up of primarily of non-Adivasis, the association of Adivasi movements for autonomy with armed insurgency has a long history in Jhilimili and in the hilly tracts of eastern India more generally. As village headmen and councils lost their rights to negotiate for forests, lands, and water resources with colonial authorities, and following various armed insurrections, colonial, and postcolonial police authorities increasingly started to associate demands for forest, land, and water rights by Adivasis as criminal acts. In fact, as historians such as Ranabir Samaddar (1998) have noted, in regions such as southwest West Bengal, during the late colonial period, police started attributing criminal acts and revolts to community rather than to individuals (hence the "Bhumij" rebellion or the "Santal" Hul) and soon community after community, the entire region of the Jangal Mahals became criminalized.[16]

As part of the restive Jangal Mahals region, the Jhilimili area has long had an association with criminality, even before the most recent Maoist insurgency that was occurring in the region at the time of my fieldwork. Periodically, during the Naxalite movement in the 1970s, or at various points during the Jharkhand movement, the region has been subject to intense state surveillance. In fact, the armed CRPF encampment has been present in Jhilimili for decades, since the first stirrings of the Jharkhand movement. Thus, the rise of the Jharkhand movement and the politics of autonomy, though in many ways distinct from radical left-wing insurgency, have continually been incorporated into the discourse of criminality by the state. This is evident by the way the state chooses to deploy the Santali language, absent in other contexts, when addressing the Santali-reading population as potential informants or as insurgents willing to be reformed. By omitting Santali from its own durable institutions, but by deploying it on posters related to the ongoing Maoist insurgency, the state orders Santali language, the Ol-Chiki script, and the politics of autonomy on a scale of "counterinsurgency." This scale emerges through the interface of police agencies and discourses of criminalization and manifests itself in the state-sponsored, Santali language posters in both the Eastern Brahmi and Ol-Chiki scripts that were put up in 2010 at the peak of state counterinsurgency operations in Jhilimili (Figures 3.21 and 3.22).

Figure 3.21 appeared in Jhilimili bazaar and around the villages of southwest West Bengal after an act of sabotage on the railway track resulted in the derailment of the Gyaneshwari Express, a long-distance train that was going from Calcutta to Mumbai on May 28, 2010. The derailment resulted in a collision with an incoming freight train; 148 people died and over 200 were injured.[17] As the sabotaged track lie in the district of West Midnapur, which at the time was one of the central locations of Maoist insurgent operations, state and central authorities accused local political groups who were alleged to be allied with the Maoists. The posters, placed by the Central Bureau of Investigation, the central government's investigation arm, read, in Santali (Eastern Brahmi): "*See. Bee. Ai. [CBI] renak' wanted (sablagito): gyaneshwari express renak' case do*" "CBI's wanted (wanted), in the case of the Gyaneshwari Express."

Though these posters were also there in Bengali, the fact that that the central government chose to disseminate this information in Santali is notable, considering that any other central or state government-sponsored scheme or notices are usually not written in Santali at all. Announcements for government schemes or government events that I saw advertised in the bazaar are always related in Bengali in Eastern Brahmi, which followed from state and state institutions' directive to use the mandated regional script (Table 3.1). However, only when it came to operations of counterinsurgency, where Santals were specifically addressed communally as an insurgency-prone population, did the state deploy Santali. The implication of the message is that, despite the fact that nobody on the on the "wanted" list is Santal by caste, Santals were, by state directive, to be targeted as allies for information in the fight against insurgents, since tribal populations like the Santals are seen by government officials as generally sympathetic to insurgent groups or anti-state actors.[18] The Eastern Brahmi script localizes a directive from a remote central government agency (the CBI), and the Santali code targets a Santali-speaking/-reading population

Figure 3.21 *CBI renak' wanted* poster outlining the suspects in the Maoist derailing of the Gyaneshwari Express on the railway line near Jhilimili, Central Bureau of Investigation, Government of India (in Santali (Eastern Brahmi script)). Photo by author.

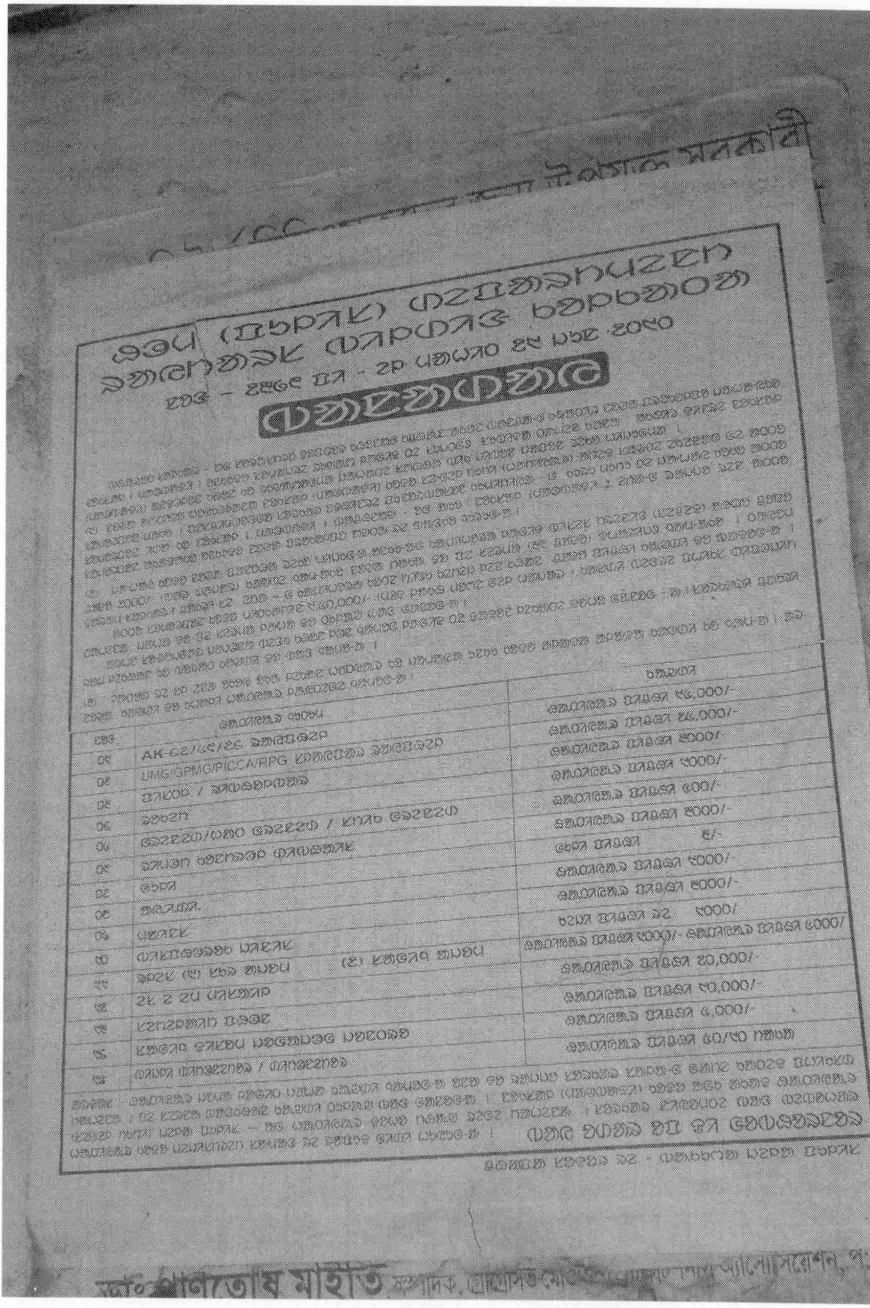

Figure 3.22 Poster outlining arms-for-cash exchange targeted at Maoist insurgents around Jhilimili area, Home (Police) Department, Government of West Bengal (in Santali (Ol-Chiki script)). Photo by author.

as the prime population that would have knowledge or collaboration with the insurgent groups. The use of Santali in Eastern Brahmi script, unlike in other contexts such as drama posters, enacts a different, and on a more ominous scale, linking the language, and the regional forms of autonomy it indexes, with national counterinsurgency/counterterrorism strategies and the police powers of the state.

On an adjacent wall (Figure 3.22) is another government directive poster, labeled *Home (Police) Department, Writer's Building, Kolkata, [in black background] Banaday* ("Home (Police) Department, Writer's Building, Kolkata, Money Exchange"). This poster is also marked on the surface because it is in Ol-Chiki script (perhaps the longest and most detailed Ol-Chiki notice on the surfaces of Jhilimili bazaar), as it is a government notice, a genre in which use of the Ol-Chiki script is otherwise nonexistent. The poster announces an arms exchange program started by the state government of West Bengal whereby armed Maoist insurgents are able to exchange arms-for-cash rewards. The poster also lists the names of arms and how much money one can get for exchanging them. In the first row, exchanging AK 46/47/48s will bring Rs. 15,000 (around $200) while in the second row, sniper rifles will bring in Rs. 25,000 (around $350). Unlike the poster in Figure 3.21, which targets Santals as allies of insurgents (or general carriers of information on insurgent activities) Figure 3.22 targets a politically aware Santali-speaking/reading population as the insurgent group itself. In this poster, Santals are discursively interpellated as not only carriers of information, but also as carriers of the arms that make the insurgency possible. Thus again, state intervention into the Santali public sphere inscribes the scale of "counterinsurgency" onto the landscape, where Ol-Chiki is used to address Santals as anti-state (or "criminal") actors, attempting to subordinate them to the so-called rule of law through cash incentives.

The extensive use of Ol-Chiki in this directive raises the question as to why the state chose to publicize its arms-for-cash program in a script in which there is limited literacy to begin with? One reason may be, unlike the "wanted" poster that is in Eastern Brahmi, the use of Ol-Chiki in the poster in Figure 3.22 may be a way for the state government, which is associated with the Eastern Brahmi script, to incorporate counterinsurgency within networks of tribal autonomy, for which the Ol-Chiki script is the salient emblem. Yet, the uniqueness of such efforts suggests that the state is only willing to make connections with these networks in the context of combating insurgency and thus views demands for tribal autonomy as connected to "terrorism" and anti-state activity. The use of the Ol-Chiki script to target insurgents implicitly links the movements for Santal autonomy and the trans-regional scale to which this movement is evaluated with the ideology of Maoist insurgency, which, as a national movement across India, also transcends regional boundaries.[19] The curious use of Ol-Chiki script to issue a directive about arms exchange fits within a historical pattern of criminalization of the Santal (or in general, Adivasi) demands by the state, whether in the cultural domains of rights to language and script, or in the economic domains of rights to land, forests, or water.

The posters in Figures 3.21 and 3.22 create an interscalar assemblage that draws on the semiotic media (Ol-Chiki, Eastern Brahmi, and the Santali language) deployed within signboards connected with Santali autonomy (such as in Figure 3.4), yet in doing so aligns "counterinsurgency" with Santali demands for autonomy. In this approach, the state links trans-regional scale that Ol-Chiki projects with the Maoist insurgency, which the prime minister at the time, Manmohan Singh, called India's "greatest internal security threat,"[20] a sentiment echoed by the ruling Communist Party of West Bengal. Thus, aligning language, script, and counterinsurgency, the state evaluates the Santali demands for autonomy as a local, regional, and national "law-and-order" issue, while at the same time attempting to incorporate these networks and scales into the coercive apparatus of state power. Unlike the scalar assemblages of autonomy, posters such as these create a scalar network in which Santals are, in Erving Goffman's terminology, neither "authors" nor "principals," but figure primarily as insurgent-prone "addressees."

Conclusion

Jhilimili bazaar is a place where most villagers visit regularly to carry out their daily activities; it is the site where goods, services, and people circulate. It forms the spatial interface between the outlying hamlets, which are predominately Santal and tribal-dominated, and other parts of the region, country, and world.

Yet, in addition to goods and services, the bazaar also forms a site for the circulation of semiotic media as well as political solidarities and antagonism. Given that graphic media, particularly script, since the time of the Jharkhand movement, and especially following the creation of the Jharkhand state, has taken on heightened political salience, the chapter focused on the visual and material as a primary site where politics in the bazaar occurs, mapping contested notions of territory, temporality, and administrative regimes onto the built environment. This politics, the chapter has claimed, is not one that is explicit, yet, in the myriad of signs, posters, and graffiti that cover the surfaces of its shops, homes, and offices, forms the literal backdrop for all other activity.

Following the sociolinguistic traditions of studying material manifestations of language on the built environment (known as linguistic landscape studies), the chapter tracks the various assemblages of script and code and how they are evaluated by both Santals and non-Santals according to specific scalar ideologies. Santals, having been involved in the Jharkhand movement for many decades, and having seen Santali attain constitutional recognition, have an acute sense of Santali as a language that transcends their particular location in Jhilimili or its status as a lower caste dialect. On the other hand, caste Hindus as well as state organizations have continued to marginalize the language. This is evident especially through the lack of visibility of Ol-Chiki script on official signboards, which for Santals, has become emblematic of a trans-regional politics of autonomy that imagines Jhilimili as part of a larger Santali-speaking community dispersed throughout eastern India. This modality manifests itself in a number of different tokens that form a visual network in the bazaar, such as signs for the Santali social administrative offices, "All-India" Santali organizations, and Santali film posters.

A visual survey of the bazaar also shows how script use, as well as autonomy itself, is more complicated than simply appealing to an alternative discourse of the nation. Instead, we see how the politics of autonomy is also entangled in conceptions of the local and regional, made manifest in such as in signs for the Jharkhand Party, which uses Eastern Brahmi script and the Bengali language to contest for local elected political office, or posters for Santali-language dramas, which present transregional performance through the Eastern Brahmi script. This shows how Santali attempts to claim the bazaar and link the bazaar to other Santali speakers both challenges the state boundaries, yet also firmly acknowledges Santali speakers' connections to their villages and the region of southwest West Bengal (neighboring Jharkhand) in which they reside. However, scales gain meaning not only from the linking of Santali with different scripts, but also from social evaluations of the participants involved in making such connections. Santals are skeptical of caste Hindu usage of Ol-Chiki or Santali, as they do not scale the language in terms of a politics of autonomy; in addition, state usage of Santali presents a new scale, characterizing autonomy in terms of national and regional discourses of insurgency and counterinsurgency.

The bazaar is a fluid, open, and dynamic space where multiple scalar assemblages interact. However, an analysis such as this one, while presenting a broad overview, provides only a surface view. How graphic politics and scalar projects of autonomy interact within actual institutions will be investigated further in the following chapter.

4

Caste, Community, and Santali-Language Education

M.A. B.A. bạbu-m pas keda,
Bajar-sahar babu-m, dolan keda.
Opis rem cạkri, diku tem roṛa,
janam pạrsi bạbu-m bohoy keda.

Pạrsi tamem at'-leda,
lakcar tamem bohoy leda
eṛẹl tulạm lekam otang-a.

—Dong seren' [wedding song] Motilal Hansda (*Sarjom Umul* 2:2, Jan.–March, 2011 p. 7) Purulia, West Bengal

[Oh my son, you've passed your M.A. [Masters],
you've passed your B.A. [Bachelor's]
You set up a house in the bazaar
You work in an office, you speak in *diku*
Your birth language has whisked away in the wind.

Your language is lost,
Your culture has wafted away,
Floating away in the wind, like a piece of cotton.]

It was a hot afternoon at the Jhilimili high school; lunch had just been served and class 9 students, boys in their red pants and white-collared shirts, girls in their white *salwars* and red *dupattas* huddled together on their benches. The teacher called the roll and then started writing on the board, stroke by stroke, the Ol-Chiki letters, commenting on how efficient the script was to write and how beautiful it looked in the handwritten style. Though these students had grown up speaking Santali at home, this was their first encounter with Santali in the classroom, and they had to learn a new script from scratch after having studied Bengali and English for nine years. Yet the classroom overflowed, and the students, despite the heat and their full stomachs, were fully attentive as they learned, stroke by stroke, their native language anew.

It had been seven years since the high school implemented Santali language as an elective subject, and that too, only from class 9. English and Bengali, on the other hand, were taught from class 1, and all other subjects were taught in Bengali. Thus, up until class 9, students studied exclusively in Bengali (with exception of the compulsory English subject) and retained the option of continuing with the Bengali language elective as their "first language" course of study. In fact, when Santali was initially introduced, many students chose just that; the first Santali language class at Jhilimili only had nine students, with many students wary of learning a new language after so many years of Bengali-language study. Yet at the time of my fieldwork from 2009 to 2011, the situation had changed dramatically. Despite Santali still only being offered from class 9, and the fact that this was the first time many students would learn to read and write the Ol-Chiki script, the enrollment in the class 9 Santali course alone had shot to over a hundred students. This was in addition to the relatively large enrollments in classes 10–12. As one caste Hindu schoolteacher told me, he "never saw" his students "as excited as they were about their *script*."

The enthusiasm for Santali baffled many caste Hindu residents. Older people, even many who worked on the school grounds, continued to refer to the language as *ṭhar*, refusing to acknowledge Santali as anything other than an incomprehensible, low-caste dialect. The younger generation also expressed their puzzlement, with many wondering about the educational value of learning Santali. A caste Hindu resident of Jhilimili who was at the time enrolled in a doctoral program in the United States, and thus, by the standards of the community, highly successful, expressed genuine curiosity, asking me why Santali speakers were so enthusiastic about learning their language when to him, and to many others like him, it was clear that English was much more important for academic success.

This chapter argues that the enthusiasm that lies at the heart of the students' embrace of Ol-Chiki, and which has informed the struggle to implement Santali-language education, is rooted not in dominant discourses of academic or financial success nor in the practical utility of the language itself. Instead, it derives from one of the historical aims of the Jharkhand movement, which sought to refigure Santali speakers (and other Adivasi communities) from that of a hierarchically subordinate and "backward" *caste* community to one of an autonomous *language community* equally situated within the liberal and institutional framework of the postcolonial developmental state. The terrain on which this semiotic struggle occurs is not that of language in its denotational sense (code) or as a spoken modality (speech), both of which remain entrenched in relations of caste distinction, but in its written, graphic modality (script).

In Jhilimili, script affords an alternative "axis of differentiation" (Gal 2016) from spoken language. Santali speakers associate Santali speech *(roṛ)* with the community of Santals *(hoṛ)* as well as community-internal social practices, such as songs, ritual, and the telling of Santali histories. Bengali, or other Indo-European languages, though spoken by all Santals, is associated with non-Santal (or non-Adivasi) persons *(diku)* and community-external practices, which include education, as the song at the outset of the chapter poetically expresses. At the same time, from the perspective of caste Hindus, spoken Santali, referred to as *ṭhar* or sometimes as "Adivasi," is, unlike Bengali or English, not seen as a language at all. In associating the Santali language with caste, speakers reinforce the perception of Adivasis as lower caste or primitive and caste Hindus as educated and developed.

Script, however, provides a different axis of differentiation for Santali speakers, allowing them to pursue a politics of autonomy within liberal institutions such as the school. On the one hand, script continues to signify the pole between "Hoṛ" and "Diku," with Ol-Chiki script articulating Santal-specific temporalities, ritual performance, kinship, and territoriality. Yet, on the other hand, the political project of Ol-Chiki is also tied to the developmental discourse of the state, the lynchpins of which are literacy and education. By asserting the use of Ol-Chiki as part of an educational project, Santals align a politics of autonomy with a project of emancipation from caste hierarchy and institutional equality, both of which are liberal ideals of citizenship promised by membership in Indian democracy through which they may publicly contest caste subordination and institutional exclusion. At the same time, given its emergence within the community and its associations with Santal-specific narratives and practices, the use of Ol-Chiki also creates within caste-demarcated spaces such as the school a sphere of "intimacy" associated with the community and language.

The chapter will first outline the frameworks of caste and community present in Jhilimili and relate them to the axis of differentiation between spoken and written language. Then, drawing on fieldwork conducted at Jhilimili high school between 2010 and 2012, it will show how the school, the major institutional site of literacy socialization in rural India, provides the literal surfaces on which young Santali students enfigure community through visible use of script repertoires. These figurations create intimate spaces of autonomy while also publicly staking claim to institutional equity and multicultural citizenship. Finally, I suggest that the alignment between autonomy and education through the medium of script, while successfully resignifying distinctions between castes, has also resulted in the creation of new hierarchical distinctions within the Santali-speaking community on the basis of written and spoken language, showing the limits of an institution-centered project for a broad-based politics of autonomy.

Caste and Community in Jhilimili

Caste has always been a difficult concept to define and apply in tribal areas such as Jhilimili. Colonial administrators and Indian intellectuals often saw resident communities such as the Santals as not fully included in the caste system. This differing experience, or inexperience, with caste led the famous Dalit scholar and activist B. R. Ambedkar, the author of the Indian Constitution, to assert that Adivasis lacked the "political sense" to become incorporated fully into the anti-caste struggle (Ambedkar 2014: 248).[1] However, as sociologist André Béteille has repeated, the dividing lines between what are considered "tribes" and "castes" are blurry and often difficult to distinguish (Beteille 1986, 1998, 2006). Perhaps what has been more relevant than any given social distinction between tribe and caste has been what Amita Baviskar has called the "strong spatial dimension" to the categorization of "indigeneity" in India that has linked the culture of groups like the Santals to the ecology in which they inhabit (Baviskar 2007: 35). Indeed, proponents of the Jharkhand movement such as the scholar-activist Sanjay Basu Mullick have transposed the spatialization onto the territory of Jharkhand itself, arguing the due to the prevailing Adivasi culture, "in Jharkhand, the caste system was never a dominant social reality" (Mullick 2003:vii).

Yet from what I saw in Jhilimili most caste Hindus, particularly upper and artisanal castes, viewed the Santals and other Scheduled Tribes as ritually polluting (*achut*). For instance, they would not share vessels with Santals, as the dietary habits of many Santals included consumption of beef and pork, which were considered impure. In addition, upper and artisanal castes were also critical of the fact that for many Adivasis, physical relations between unmarried men and women were tolerated, liquor had greater acceptance, and ritual involved animal sacrifice. These traits were considered evidence of general "backwardness," which they attributed to their "culture." In this discourse, Adivasis such as the Santals were forever locked into a backward status that, in everyday social relations, created many of the same effects as subordinate caste status.

Yet the most frequent way I heard caste discussed in Jhilimili was in relation to people's interactions with state institutions and agencies. When asked what about one's "*caste*" (most often the English word "caste" is used in this reference, as opposed to Indic terms like *jati*), one usually responds with the terms "general," "Scheduled Tribe (ST)," "Scheduled Caste (SC)," or "Other Backward Classes (OBC)." These terms refer to the legal designations of persons based on patrilineal lineage that shape their relation to state institutions and electoral politics.[2] In West Bengal, as in Jharkhand, Odisha, and Bihar, Santali speakers are considered "ST" or "Scheduled Tribe." ST communities are labeled as "socially or educationally backward" according to the Article 340 of the Indian Constitution,[3] legally enjoining the state to uplift these communities into the "mainstream" society through targeted reservations. The concessions to these communities include special quotas to increase their enrollment and success rate in schools, reserved seats in elected bodies, eligibility for government stipends, and quotas in government jobs. Reservations are also extended to members of Scheduled Castes (often known in India as Dalit, but including a wide range of communities), and to a lesser extent groups classified as Other Backward Classes (OBCs).[4] Communities for whom reservations are not extended are termed as "general," and in Jhilimili, they comprise caste Hindu groups such as Brahmins and Vaishnav ("Das").

One of the primary ways the Santals interface with state institutions is through their legally designated caste category of "Scheduled Tribe." This category is embraced by Santals in that it guarantees the benefits, financial and otherwise, that allow their children, many of whom come from poor, marginalized families, to attend school in the first place. Yet the categorization of "ST" inherently carries the connation of underdevelopment and primitiveness, and interactions with state agencies therefore occur in the context of state efforts at social improvement. Consequently, while the ST status guarantees benefits, it does not necessarily guarantee equity within state-run institutions. In this paradigm there is no room for the Santali language, nor is there any imperative for caste-Hindu schoolteachers or administrators, who see their job in part as one of development, to consider such demands. In fact, teachers often echoed the sentiments of many caste Hindus in Jhilimili; while the new generation of teachers supported Santali-language education at the school, they thought that it was Bengali or English that would ultimately guarantee success in integration with the larger society.

At the founding of the Indian state, caste discrimination was seen as a social ill inherited from premodern times, and designations such as Scheduled Caste and Scheduled Tribe, and the benefits they entailed, were offered as a liberal solution for what was essentially an illiberal problem.[5] Yet in doing so, the government established a new operative hierarchy within the liberal state structure in which performances of "backwardness" became necessary to guarantee benefits and privileges from within the state structure.[6] However Article 29 of the Indian Constitution provided for another educational imperative that stated that "any section of the citizens of India . . . having a *distinct* language, script, or culture of its own shall have the *right* to conserve the same" (my emphasis).[7] Unlike caste, therefore, which addresses inherently unequal distinctions framed around temporal lag ("backward"), language and script guarantee the preservation of distinctions applied *equally* to "any section of the citizens of India." The Indian Constitution therefore understood society as divided into hierarchically organized castes, which had to be managed through a differential regime of reservations and what linguistic anthropologists have called "language communities" (Irvine 2006),[8] groups that despite de facto multilingualism ideologically align with a bounded linguistic code in order to be recognized as a distinct community.

However unlike "caste," recognition as a "distinct" community is not a legal designation in that it does not officially determine access to resources or institutions. Instead, in order to be recognized as a community, one had to assert one's rights within the multicultural framework of the state. This involved what Akio Tanabe, in his study of a caste-demarcated village in Odisha, has called a "moral" assertion: a "reinterpretation of the community principle from one based on the hierarchical values of hegemony and domination to one based on the subalternate value of ontological equality" (Tanabe 2007: 569).[9] Yet this reinterpretation also comes with a new commitment to renew the "sacrificial ethics of cooperation" (ibid.), within the local democratic structure, which means a commitment to push for ontological equality while also maintaining more intimate community ties and bonds. In this way, autonomy, which forms the basis of the community of "people" (*hoṛ*) for the Santals, becomes operationalized within caste-delineated societies and institutions as a politics of equality.

This chapter suggests that the assertion of an ontologically equal, yet autonomous, community among the Santals in Jhilimili takes place not along the axis of spoken language, which is entrenched in relations of caste hierarchy and paradigms of inclusion/exclusion, but on the axis of written language, tied to notions of development, citizenship, and institutional equity. Schools are particularly critical sites for the examination of such politics, as they are tasked with the duty to disseminate developmental paradigms while also having to respond to local political pressure in a more immediate way than other state institutions. Although school policy and administration in many ways continue to perpetuate caste hegemony, the institution also is subject to a dialogic process of contestation, evident in the ways students transform their spaces through the deployment of script.

Differentiating the Oral and the Graphic

As my quarters were located next to the village high school, over the course of my fieldwork, I developed a strong relationship with the students and teachers there. One day, after giving a guest lecture on the difference between Indian and American education, I was chatting with the students. They were telling me how they were happy that I spoke Santali, and how my presence was causing a slight stir in the village, especially among caste Hindus. I asked them to elaborate, and they said that the caste Hindu shopowners were very confused by me since I was also of caste Hindu background (though from a different region of India), spoke English, and had a preference for vegetarian food, yet I still *spoke* Santali. For the caste Hindu residents of Jhilimili, these qualities did not align, and Santali-speaking students, who were more perceptive about caste relations than I, clearly noticed the discrepancy in behavior.

Thus, for caste Hindus, spoken Santali was clearly associated with certain "qualities," to which I did not fit. The fact that they referred to Santali as *ṭhar* meant that it was not considered a legitimate "language" (*bhasha*) unlike Bengali or English. In addition, it was associated with other qualities that marked Santali bodies, such as the consuming of beef and pork, manual labor, and the pursuit of "pleasure" activities like drinking or dancing. Spoken Santali then was synonymous with either a lack (*ṭhar*) or a caste-delimited identity ("Adivasi" language), and not considered a language that would be spoken by an outsider, much less be the subject of academic study.

Spoken Santali therefore existed on what linguistic anthropologist Susan Gal has called an "axis of differentiation" with Bengali or English,[10] a "relation of contrast between signs/registers . . . organized according to the *qualities* picked out as shared by the expressive features that make up the register and also by the persona it indexes" (Gal 2016: 121).[11] The "feeling" of sameness between language and persons is a semiotic process Gal calls "rhematization" (122), a term adopted from Charles Sanders Peirce (1955) to describe the interpretation of indexical signs (contiguity) as iconic signs (resemblance). Hence, due to the indexical fact that persons who are by caste Santal speak Santali, the same caste qualities of Santal persons are iconically extended to the spoken register of Santali.

Santals, however, view their language on a different axis of differentiation. Santals refer to themselves as the community of "people" (*hoṛ*) and the language as *hoṛ roṛ* or "speech of the people." Hoṛ is a positively valued term, carrying connotations of honesty, diligence, and struggle. Bengali, on the other hand, is referred to as *diku roṛ*, or the speech of the "Diku." Diku is associated with persons who are deceitful, vain, and not to be trusted. The "speech" of the people (*Hoṛ*) has accompanied the Santali-speaking community from their origins to the present day, and, in the dominant conception, has remained constant throughout periods of historical transformation and disruption. Despite the fact that all the Santals in Jhilimili speak Bengali fluently and often, with even some predominately speaking Bengali, they distinguish persons and registers along this axis of differentiation. As one predominately Bengali-speaking Santal in Jhilimili told me (in Santali), "we are Hoṛ though we speak in Diku."

Spoken Santali is semiotically evaluated along two different axes of differentiation in Jhilimili. One is on the axis of caste differentiation: caste Hindus view Santali as underdeveloped and inferior to legitimate languages such as Bengali or English, much in the way they view Santal persons as of lower-caste background. Santals on the other hand view their "speech" (*roṛ*) as coterminous with positively valued qualities of the Santal persons and as an "intimate" practice,[12] whereas certain other registers, even though they are part of Santali speakers' repertoires, are felt to be external. On both axes of differentiation therefore spoken Santali is evaluated in terms of intercommunity (or intercaste) relations, which leads to an ambivalence toward caste Hindu-dominated institutions such as schools. In fact, were it not for graphic politics, the situation could appear similar to the one Garcia (2003) describes in highland Peru, where indigenous Quechua speakers resist the imposition of Quechua language education in schools since Quechua is negatively valued by the more dominant, Spanish-speaking mestizo society. On the other hand, speakers value Quechua as a community-internal marker of intimacy, and thus desire that it should remain outside of community-external spaces such as schools.

In Jhilimili, the situation differs from the one analyzed by Garcia because of the differentiation between spoken and written language, mediated by a graphic politics of autonomy. In India, as in many parts of the world, official policy promoted the acquisition of "literacy" as a way to create a modern, universal citizen-subject[13] capable of participating in the state project of development.[14] This goal echoed international development policy, such as that stated in The *United Nations Educational, Scientific and Cultural Organization's* (UNESCO) "Literacy for All" campaign in which the acquisition of literacy was understood as a key component in the eradication of child poverty, curbing of excess population, and "sustainable development, peace, and democracy."[15] Echoing this formulation, the well-known development economists Jean Dreze and Amartya Sen (2002) suggest that lack of literacy is one of the primary reasons India lags behind its Asian neighbors in most of the relevant development indicators, including "participation" in democratic processes.

Unlike spoken language, which is entrenched in relations of caste and intimacy, the Indian state, and the supporters of its developmental logic, view literacy as a way to realize oneself as an equal citizen of the state, free from illiberal caste hierarchies. This framework extends not only to the state but also to social movements and developmental organizations. In his study of literacy activism in the South Indian state of Tamilnadu, Francis Cody (2009, 2013) discusses how activists sought to teach lower-caste Dalit villagers to read and write so that they may learn to petition state institutions to request interventions in situations of exploitation by middle and upper castes and guarantee their rights as equal citizens. However, as Cody demonstrates, despite activists' belief that the knowledge of writing would facilitate access to bureaucratic institutions, the interactive structure and opacity of bureaucratic practices reinscribe caste hierarchy regardless of petitioners' writing ability or awareness of rights under the law, revealing the limits to literacy as an emancipatory tool.

Cody's study shows that the acquisition of literacy alone does not transform caste relations. However, in Jhilimili, activists call for a different type of project: one in which the acquisition of literacy in a script autonomous from bureaucratic institutions and entrenched caste relations will serve as a way to refigure caste into community. This goal was made clear in Raghunath Murmu's original campaigns to promote Ol-Chiki in the West Bengal state, where, at a 1978 gathering, he stated that "in our country they [upper-castes] call [our language] *ṭhar* . . . you must have heard it all before, but it is a language [*bhasha*], not some unformed speech . . . as old as Sanskrit . . . and so it must have a script [*ol*]" (Murmu [1978] 2011: 14). In speeches such as these, Murmu sought to equate Santali, hitherto referred to as *ṭhar* or "unformed speech" with a language or *bhasha* such as Sanskrit, the classical language of India, or Hindi, Bengali, or English. Thus, Murmu introduced a new axis of differentiation in which the Santali language, in its written [*ol*] form, visually enfigured an independent community that existed not only in the present, but also in history, at an equal level with Sanskrit, the classical language of caste Hinduism.

In order to promote the script, Murmu set up his own organization, the Adivasi Socio-Educational Cultural Association (ASECA), which printed and distributed primers in the script and set up informal schools to teach the script in both rural and urban areas. These programs followed the structure of formal government schooling, including a formal syllabus "lower," "secondary," and "higher" levels, examinations, and degrees at different levels of completion.[16] However, unlike in government schools, which were characterized as Diku-dominated institutions, in these schools, the learning of script was suffused with the intimate relations of the community of Hoṛ. When I attended weekend classes at an ASECA school on the outskirts of Kolkata, we started the class with a prayer (*nehor*) to Bidhu and Chandan, the heroes of Murmu's play, who used the script to communicate their intimate feelings to one another and to which no outsider could access. Some classes were devoted to the learning of rituals or the singing of "culture songs" (*lakchar seren*') in addition to the learning of grammar and Ol-Chiki. Classes ended with a song that exhorted us to "sharpen" both our knowledge and devote oneself to the community. The enlightenment discourse of literacy therefore was explicitly and institutionally linked to the intimate relations between Santali speakers as well as to a refiguration from caste to community. These schools prepared a young generation of Santals to enter the formal education system with an already developed sense of a politics of autonomy, in which the Santali language, in its written form, signified both equality and intimacy. In Jhilimili, where, as we will see, the formal institutionalization of Santali was a politically wrought issue, the first teachers of the language at the government high school were all graduates of this alternative educational system, and its influence extended to the incoming students as well.

Graphic Politics and Santali-Language Education

When I first came to Jhilimili, I was excited to learn that the local high school had recently started Santali as a first language subject from class 9. I went to the headmaster of the school, a Bengali-speaking Brahmin and Ph.D. in English literature. He explained to me (in English) that he was very proud of the school's "multilingual philosophy" in which three languages,

"Bengali," "English," and what he called "Ol-Chiki," all were supported equally. These comments echoed the liberal multiculturalism enshrined in provisions such as Article 29 of the Indian Constitution, in which the state was enjoined to guarantee equality to minority languages, and subsequent education policies that stated that all students had a right to education in their mother tongue.[17]

Yet the institution of Santali was not so straightforward as the headmaster's comments seemed to suggest. Schools in rural West Bengal, in addition to their bureaucratic function, serve a political function as well. As Arild Ruud (2003) discusses, from the late 1970s, schools and schoolteachers spearheaded the spread of Communism in rural areas by enmeshing politics with the metropolitan literary culture of the urban, Calcutta-based middle class (*bhadralok* or respectable people).[18] Hence rather than establishing a hegemony of class-based struggle, the rise of Communism established new classes of what Ruud calls "rustic *bhadralok*" (Ruud 2003:73), intellectuals of various caste backgrounds who aligned with metropolitan Bengali language and literature, using their cultural and political capital to ensure uninterrupted Communist rule in the state from 1977 to 2011.

As editors of a recent volume on caste in West Bengal suggest, discussions about caste in West Bengal are often obfuscated by what they call the "*bhadralok* hegemony" of metropolitan Bengali language and culture (Chandra et al. 2015: 2), an upper-caste directed[19] hegemony propagated in large part by the system of education. The school, however, as a political space also played a crucial part in Jharkhand politics and the rise of activism. Raghunath Murmu was for example a schoolteacher who gained his position in part due to his status as ST (Scheduled Tribe), but was then tasked with teaching his students the "mainstream" literary culture. In addition, most of the Jhilimili region's famous Santali-language poets, such as Sarada Prasad Kisku, who was extremely influential in establishing Santali literature in the region and was a graduate of Jhilimili High School, were also schoolteachers. Hence, the school itself served as a dialogic space, where caste hegemony (in the form of Bengali *bhadralok* politics) was both perpetuated and contested. Moreover, like the spread of Communism, the school also became a place where a Jharkhand-inspired politics of autonomy was elaborated, and from where the Santali language was endowed with qualities akin to Bengali, which then became materialized in the form of writing and circulated back through the villages.

Following the creation of the Jharkhand state, and the rise of a more militant Santali-language activism among a younger generation of Santals, there were new demands made on the West Bengal government that schools in Santal-plurality areas should begin offering Santali as a first-language subject. After persistent neglect by the Communist-led government to implement the courses, organizations such as the All India Santali Students Association, ASECA, and others filed a series of court cases in the 1990s demanding that posts be created as per government law. The court agreed and enjoined the government to advertise posts at a handful of schools, including Jhilimili.

In 2002, the first Santali-language teacher was hired at Jhilimili. Hailing from Jharkhand state himself, he was active in Jharkhand politics and was part of the students' organization that agitated for Santali implementation in schools. He had also graduated from ASECA schools and learned the Ol-Chiki script. However, when it was finally time to begin the classes, he told me in an interview that the headmaster refused to implement the court order, saying he lacked permission from the school managing committee. The managing committee was an elected body of local community members that managed school affairs and community relations, and, especially since the rise of Communism, had become affiliated with party politics. At the time of Santali's implementation, caste Hindu members of the Communist Party dominated the managing committee.

When asked why the managing committee refused to give permission, the teacher shrugged his shoulders and said, in a matter-of-fact manner, that there was "a lack of interest." This answer appeared to me at first strange, but it became clearer once I realized that for caste Hindus Santali was not considered a legitimate language but rather an unformed dialect of lower-caste persons. If that were the case, then why would they take an interest in implementing it into the education system, the purpose of which was to transform rural citizens into a "respectable" class (*bhadralok*) through the exposure to Bengali metropolitan literature? Consequently, though the teacher was hired to teach Santali, he was instead assigned to teach what was considered more desirable and necessary subjects by the committee, such as maths or Bengali.

The issue, according to the teacher, became highly politicized. Groups allied with the Jharkhand movement such as the Jharkhand political parties and the local branch of ASECA regularly held demonstrations protesting for the immediate implementation of Santali language and the use of Ol-Chiki script inside the classroom. Classes and normal school activities were disrupted, but still the stalemate continued. Finally in 2003, the Calcutta High Court ordered that Santali classes resume without delay and provided the teacher with police protection. Under the eye of the state government, and with the school administration and committee members watching, he taught his first class with only nine students in attendance.

At present, one would never suppose that the implementation of Santali was such a highly politicized issue. Yet if one were to view the "official" surfaces of the school buildings, like in the bazaar discussed earlier, one would see very little trace of the institutionalization of Santali or the Ol-Chiki script. In fact, despite the school's "multilingual" philosophy, the visual displays perpetuate a *bhadralok* hegemony grounded in metropolitan Bengali language and literature in which Santali is clearly omitted. Yet sitting barely ten meters from the school buildings are the hostels, provided to SC and ST students for their lodging. There the students, even those who are not enrolled in the Santali-language class, have brought with them the ideology of the Jharkhand movement, prominently displaying the Ol-Chiki script and Santal-specific histories on the surfaces of their buildings. In embracing the politics of autonomy on the school grounds, they are creating a space of intimacy while publicly repositioning themselves from a "caste" in need of development to a "community" with equal stake in the institution and bureaucratic apparatus.

Inscribing *Bhadralok* Hegemony

The school lay at the intersection of state-level bureaucracy and the local political structure. Teachers from throughout the district and the state of West Bengal were sent to Jhilimili and allotted positions based on results of a statewide competitive examination. For many of the teachers, this was their first-time encounter with Santali in their life apart from the way it had been portrayed in Bengali-language literature and media. The school's position as a state institution led to a valorization of the Bengali language on all official

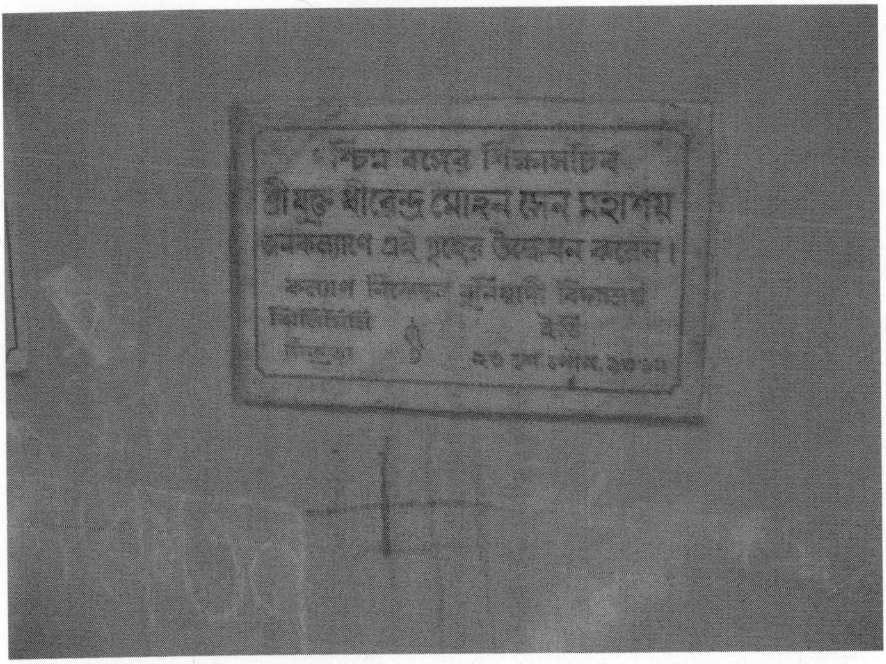

Figure 4.1 Plaque outside the staff room, administrative building (Bengali/Eastern Brahmi script). Photo by author.

signage, despite Santali's position as both a state and nationally recognized official language. For instance, all school buildings, including the hostels for the ST students, were named with official plaques in Bengali describing the date of their inauguration (Figure 4.1), in which a minister took part. There was no attempt to use Santali or Ol-Chiki for this purpose.

The sign is rendered in an official variety of Bengali and mentions the "Paschim Bangla Shikhasachiv" or the official secretary of the West Bengal department of education, who inaugurated this teacher's room for the Jhilimili Kalyan Niketan School. Signs like this, through the use of Bengali language and script, connect the school to the state government in Kolkata and an all-West Bengal framework for education and bureaucratic protocol in which the sole language is Bengali.

When I first arrived in Jhilimili, most of the school buildings, with the exception of the dedication plaques, were a blank orange color with no inscription at all. In an effort to enliven the environment, the teachers, many of whom were young caste Hindus who were experiencing life in a forest area for the first time and took their charge of education seriously, decided to name the buildings. They chose to name the buildings after famous personalities of the "Bengali Renaissance," which refers to the late nineteenth and early twentieth century flowering of metropolitan Bengali literary and scientific culture. Buildings were named after famous caste Hindu Renaissance personalities such as the renowned chemist Prafulla Chandra Ray (see Figure 4.2), the nationalist modernizer Swami Vivekananda, and the Nobel-prize winning author Rabrindranath Tagore. While one building was named after the Adivasi hero Birsa Munda, no mention of any Santali author or historical figure was painted, despite many hailing from the local area in and around Jhilimili. This effort thus perpetuated the *bhadralok* hegemony in which metropolitan Bengali and its literature was institutionally valorized and endowed with qualities of enlightened knowledge associated with education, while Santali was considered an external, caste-delimited local dialect.

In addition to drawing in the metropolitan Bengali culture that underlie the expansion of education and state power in West Bengal, the school grounds also featured local displays of caste hegemony. For instance, wealthy Utkal

Figure 4.2 Classroom building named after famous Bengali chemist Prafulla Chandra Ray (1861–1944). The sign reads "Acharya [teacher] Prafulla Chandra Bhobon [hall]" (Eastern Brahmi script). Photo by author.

Figure 4.3 Entrance gate to Jhilimili high school, donated by a Brahmin family featuring Saraswati, Hindu goddess of learning. Photo by author.

Brahmins donated the school grounds, and, in the initial years, oversaw the education system. Utkal Brahmin residents still played an important role in the school affairs, although with the rise of electoral politics, their influence diminished. Yet, even on entering the school itself, one sees signs of their influence and largesse, for instance, the majestic gate at the entrance, which prominently displays Saraswati, the Hindu goddess of learning. The gate frames the school, though nominally secular, as an officially caste-Hindu space (Figure 4.3).

Refiguring Writing

On the school buildings writing enfigured caste-Hindu, *bhadralok* qualities, which the education system in West Bengal (and in the Bengali language) sought to endow in students. However, the school space contrasted with the space of the student dormitories or "hostels," located immediately adjacent to the classroom and administrative buildings. These hostels were reserved for members of Scheduled Tribes and Scheduled Castes, and thus Santals formed a plurality within them, though there were also other castes such as Munda, Bhumij (ST), and Mandal (SC). In these hostels, writing, through the use of Ol-Chiki in particular but also in the use of multigraphic repertoires of the Santali language, was refigured. Enlightenment ideals associated with education such as knowledge and good character were de-linked from the figure of the *bhadralok* and attached to Santal-specific histories, practices, and intimate domains.

In order to accomplish this, students, like the teachers did with the school buildings, would inscribe the interiors and exteriors of their quarters. Some of these inscriptions were in Bengali language and script, but they marked out an alternative history of writing and education to the one endorsed on the grounds of the nearby school. For instance, at the front of the class 8 hostel, students named the adjacent hostel quarters "Sidhu–Kanu bhobon" (Sidhu Kanu Hall, Figure 4.3) and "Pandit Raghunath Murmu koksho" (Pandit Raghunath Murmu Room, Figure 4.4). Placing the warriors Sidhu–Kanhu and the founder of Ol-Chiki script side by side, they hearken back to a history of writing, discussed in Chapter 2, that extends beyond the halls of the schools and articulates the history of insurrection and the Jharkhand movement.

In addition to a small number of Bengali tokens, students were also enthusiastic about decorating their building exteriors with Ol-Chiki. For instance in the class 8 and 9 boys' hostel, the entrances were decorated with odes to "*Biddạ Ayo*" (Mother Knowledge, Figure 4.5) and the introductory

Figure 4.4 Sidhu Kanhu Bhobon, class 8/9 boys' hostel in Bengali/Eastern Brahmi. Photo by author.

Figure 4.5 Pandit Raghunath Murmu Koksho, class 8/9 boys' hostel in Bengali/Eastern Brahmi. Photo by author.

Figure 4.6 "*Biddạ Ayo*" (Mother Knowledge) in Santali/Ol-Chiki script, class 8/9 hostels. Photo by author.

prayer to Raghunath Murmu's play about Ol-Chiki script *Bidhu-Chandan*, describing the patron spirits of Ol-Chiki "spreading knowledge" (*biddạ chachalakin*, Figure 4.6). The students in these hostels thus imbued Ol-Chiki with "enlightenment" tied to literacy within the multicultural, developmental state, but in this case the enlightenment is also tied to Santali-specific histories and the trajectory of the Jharkhand movement. The writing also serves as a form of affective socialization, aligning Ol-Chiki with the educational project, especially for younger students who are not yet old enough to enroll in the Santali-language course.

The upper-class boys' hostel also featured the use of Ol-Chiki on the entrances. For instance, the doors, decorated with patterns seen on entrances in village homes, are prominently labeled in Ol-Chiki with the words "*Sagun Daram*" "Welcome," and "Jhilimili" (Figures 4.8 and 4.9). Many of the students in classes 10–12 are enrolled in the Santali course, but even in my conversations with Santali-speaking students who opted for Bengali, I saw that

Figure 4.7 "*Bidhu Chandan kin Johar, Biddạ chachala kin.*" Salutations to Bidhu–Chandan, who spread knowledge." Class 8/9 hostels. Photo by author.

Figure 4.8 *Sagun Daram* (Welcome) on the class 10–12 hostel doors, Santali, Ol-Chiki. Photo by author.

Figure 4.9 "Jhilimili" in Ol-Chiki script, class 10–12 hostel doors, Ol-Chiki. Photo by author.

increasing use of Ol-Chiki on the hostel grounds created an enthusiasm and identification with the script. One Santal student who had opted for Bengali language as his "first language" was the first one to point the doors out to me, remarking on how nice the doors to their room looked with the Ol-Chiki script

Figure 4.10 "Sagun Daram" in Santali/Roman, class 10–12 hostel doors. Photo by author.

inscribed on them. Finally, a third door (Figure 4.10) is labeled with the words "*Sagun Daram*" or "Welcome" in Roman, echoing similar patterns in the bazaar discussed in Chapter 3, where Roman/Ol-Chiki combinations project a trans-regional scale that recalls the calls for larger Jharkhand. In echoing these patterns, the students are placing the school, which administratively is tied to the state of West Bengal, to the larger spatial network that expands beyond the borders of the administrative region.

Consequently, while the hostels are nominally caste delimited spaces in that they are reserved for the development of Scheduled Tribes and Scheduled Castes, the presence of Santali and Ol-Chiki on the hostel's visible exteriors transforms them to venues for the assertion of Santali aspirations for institutional equity and community autonomy. However, the transition from caste to community is not simply a process of public display or demanding recognition, but also entails a certain configuration of values in which the Santali language and the Ol-Chiki script align with the desirable qualities of education. These more intimate displays take place on the interiors of the hostels and in different forms. For instance, every day in the girls' hostel, which unlike the boys' quarters is cut off from the campus by a boundary wall, the senior students would organize the daily evening prayer. Yet, instead of a prayer to the Hindu goddess Saraswati, or general prayer, the prayer was the opening hymn for Raghunath Murmu's play, *Bidhu-Chandan*:

Transcript 4.1 Evening prayer, girls hostel, Jhilimili high school

Student 1: (in Bengali) Prarthona shuru koro	Please start the prayer
All students: (in Santali)	
1 Johar, Johar Bidhu-Chandan	Salutations to Bidhu Chandan
2 Gun biddạ chachalakin	Who spread knowledge of good qualities
3 Ol biddạ geyan chachal [akin]	Who spread knowledge of writing (ol)
4 Buddhi geyan khaṭo getin'	My knowledge and understanding is lacking
5 Dhi dare bale getin'	The power of my intelligence is untapped
6 Dese in' ho disạ emạn'bin	[Bidhu-Chandan] offer me direction

The hymn imbues the knowledge of writing (*ol*) with the knowledge of good "qualities" (*gun bidạ*), such as intelligence (*buddhi*), understanding (*geyan*), and ability (*dhi dare*). However, because the spirits referenced are Bidhu and Chandan, who are the patron saints of Ol-Chiki specifically, "writing" here

Figure 4.11 "Here you do not have a chance to look at yourselves." Santali/Ol-Chiki. Class 10–12 hostel. Photo by author.

is not understood simply as knowledge of literacy but also knowledge of the Ol-Chiki script. The script, and the interdiscursive networks of affective performance in which it is embedded, serve as a way of alternative language and literacy socialization, bringing Scheduled Caste and Scheduled Tribe girls, some of whom are not even Santali speakers, into an intimate, and affectively charged relation with writing.

While songs such as this are not performed in the boys' hostels, the boy students decorated the inside of their rooms with proverbs and edicts in Ol-Chiki script that exhort the students to assume positive qualities associated with education and knowledge cultivation. For instance, on the windowsills are two edicts, framed as prohibitions that say, "Here you (pl) do not have a chance to look at yourselves" (Figure 4.11) and "Suspicious looks, sarcastic smiles, and haughty walks are prohibited here" (Figure 4.12). By relating these proverbs in Ol-Chiki, the students link the script with an intimate, community-internal morality and ethics.

Yet the interior of the upper-class boys' hostel also displayed proverbs and posters in Santali in Eastern Brahmi script, contrasting with the exteriors, which only displayed Santali in Ol-Chiki or Ol-Chiki/Roman combinations.

Figure 4.12 "Suspicious looks, sarcastic smiles, and haughty walks are prohibited." Class 10–12 hostel. Santali/Ol-Chiki. Photo by author.

As noted, some of the Santali-speaking students, and most of the other students from different SC/ST groups, did not take the Santali language class and thus were not familiar with Ol-Chiki. In addition, many Santali students, even if they did take the Santali class, preferred writing Santali in the Eastern Brahmi. For instance, old discarded notebooks scattered around the school grounds showed students writing love letters to their Santali-speaking girlfriends, Santali-language drama scripts, or songs in Santali/Eastern Brahmi. As one student told me, while most students liked the idea of Ol-Chiki, Eastern Brahmi was easier to write, and both in the classroom and in daily writing they used it more. Yet, unlike Ol-Chiki, no student showed enthusiasm about Eastern Brahmi or referred to it as "our" (*aboak'*) script. Thus, Eastern Brahmi was still associated with the dominant Bengali language and reinforced the subordination of Santali. This could be one reason for its absence on the exterior of the hostel, even though its association with intimate writing practices resulted in its continued use on the hostel's interior, away from the public gaze. Figure 4.13 displays an example of Santali language proverbs on their walls written in Eastern Brahmi so they could be easily readable; also on the hostel walls students had pasted posters of their favorite Santali-language dramas (in Eastern Brahmi script), of which they were avid fans.

Figure 4.13 "Jhilimili" in Santali/Ol-Chiki at the foot of the headmaster's office. Photo by author.

The surfaces on the hostel's exteriors and interiors, as well as affective socialization around script, refigure notions of caste of and intimacy through the deployment of graphic politics. However, these practices differ depending on which axis the graphic politics are operating. On the intercommunity axis of differentiation, in which recognition determines a status as caste or community, refiguration occurs through the valorization of Ol-Chiki script alone, emblematic of a distinct Santali-speaking community equal under the multicultural eyes of the state. Yet on the axis of intracommunity differentiation (or intimacy), writing assumes relevance through its endowment with community-internal values, which is accomplished through the deployment of a multiscriptal and multimodal repertoire.

From Caste to Community

Walking out of the staff room, I passed by the headmasters' office, when I saw at the foot of his door the words "Jhilimili" scrawled in Ol-Chiki script

(Figure 4.13). The Santali teacher at the time laughed when he saw this saying that the students were writing a lot these days. In fact, it was true, students had started writing Ol-Chiki messages in graffiti, usually simple words or phrases, not only on the walls of the hostels but on the main school buildings as well. While the teachers did not explicitly comment much about it, in practice it constantly forced them to recognize the presence of Ol-Chiki on the campus.

It had been nearing a decade since the first Santali-language class was instituted at the school. By this time, the political movement and student-led efforts to increase the visibility of the Ol-Chiki script had started to alter the evaluation of Santali within the institution. However, the acknowledgement of Santali came not in the form of spoken language, which was still viewed in negative caste terms, but strictly in its graphic form. Hence the headmaster who was describing the "multilingual" philosophy talked about "Bengali, English, and *Ol-Chiki.*" Non-Santali teachers consistently referred to the Santali-language class as the "Ol-Chiki subject" and whenever caste Hindus in the school mentioned the name of the language in reference to its instruction, they referred to it as "Ol-Chiki" rather than the caste-based references they used to refer to the spoken language (*ṭhar* or *adibasi*). Consequently, through a foregrounding of script, and through the endowing of script with the qualities associated with institutional education, students and activists had started to change the conception of Santali more generally from a spoken caste-based variety to an equal, autonomous register known simply as "Ol-Chiki."

Many Santals I talked to had reservations about this refiguration. One writer said that the "Dikus" call it "Ol-Chiki, but that is the name of the *script* not the language (*bhasha*)." Ol-Chiki script itself was not universally accepted among Santals in Jhilimili, especially those of the older generation who were not proficient in the script, and had grown up reading and writing Santali in Eastern Brahmi. They argued that Santali in Eastern Brahmi was legitimate as well, and indeed it was much more widespread than Ol-Chiki, both in everyday written practice, in the bazaar, and within the school itself. Even for the younger generation, most of who supported Ol-Chiki, such as the Santali-language teacher at the school, the constant referral to the language as "Ol-Chiki" was met with ambivalence.

Yet even with these reservations around the conflation of script and language, it seems as if the qualities endowed the Ol-Chiki script did, in fact, impact Santali speakers' perceptions and evaluations of their relationship to their own language and general ideas of literacy. When Santals learned that I studied "Ol-Chiki," I assumed a certain respect in the community, and some even called me "Ol-Chiki master," which was a respectful term used for teacher. One of my interlocutors who lived in a village near Jhilimili, a native-speaking Santali woman who had studied up until class 10 (in Bengali) once remarked to me how I was more proficient in "Santali" than she or her family because I knew to read and write Ol-Chiki script. This is despite the fact that I was clearly much less competent than her in the spoken register of Santali. Conversations such as these indicate that as Ol-Chiki started to signify (or "rhematize") institutionally sanctioned literacy in Santali-speaking communities, speakers started to align Santali proficiency with Ol-Chiki script rather than the speech of the Hoṛ.

My conversations also demonstrated the effects of the refiguration of Santali language on an axis of differentiation that valorizes writing *over* speech within the community. The opposition between Hoṛ and Diku on the axis of differentiation within the spoken language intimately binds the Santali-speaking community together regardless of their schooling or literacy levels. However, the importation of a developmental logic of literacy in which Ol-Chiki is the primary icon of the "community" has the unintended consequence of constructing a hierarchy between written and spoken varieties, inadvertently instilling a feeling of illiteracy among Santali speakers in relation to their own language where none existed before. This process is similar to what Barbra Meek has observed in her study of First Nations language revitalization efforts in northwest Canada, where she suggests that the "merging of bureaucratic logics with in-group distinctions" creates a "disruption" of the intimate domains previously typified by indigenous language use (Meek 2014: 80–1).

Conclusion

Visiting Jharkhand state, one now sees a renewed push by activists among different Adivasi communities, such as the Ho and Oraon, to institute their script as part of the school education. The case in Jhilimili offers some insights into both the possibilities and limits for indigenous language, and importantly, indigenous script as a medium for education. On the one hand, script challenges prevailing hierarchies, which, in relation to Adivasis such as the Santals, functions on an axis of differentiation in which language is fused with embodied qualities of personhood. By valorizing script, Santali speakers were able to refigure Santali as a written language with an independent script, endowing this script with qualities that aligned with the developmental ideals of state-driven education and literacy. Hence, Santali was cast as autonomous, and therefore, equal, in the multicultural framework of the state, challenging the caste hierarchies associated with the spoken register.

Yet as I also showed this was not simply a matter of recognition, for as Garcia's account of the rejection of indigenous language schooling by community members in Peru suggests, state recognition alone does not guarantee success or salience, especially when the community does not embrace it. Ol-Chiki at the school had to be co-articulated with extrainstitutional practices of autonomy such as Santali-specific histories, oral performance practices, and as part of a multiscriptal repertoire. This meant that within the institution, Ol-Chiki accrued both an external, intercommunity function, and an intimate function in which the politics of autonomy could persist even in a Diku-dominated space, creating what Tanabe called a moral foundation necessary for the contestation of caste inequality in modern Indian democracy. The dual function of Ol-Chiki on the school grounds therefore aligns with the larger Jharkhand project, in which Adivasis maintain autonomy in relation to state institutions, from both within and without, and through that autonomy assert equality within the field of caste relations.

However, I also showed the limits of such a project. By linking Ol-Chiki with discourses of development, "language community," and institutionalized education, the project elevates the graphic over the spoken register, resulting in new feelings of illiteracy within the larger Santali-speaking population. This in turn creates a certain limitation on the Jharkhand project and the politics of autonomy, which in the larger community is about much more than the Ol-Chiki script. In fact, as the students' own writing practices show, Ol-Chiki exists in a certain relation with other scripts and languages, all of which allow a more complex idea of Jharkhand to emerge. The school is limited in that its institutional structure only creates space for certain version of the project. That is why we turn to a place where we can chart the multilingual, multiscriptal historical and intergenerational networks—the vibrant field of Santali-language media.

5

Santali-Language Print Media and the Jharkhand Imagination

During my fieldwork, I remember sitting on the stoop of the bicycle garage at the crossroads on the way to Jhilimili bazaar and seeing a deliveryman on a bicycle come and deliver copies of the Bengali-language newspapers *Anandabazar Patrika, Bartaman* (Present Day), and *Pratidin* (Daily). *Anandabazar Patrika* came daily in the morning from Kolkata, although different insets would be placed inside depending on which part of the state it was being distributed. It was the more highbrow of the three and was the most common paper read by the Bengali metropolitan middle class. *Bartaman* and *Pratidin* had branch offices in the district towns, and their headlines were bolder and more sensationalistic. As the papers were delivered, a steady stream of people would come to the stoop and begin to read, handing out sections to one another and discussing the daily news events.

As the conflict between the Maoist forces and the state paramilitary forces stepped up, people's interest in the news piqued, and headlines frequently became topics of conversation. Politically motivated killings, calls for general strikes, and news of battles between Maoists and state forces made the daily delivery of the newspaper an eagerly awaited event, even if now in most villages there were at least a few households with access to multiple twenty-four-hour Bengali-language news networks. The hotly contested 2011 state elections in West Bengal, in which the Communist Party of India (Marxist) lost power in the state elections for the first time in thirty-eight years, compounded the heatedness of the present moment. People crowded around copies of the paper as they were delivered each morning, reading out the headlines and passing different sections around so everyone had a chance to look. Depending on who was present, opinions were frequently solicited and then contested. After the Democratic Party in the United States lost the 2010 midterm elections, people would often point to the paper and discuss these events with me, asking me questions about the American political system.

Saturated with Bengali-language media, Jhilimili could be easily seen as incorporated within, to cite Benedict Anderson, the Bengali "imagined" community.[1] In fact, a growing stream of literate readers, educated in the metropolitan variety of Bengali, and given the importance of statewide politics for the daily lives of the readers meant that residents of Jhilimili and other areas of West Bengal consumed the news from the metropolitan centers in much the same way that their other Bengali-reading and -speaking contemporaries did elsewhere in the state.[2] Even the news about their own region was primarily channeled through this metropolitan reportage, a fact of which residents were keenly aware. For instance, everybody laughed when it was reported in one of the newspapers that Adivasis in the Jungle Mahal were so poor that they had to eat red ants, despite the fact that red ants, which had a strong flavor, were known to be a delicacy in the area.

Such kind of reporting, which characterized the "Adivasi" as mired in extreme poverty and the forested area where they resided as exotic and politically unstable perpetuated the notion of Jhilimili, and the whole region, as a marginal location in the metropolitan Bengali imagination. Yet residents of Jhilimili reflected on themselves or their region not only through the lens of the metropolitan press. The history of the Jharkhand movement, the resulting political identity of "Adivasi," and the growth of writing in Santali in multiple scripts created the conditions for a proliferation of locally produced, multilingual, and multiscriptal media that addresses readers not simply as residents in a delimited state or territory, or members of a vernacular or regional language community, but as subjects involved in the production of autonomous domains that cut across lines of territory, caste, and linguistic affiliation.

The chapter begins by detailing what I call the Jharkhand imagination[3] in relation to popular frameworks of Indian nationalism. I suggest that this imagination, based not on unity but on difference, challenges both Benedict Anderson's notion of print capitalism as creating unified, "mono-glot" publics, as well as theories of Indian nationalism, which posit publics as fragmented through distinctions between cosmopolitan and vernacular language media.

Instead, Santali-language print media project images of publics that both assert difference, yet also attempt to bridge these differences to create "trans-ethnic" political platforms. In analyzing both monolingual, multiscriptal Santali-language magazines and bilingual, multiscriptal Santali–Bengali newspapers, in the chapter I argue that the multiscriptality and multilingualism embedded in this media form engenders new political affiliations that project aspirations for autonomy for the Santali-speaking community as well as the region as a whole. While the focus of this chapter is on print media, I will briefly discuss how these aspirations also shape online communication as well.

Autonomy beyond the Vernacular

Binaries between cosmopolitan registers ("English") and the so-called vernaculars such as Hindi, Bengali, and Tamil, have often informed studies of nationalism. For instance, in his criticism of Anderson's monolingual and mono-directional conception of nationalism, Partha Chatterjee (1993) suggests that the bilingualism of Indian elites resulted in a dichotomy between a "material" form of nationalism that more closely resembled Anderson's progressive and Western-like imagined community, and a "spiritual" form in which European models of nation were rejected for traditional and timeless "Indian" conceptions. Chatterjee argues that the material domain was articulated through innovation in indigenous writing in English, while the spiritual was cultivated through the standardization and creation of new literary genres in vernacular languages such as Bengali. In a similar vein, Sudipta Kaviraj (1992) discusses how national elites leveraged English as the language of an interregional nationalism, while delimiting identities through standardization projects of regional vernaculars. The maintenance of this English/vernacular dichotomy ensured, according to Kaviraj, that subaltern political aspirations would be limited to regional political formations, and the disavowal of a previously rich multilingual culture resulted in a "thin" (Kaviraj 1992: 50) nationalism at the level of the larger Indian state.

In recent times, the "vernacular" has started to become to be taken more seriously as a medium and modality of nationalist politics, particularly in relation to media. For instance, in a famous study, Rajagopal (2001) discusses how Hindi-language media aided in the rise of the Hindu right in the late 1980s and early 1990s in India, a phenomenon that was inadequately understood by the national-level English-language newspapers. Rajagopal characterizes this as a "split public," where populist (and fundamentalist) aspirations are manifested in the vernacular language, while the English-language media remains tied to a "political and legal framework." Rajagopal's analysis reveals a polity fractured along the lines of two monolingual interpretative communities, which, without any kind of interaction, has led to a pernicious and dangerous form of nationalism.

Thus, even in outlining the ways in which linguistic and cultural diversity interrupts Anderson's "modular" conceptions, scholars of Indian nationalism continue to rely on what Michael Silverstein, in his critique of Anderson's work, calls a certain assumption of "we-ness" (Silverstein 2000:117). Silverstein argues that in order to "imagine" that the reader and writer are speaking in one and the same voice, analysts must take for granted the institutions and power relations that guarantee that addressor and addressee share a similar spatiotemporal frame in the use of any given language. The concept of split or fragmented publics still assumes the use of English as invoking a cosmopolitan and state-centric stance, while the vernacular indexes regional and popular perspectives.[4] Yet as the episode of Jhilimili residents' reactions to the Bengali-language newspapers' discussion of "the poor, red-ant eating Adivasis" illustrates, the use of a common language regularly fails to align addressor and addressee in a unified "we."

The Jharkhand movement has offered a different vision of "we"-ness than the linguistically informed nationalism in which language became a marker of ethnic and territorial unity. As the Marxist scholar Javeed Alam notes, the movement for Jharkhand, led by no dominant linguistic or ethnic group, was informed by a combination of certain tribal communities demanding "recognition as a distinct group" while also organizing "trans-ethnic political platforms" (Alam 2003:196). These platforms saw members of different tribal communities (under the name "Adivasi") collaborating with non-Adivasis to forge a political alliance in relation to perceived "others." As Alam suggests, the demands for autonomy did not seek to guarantee special privileges for a particular region, language, or ethnic group, but instead aimed to create platforms in which difference was recognized between individual groups as well as between the totality of these groups and perceived others: "there grows a sense of 'we together' are a different people with a trans-ethnic dimension" (197).

The voice of "we-together" has faded, as many have suggested from the state-centric politics of the current Jharkhand state,[5] yet I argue that it is this voice—one that allows for disjuncture[6] rather than presupposing an imagined alignment—that emerges in the locally produced multilingual and multiscriptal media of southwest West Bengal. This part of West Bengal differs from other parts of Jharkhand state in that, even though it is comprised of a variety of ethnic groups, the plurality of the Santals and their leadership in the local Jharkhand movement has resulted in Santali becoming the primary linguistic register through which an Adivasi political affiliation is articulated, with Bengali acting as a link language with different communities, both Adivasi and non-Adivasi. Hence the media discussed here include Santali "literary and cultural journal," monolingual, multiscriptal magazines, which have helped create an independent Santali literary sphere, and bilingual Santali–Bengali newspapers written in Eastern Brahmi and Ol-Chiki that link the Santali language with a larger conception of Jharkhand. Despite the relatively small circulation of these media artifacts, the use of different scripts and languages, I suggest, allows media producers to scale multiple conceptions of territory (local, regional, trans-regional) and address different audiences simultaneously. Santali in the Eastern Brahmi script, for instance, can be used to invoke a locally based politics of autonomy that evolved from region-level organizing, while the Ol-Chiki script invokes the project of "unity" with other Santals throughout the breadth of eastern India. The use of Bengali language, on the other hand, far from aligning Santals with a metropolitan chronotope, is used to invoke a trans-ethnic vision of a Jharkhand public that invites participation from various communities while also addressing so-called others such as the state government.

I will first outline the media ecology of the region and then focus on the two major genres of locally produced Santali-language media, the "literary and cultural journal" and the "news." I will chart how an evolving politics of autonomy and changing nature of the conception of Jharkhand has influenced the organization of these media artifacts and their circulation and reception. Contrary to the "voice" of nationalism, I argue that these periodicals, projecting several distinct graphic and linguistic ideologies, envisions a polity encompassing separate, but overlapping political identities and alliances that exist both within and beyond national borders. This vision of autonomy, what here I call the Jharkhand "imagination," emerges at the interstices of the material and the political.[7]

Mediating Jharkhand in Southwest West Bengal

The Jharkhand imagination in southwest West Bengal, a region popularly known as the Jangal Mahals, has evolved through a shared history of migration, expropriation, and revolt. The "Jangal Mahals" was a former colonial district that covered a wide area in the erstwhile Bengal presidency, encompassing parts of the current states of Jharkhand, West Bengal, and Odisha. Ecologically, the region could be characterized by its hilly and forested terrain and precarious cultivation cycles; demographically, it was inhabited by highly mobile populations in which headmen negotiated with local zamindars to cultivate land and access the forests. These populations included several Scheduled Tribe communities now called Adivasi, including Santals, Kheria, Bhumij, Munda, and other castes who claim to be Adivasi, such as Mahato. Surviving on irregular cultivation supplemented by forest produce, the lives of these communities crucially depended on forest access and entrenched systems of patronage and community-level governance that allowed them to freely migrate between settlements in times of scarcity.

During the colonial period, the British attempted to intervene in this geography of movement and settlement with the passage of tenancy laws (the infamous "Permanent Settlement" of 1793)[8], requiring landlords to collect fixed revenue from the individual cultivator, bypassing the village headmen. This resulted in large-scale displacement of the tribal communities, massive transfers of land, and the breakdown of the headman system. However, in response to Permanent Settlement, headmen from various communities began to orchestrate revolts throughout the region, starting with the 1799 Chuar Rebellion, which occurred in and around Jhilimili, and the 1832 Bhumij Rebellion in Purulia district, near Jhilimili, followed by a series of similar rebellions.[9] These revolts were also connected with insurrections in nearby areas such as the 1855 Santal Hul, which originated in Dumka district in northern Jharkhand, or the *deshgaro* ("seize the country") rebellions of 1920 and 1924 activated by Santal unrest in Odisha. Despite the British attempts to divide and delineate territory, as well as criminalize various communities, the revolts resulted in what Rannabir Samaddar calls a "territorial" memory (Samaddar 1998: 144) of regional autonomy and trans-ethnic collective action that continues to animate the life and politics of the people of the region.

During the time immediately before and after Indian Independence, this territorial consciousness emerged once again in the call for Jharkhand. Jharkhand was at once about a demand for independent statehood within the federal structure of independent India, while at the same time a political project that aligned this territorial consciousness with an emerging national-level identity (Adivasi) and demands for equal citizenship in a democratic polity. These alignments are most pointedly articulated in a popular slogan made famous by one of the Jharkhand movement's most notable early personalities, Jaipal Singh, in his famous speech to the All India Adivasi Mahasabha in Ranchi in 1948 titled "Jai Jharkhand! Jai Adivasi! Jai Hind [India]!" (Singh 2003: 2).

In addition to a territorial consciousness fomented through rebellions and political movements such as Jharkhand, from the late nineteenth century, missionaries and Santali-language activists were involved in cultivating a reading public that was linked together across a wide expanse of eastern India through the production and circulation of Santali-language media. The first Santali-language magazine, *Hoṛ hopon ren peṛa,* (The Santal "Guest") published in 1890 in Roman script by Scandinavian missionaries, written in "the Evangelical idiom, for those educated at Mission schools, in an elaborate language" (Carrin and Tambs-Lyche 2008: 288). The magazine (later in 1922 renamed as *Peṛa Hoṛ*) served to connect activities at Benagaria with the mission's far-flung settlements in Assam and areas of the Bengal presidency in what is now Bangladesh.[10] In 1946, the Catholic Church also began publishing its own Santal language monthly, *Marsal Tabon* (Our Light), which like *Peṛa Hoṛ*, contained church news, religious information, Santali-language stories, poetry, and drama. These magazines not only connected church-affiliated Santals who were spread throughout eastern India but also offered platforms for the development and spread of written Santali. Even today, Roman-script publication continues in magazines such as *Jugsirjol* and *Nawa Ipil*, which are read by both Christians and non-Christians throughout eastern India.

Following Indian independence, states made an attempt to reach out to their minority populations through the publication and dissemination of magazines.[11] In 1947, the Bihar government started a Santali-language magazine *Hoṛ Sombad* (Saṇtali News) under the editorial leadership of Dr. Domon Sahu Samir. A caste Hindu from a Santali-speaking area, Samir was one of the first of a long line of non-Santals who became involved in the production of Santali-language material. The publication, on the one hand, strived to promote literary production in Santali while also providing an interface between Santals and the state. Since Hindi in Devanagari script had been proclaimed the official script-language of a multilingual Bihar, *Hoṛ Sombad* was published in a slightly modified Devanagari script (Hembrom 2007:186). Although its primary circulation was in the state of Bihar, the magazine was also influential in the promotion of Santali writing in many of the neighboring regions of southwest West Bengal. Senior writers and publishers in the areas around Jhilimili remarked how some of their first writings were published in that magazine. In 1956, the West Bengal state government began publishing a similar Santali-language magazine, *Galmarao* (Discussion) in Eastern Brahmi script (Bengali), later to be renamed simply *Pachim Bangla* (West Bengal) (Hembrom 2007: 216). In both these cases, the aim was to draw in a Santali literary and cultural elite into the state sphere through participation in the magazine, while also creating state-sponsored networks for the dissemination Santali-language material in the rural areas in state scripts.

Although states tried to incorporate Santali-language media production, from the 1950s onward the Jharkhand movement and a politics of autonomy created the conditions for a proliferation of alternative media network in areas such as southwest West Bengal where Santali-language writers, through considerable expense and effort, published magazines on their own in Eastern Brahmi script. These magazines were usually published through small-scale organizations (called *gaonta* in Santali) and financed by local salaried elite (such as schoolteachers or government workers). In many ways, they mirrored the rise of "little magazines," independently produced Bengali-language magazines that contributed significantly to the rise of Left politics.[12] However, while bearing close resemblance to the trend in Bengali metropolitan culture, in using Santali, and in promoting Jharkhand-related agendas, the magazines themselves represented an autonomous form of mediation. In some parts of the area, such as in Purulia district, which borders Jhilimili to the north, as early as the 1970s, there were over sixteen independently produced magazines in Santali language, which circulated along with the twenty-two locally produced Bengali-language magazines.[13] This was quite remarkable considering the fact that Santali was not taught in schools nor did it have a robust printed literary tradition or wide readership market like Bengali.

Thus, along with the creation of independent scripts such as Ol-Chiki or Monj Dander Ank, the emergent media publishing culture in southwest West Bengal rendered written Santali, in particular the Santali print artifact, a critical component of a politics of autonomy. Unlike the Roman-script magazines of the Christian mission or the state-sponsored publications, the magazines, produced locally and consumed only by a small readership, were not affiliated to any institutions (such as the Church) or governmental organizations. Instead they circulated a territorial imagination that was rooted in regional histories and experiences, yet at the same time aligned with the larger project of Jharkhand and the movement for autonomy. In Purulia district, one of the centers of publishing in the region, a senior writer told me that his writing and publishing were connected to the historical experience of his area being wrested away from the state of Bihar and of losing access to the Chota Nagpur Tenancy Act, which guaranteed land rights to Adivasis when the erstwhile Manbhum district became part of Bihar. The strong networks of Santali-language magazine publication, while explicitly connected to the cultivation of Santali literature, was nevertheless, intimately involved in the crafting of circulatory domains where aspirations for autonomy could be enacted and promoted.

Santali-Language Media in Southwest West Bengal

During my time in Jhilimili, I collected various examples of locally produced media that contained Santali, either found lying around the grounds of the village high school, or given to me by subscribers, or writers, or publishers, or bought at village fairs. These publications fell in two broad categories: the

Table 5.1 Santali-language Media Genres present in the region of southwest West Bengal

Genre	**Language**	**Script**	**Circulation**
Literary and cultural journal	Monolingual	monographic	Monthly, quarterly, annually
News	Bilingual	Monographic/digraphic	Fortnightly, monthly

"literary and cultural journal" and what was referred to simply as "news." Literary and cultural journals are magazines, published monthly, quarterly, or annually, and only in the Santali language, though they are written either in Eastern Brahmi, Ol-Chiki, or Roman scripts. They are produced in booklet form with a cover page that contains the title of the magazine and usually different painted artwork. "News," on the other hand, is printed on broadsheet newsprint and is circulated fortnightly or monthly. Most "news" is printed in Santali and Bengali, using Eastern Brahmi and Ol-Chiki scripts (see Table 5.1).

While I have covered the history and the generational divides that characterize the production of the literary and cultural journals extensively elsewhere (Choksi 2017), I provide a brief overview of the genre here in order to show how Santali writers and editors have been involved in creating an independent sphere of Santali literary activity in order to provide the language legitimacy both within the community and across the region as a whole. Magazines have acted as crucial vectors for establishing this legitimacy, particularly given the fact that Santali was not taught in schools nor in use in any institutional or governmental setting.

The durability of this form of circulation can be seen in two of the most popular Santali-language magazines that circulated in Jhilimili, *Tetre* (Marriage Anointer) and *Sili* (Hair-rope), both published from nearby Bandowan, some ten kilometers north of Jhilimili. *Tetre* was started in 1976 and recently restarted circulation, while *Sili* is being published continuously every month for thirty years. The magazines' editors considered themselves acolytes of the famous local Santali-language poet Sarada Prasad Kisku, a schoolteacher and graduate of the Jhilimili High School, who had written numerous poems related to autonomy and the Jharkhand movement and had edited his own magazine *Susạṛ Ḍahar* (Road to Social Welfare). This movement was closely linked with the movement for an independent

Jharkhand. Many of them, who were influenced by this local magazine culture, later became leaders of political parties, such as Aditya Kisku, who started his own printing press and Santali-language magazine before entering formal politics..

Tetre and *Sili* are both published in the Eastern Brahmi script. As digital offset presses only became available recently, the only way to publish them was through manual typesetting and of course only Eastern Brahmi script was available in presses. In addition, as the editor of *Sili* told me, the issue for himself and others involved in Santali-language publishing was to generate interest in the Santali *language* and not to promote any particular *script*. Eastern Brahmi was therefore cast as the most neutral and easily accessible script to build up and circulate Santali-language publications. However, following Salkhan Murmu's visit to West Bengal and the establishment of the "*Bhasha Morcha*" (language movement), where he wedded the idea of Jharkhand with the Ol-Chiki script, readership, according to the *Sili* editor, became increasingly vocal in its demand that Santali-language publications use some form of Ol-Chiki script. In the early 1990s, local members of the local ASECA branch said that they would boycott *Sili* if the magazine did not make some kind of acknowledgment of Ol Chiki. In response, the editor decided to write the title page in Eastern Brahmi and Ol-Chiki, along with Roman transcription (see Figure 5.1). This format has become the standard for most title pages of Santali-language "literary and cultural journals" published in Eastern Brahmi script.

For the editor of *Sili* and others of his generation, the rise of Ol-Chiki was seen more as a distraction and a hindrance to the work they were trying to do in establishing the legitimacy and continuity of Santali-language literature and publication. Yet, as he noted, the addition of Ol-Chiki was a reader-demanded initiative, for which the publishers had to respond in kind. The multiscriptal cover pages diagrams a graphic record of the development of the Santali language in southwest West Bengal, while also, in its continued publication and circulation, offers a certain visual image of Santal autonomy. On the one hand, the Eastern Brahmi script delineates an autonomous domain for the Santali language within the territory of West Bengal in which local political actors could promote a literature and culture even in the absence of formal education

Figure 5.1 *Sili* magazine cover page in (from top to bottom) Ol-Chiki, Eastern Brahmi, and Roman (edited by Kolendranath Mandi, Shirishgora, Purulia, West Bengal).

or state support. This created the conditions under which Santali as a legitimate language could emerge in the first place. Yet at the same time, in employing the Ol-Chiki script on its cover, the magazine aligns with the demands of a new generation and vocal section of readers who imagine territory as trans-local and beyond administrative boundaries, linking Santali-speaking people throughout eastern India.

One day as I was attending a literary meeting in a nearby town, I was asked by a writer and magazine editor of my age about what I thought about Ol-Chiki script. I gave a rambling and academic answer and then I asked him his opinion. He told me very straightforwardly—he thinks Santals should have "unity" and therefore there should be only one script for writing Santali, Ol-Chiki. This editor, I later found out, also a schoolteacher, was part of the same network of authors as the editors of Eastern Brahmi script publication such as *Sili* and *Tetre*: in fact, he was on the publishing committee of *Tetre* and I encountered him again later at the home of the editor of *Tetre*. Yet unlike these editors, his journal, as well as most other journals of younger editors, including the high school teacher from Jhilimili high school, published exclusively in Ol-Chiki. Instead of basing the decision to publish in Ol-Chiki in terms of market response, he cast it in the goal of language of the future; that media *should* work toward the goal of establishing a community of Ol-Chiki readers and writers that exist throughout the Santali-speaking areas. Thus in the absence of a state, Ol-Chiki would provide a connection that establishes "unity" to Santals in the various parts of eastern India.

However, the magazine was not aligned exclusively with the monographic vision of Ol-Chiki. By embracing Ol-Chiki, the magazine was laying the groundwork for future readers to embrace the script and its associated discourse of ' "unity." But it also employed Eastern Brahmi in order to link with the local networks in which the editors and readers were enmeshed. For instance, the title page (Figure 5.2) features the magazine name in Ol-Chiki along with pictures (at the top left) of Raghunath Murmu and (at the top right) Sidhu Murmu, the leader of the Hul. These images and choice of script indexes a view of a broadly conceived Santali-speaking territory bound by a shared history (such as the Hul) and graphic register (Ol-Chiki script). Yet the cover art of the issue features the poet Sarada Prasad Kisku, one of the most important people in the local network of publication, along with his many works in Eastern Brahmi script. Images such as these and the use of Eastern Brahmi script in the interior of the magazine to advertise partner publications such as *Sili* or *Tetre* (Figure 5.3) ground the magazine in the local network and, through script alternation, the publications are aligned

Figure 5.2 *Sarjom Umul* in Ol-Chiki/Roman anchored by Raghunath Murmu, founder of Ol-Chiki, Sidhu Murmu, fighter in the Hul, and Sarada Prasad Kisku, famous local writer (edited by Ganesh Mandi, Maheshnadi, Purulia, West Bengal).

with differing imaginations of community and territory that vary across generations.

Besides the literary and cultural journal, the other major form of print media that included Santali was what people referred to as the "news." Unlike

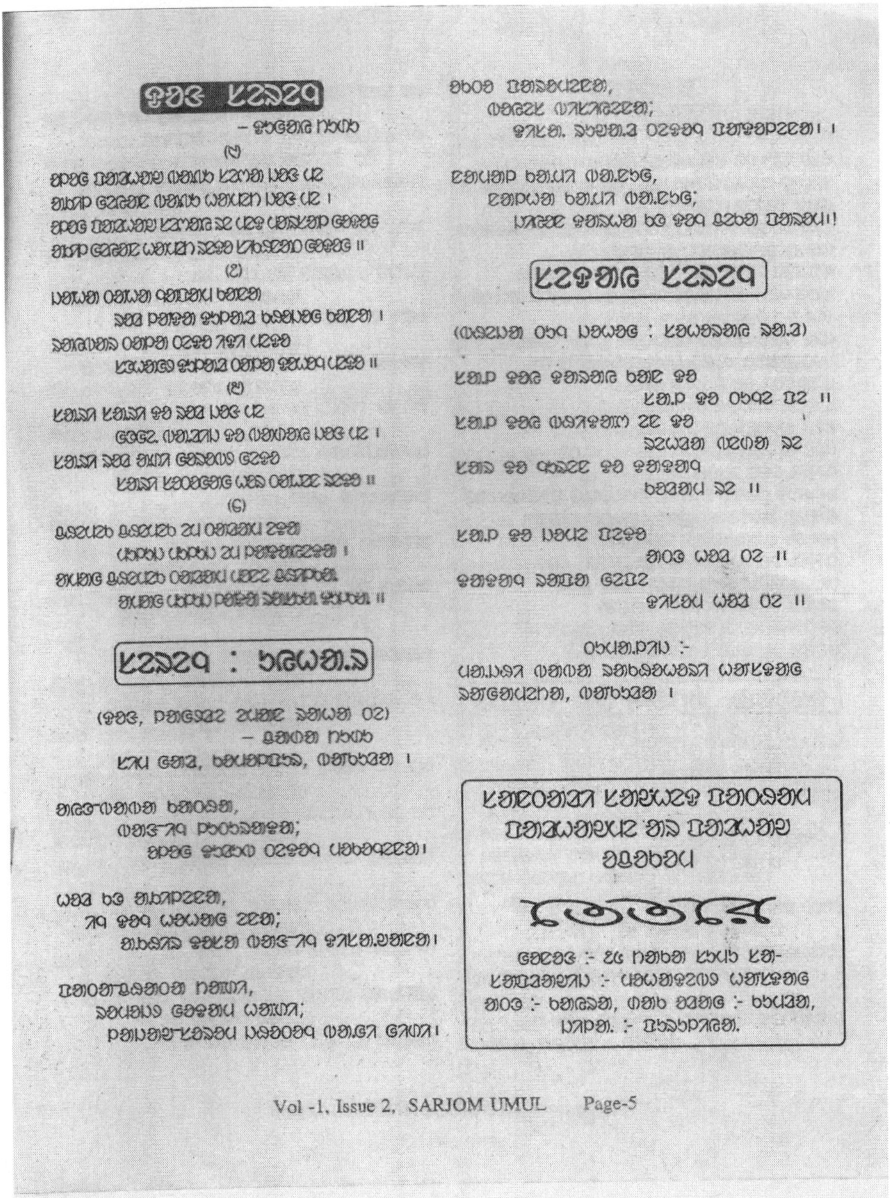

Figure 5.3 Page 5 of *Sarjom Umul* 1:2 featuring Ol-Chiki text with an advertisement for *Tetre* magazine in Eastern Brahmi script.

the magazines, the papers did not concern themselves strictly with trying to create a monolingual, Santali-reading public, but by deploying Santali in tandem with Bengali, the lingua franca of the region, the papers addressed multiple audiences simultaneously including the state administration and other castes. The papers also allied with a resolutely Jharkhand agenda, viewing newsworthy events filtered not through a metropolitan stance (which was the case with the major Bengali-language dailies) but through the lens of a Jharkhand territorial consciousness. Consequently, although the language used is Bengali, the territorial vision that results through this alignment is markedly different from the metropolitan papers.[14] With the inclusion of Santali, and the distribution of reportage between Bengali and Santali, as well as between Eastern Brahmi and Ol-Chiki scripts, Jharkhand, as a territorial conception, is scaled as autonomous from West Bengal, the administrative site of both production and consumption of these artifacts.

Like magazines, newspapers were self- or community-funded, and therefore marked by irregular circulation, with new ones appearing or disappearing frequently. However, one of the few I saw circulating regularly (fortnightly) in Jhilimili was *Sar Sagun* (Good Omen). The paper's publisher was an activist who hailed originally from the Jangal Mahal area but was stationed in the district capital of Bankura. The paper's team also comprised part-time reporters who would cross the region to report on events. The paper is in a bilingual format, containing articles in both Santali and Bengali, but all in Eastern Brahmi script.

Despite the content being displayed in Eastern Brahmi, the banner (see Figure 5.4) relates the name in Roman, Eastern Brahmi, and Ol-Chiki, following the pattern displayed on Santali-language magazines. This use of Ol-Chiki marks it as a bilingual paper, as Ol-Chiki is the most visible marker of the Santali language, despite the use of Eastern Brahmi in the paper itself. In addition the use of Ol-Chiki stakes out the paper's position vis-à-vis those readers who view Santali or Jharkhand activism as trans-regional. Indeed the paper's heading makes this trans-regional aspiration very clear, stating, in Bengali, "*Bharot-er shorbadhik Shaontali-Bangla potrika*" (India's greatest Santali–Bengali newspaper). The paper is flanked by pictures of Sidhu and Kanhu, the heroes of the Santal Hul, and asks a leading question, in Bengali, "Why isn't the Hul Day a national holiday?"

Figure 5.4 *Sar Sagun* 7/6/2011 front page. The title is in Eastern Brahmi and Ol-Chiki scripts with a small subheading in Roman (edited by Malinda Hansda, Bankura, West Bengal).

It was surprising to see that despite the relatively small circulation of the paper in a small corner of West Bengal, the paper makes a claim to speak on behalf of "India" and asks questions of "national" importance.[15] This kind of national-level operation is a claim that is not even made of the metropolitan Bengali-language dailies that have a huge circulation across eastern India and popular among the vast Bengali diaspora in the rest of the country and the world. However, claims such as these are typical of many of the newspapers circulating in this locality. This suggests that producers are involved in a scalar process that seeks to emancipate local events and the multilingual diversity of the region from the confines of marginality and cast the region as an autonomous part of the supra-state of "India." This alignment has always been critical to a Jharkhand project, both when the goal was the creation of a separate state as well as now, as the aim has shifted to enact a space of autonomy through the circulation of cultural and textual forms.

The content of the newspaper does not show any neat divide between Santali- and Bengali-language stories. The Bengali-language stories generally outnumber the Santali-language ones; in a June 7, 2011 issue of *Sar Sagun*, there were ten Bengali-language stories and four Santali-language ones, and in an issue dated March 23, 2011, there were sixteen Bengali-language stories and two Santali-language ones. These numbers are typical of any given issue. Yet despite the preponderance of Bengali-language stories, these stories are not privileged in terms of placement. The front page of the issue presented in Figure 5.4 relates Bengali-language stories about upcoming ration relief on rice or a story about a local Adivasi soccer player who excelled in a professional league. The Santali-language story, also in Eastern Brahmi script, relates how a non-Adivasi man (*diku*) molested an Adivasi-Santal woman. Other Santali-language stories in the rest of the issue discuss events like the start of the annual hunt (*sendrą*), a write-up of the festival of *mak' moṛe*, an annual five-year celebration in a village near Bankura, and a discussion about how village headman resolved a local dispute (Figure 5.5).

While all of these articles feature news items that concern local happenings in Santal villages, they do not contrast significantly in content from other news events related in Bengali. In the paper, Santali-language stories are interspersed evenly with Bengali-language stories that discuss regional and national events in relation to Adivasi concerns, and the stories were visually unified through the consistent use of Eastern Brahmi script. When I met a Santal reporter for the newspaper, I asked him (in Santali) about why the newspaper chose to publish in Bengali and why not opt for publishing only in Santali? He answered that Bengali was necessary so that "they" could understand "our" problems. By "they," he meant the government administration of West Bengal, but also non-Santali-speaking audiences such as local caste Hindus. Consequently, the paper saw itself as addressing multiple audiences with the use of script. These publications appealed to Santali audiences to whom events that were important for their communities were broadcast alongside Bengali, through which larger concerns were brought to attention.. Hence, as the reporter suggested, they could see that locally and regionally relevant "news" projected outward in a way non-Adivasis and government officials could understand. Non-Santali

দৃষ্টিহীন ভারতী হাঁসদা মাধ্যমিকে সফল

মুখ্যমন্ত্রীকে শুভেচ্ছা বার্তা

সানতাড় বাহড়িয়ী চেতান দেকো

হেরেলাঃ জাঃ জটেৎ

জাতি শংসাপত্রের

কাগজ এবং রঙ নিম্নমানের

Figure 5.5 Bottom half of front page of *Sar Sagun*. Santali story in Eastern Brahmi script (bottom left corner), other stories in Bengali.

audiences could, on the other hand, recognize Santali as an integral, and equal, part of the region.

Another one of the more popular fortnightlies that circulated regularly in Jhilimili and other nearby areas was *Lahanti Patrika* (Struggle Paper). This fortnightly is edited by a non-Adivasi who is a Bengali-speaking native of southwest West Bengal who nevertheless spoke Santali fluently and previously participated in Santali-language dramas. The paper's reporters also included non-Santal Adivasis. For instance, the reporter who facilitated my subscription to the paper belonged to the Munda, another Adivasi (ST) community living in the region. Though his native languages were Mundari and Bengali, he also could speak Santali fluently. Like *Sar Sagun*, the paper's front page featured a banner in Eastern Brahmi, Roman, and Ol-Chiki scripts (Figure 5.6) proclaiming in Bengali that it was "All-India's politically struggling Adivasis'

Ramel Group of Industries
র‍্যামেল মানেই - ভরসা আত্মবিশ্বাস প্রাণের বন্ধন

সারা ভারতের সংগ্রামী আদিবাসীদের নিজস্ব, নির্ভীক ও নিরপেক্ষ, পাক্ষিক

পত্রিকা লাহান্তি

LAHANTI PATRIKA

Govt. of India Regn. no. R.N.I. 69892/98 ★ Postal RN - SSP(BKU) / RNP - 4 / 2008 -11
Office :- Sidhu-Kanu More, Jadabpur (I.T.I.) P.O. & P.S. - Chattna, Bankura - 722132 W.B.
(FORT NIGHTLY IN SANTALI & BENGALI)

Please be a Life Member
LAHANTI PATRIKA
Editor - Swapan Kr.Paramanik (Kukmu Kuhu)
[Reciepient of Bir-Birsa Munda National Award 2006 Delhi & Dr. B. R. Ambedkar Rastriya Samman Padak 2010 Delhi]
Contact for - Santali Drama, Film & Any Printing Job
Mob: 09434650165

M : 9932464370

১৩ তম বর্ষ ১ ম সংখ্যা , ১ লা মার্চ ২০১১ (১৯৮৯ হইতে প্রকাশিত) M:- 09434650165 বার্ষিক ডাকে ৫০ টাঃ সাঃ মূল্য- ২ টাকা

ঝাড়খণ্ডে চার বৎসর স্থায়ী সরকার থাকবে

আদিবাসীদের জমি রক্ষায় ডেপুটেশন বর্ধমানে

সাঁওতালী অনুবাদ সাহিত্যে একাডেমীর প্রথম পুরস্কার ঘোষনা

বিশ্ব-ভারতীতে সাঁওতালী পি.জি. চালুর দাবী

ঝাড়খণ্ডে ৩৪ তম জাতীয় ক্রীড়া প্রতিযোগীতার বিদায়

Figure 5.6 *Lahanti Patrika* (Chatna, Bankura) featuring title in Eastern Brahmi, Ol-Chiki, and Roman, with content in Bengali/Eastern Brahmi and Santali/Ol-Chiki (edited by Swapan Kumar Pramanik, Chatna, Bankura, West Bengal).

own, self-sufficient, and non-party affiliated publication." It is anchored by pictures of leaders of various regional insurrections like Sidhu Murmu and Tilka Majhi. Hence, again like *Sar Sagun*, the banner addresses its reader, the politically engaged "Adivasis" of "all-India," as national political subjects, transforming its local domain of circulation into a national political space.

Yet unlike *Sar Sagun* and many of the other newspapers that used monographic formats, *Lahanti Patrika* employed a bilingual, digraphic format, choosing to relate Santali-language content in Ol-Chiki script. Also unlike the other papers, script and language are more closely related to particular genres: Bengali is used for news items related in a Jharkhand political register, while a single full page in the middle of each issue is written in Santali/Ol-Chiki that usually relates some kind of essay or opinion piece related to Santal society or literature. In Figure 5.6, a copy dated March 1, 2011, the top headlines read in Bengali, the "Jharkhand Government Will Remain Set for Four Years,"

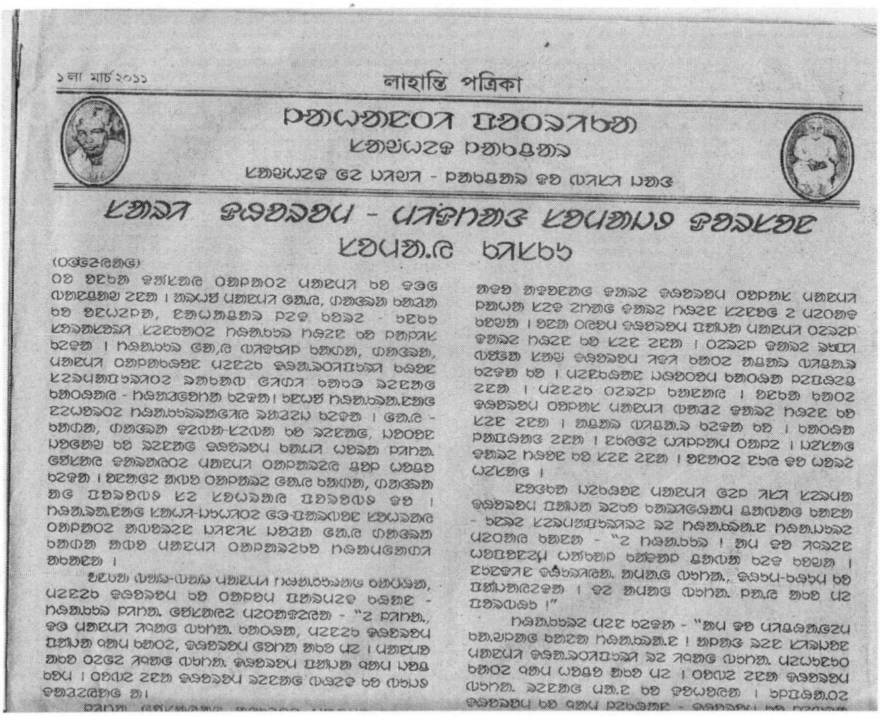

১লা মার্চ ২০১১ লাহান্তি পত্রিকা

Figure 5.7 Page 3 of *Lahanti Patrika*, entirely in Ol-Chiki script, flanked by pictures of Raghunath Murmu (founder of Ol-Chiki) and famous Santali poet Sadhu Ramchand Murmu.

an unusual feat for a state notorious for its fluctuating governments. Beside the headline is another Bengali headline: "Adivasis send a deputation for protection of land to Bardhaman [a city in West Bengal]." Appearing lower down the page is news concerning a celebration of the birth anniversary of the Santal leader of a 1784 rebellion against the Briṭish administration in what is now Bihar, Tilka Majhi (*Baba Tilka Majhi-r jonmo dibos udjapon*), related in Bengali language/Eastern Brahmi script.

The first page of the paper contrasts with page 3 (Figure 5.7), which is a distinct section entirely in Santali/Ol-Chiki script. This section has a separate banner heading, in which the name of the paper (*Lahanti Patrika*) is repeated *only* in Ol-Chiki script, and with no accompanying text in either Bengali or Roman script. Underneath the title the words *saonhet' lakcạr* (literature-culture) and in smaller font is a phrase *saonhet' ge jiwi—lakcar do bisi mang* (literature is [our] life, culture is [our] bones and blood) written in Santali/

Ol-Chiki. The banners are anchored with stalwarts of the Santali literary domain: on the left is a picture of Pandit Raghunath Murmu, the founder of the Ol-Chiki script, and on the right is a picture of Santali poet Sadhu Ramchand Murmu. The page does not display news items but features essays, such as this one looking at the "true religion" of Adivasis (in contrast to Hinduism).

The alternating use of code and script here serves multiple functions. On the one hand, echoing the reporter *Sar Sagun*, readers such as a government officer writing in an anniversary edition of the paper argued that the use of the Bengali in *Lahanti Patrika* serves to make "the public" and "the government" aware of "Adivasi problems and issues" (Kisku 2011). Unlike Bengali, which is outwardly directed toward the "public" and the "government," the use of Santali in the paper discusses community-internal, cultural concerns related only in the Ol-Chiki script. The use of Ol-Chiki in the paper diagrams the distinction between "literary and cultural journals," which are monolingual and now increasingly written using Ol-Chiki, and Bengali-language, Jharkhand-oriented "news" within the newspaper (see Table 5.2). In addition, the sole use of Ol-Chiki for writing Santali also creates an affiliation between the paper and a presupposed Santali-speaking Adivasi reader whose affiliation transcends their regional location in West Bengal and their bilingualism in Bengali.

Despite the preponderance of bilingual papers, there were also some attempts to create newspapers completely in Santali/Ol-Chiki script. Sometimes in Jhilimili bazaar, or at village fairs, I would see the distribution of Santali newspapers from the nearby city of Jamshedpur (in Jharkhand) or from Odisha, which were completely in Ol-Chiki. These were offered usually as part of a general activism for the promotion of Ol-Chiki in West Bengal. For instance, once I saw some youth handing out a copy of the Jamshedpur-based

Table 5.2 Distribution of scripts and codes in *Lahanti Patrika*

Script/language	Imagined addressee
1. Bengali/Eastern Brahmi	"Government"/West Bengal state Non-Santali-speaking/reading public Adivasi bilinguals
2. Santali/Ol-Chiki	‘"Monolingual/monographic" Adivasi reader; national Santali-speaking audience; literary and cultural journal/audience

newspaper *Setak'* (Morning), which is published entirely in Ol-Chiki, along with pamphlets in Bengali outlining why Ol-Chiki was not being implemented at the state-government level. The availability and distribution of these newspapers remind readers that their community stretches far beyond the borders of West Bengal.

However, despite the enthusiasm for monolingual newspaper publishing, the format does not seem to have been successful in southwest West Bengal. For instance, in the summer of 2012, after having returned to Jhilimili, I was surprised to see the long-running regional Bengali-language newspaper *Manbhum Sombad* (Manbhum News) come out with an exclusively Santali edition in Ol-Chiki script. *Manbhum Sombad*, titled after the old name of Purulia district before the region was annexed to West Bengal, was a pro-Jharkhand-oriented Bengali daily published from the city of Purulia.

The project was ambitious, and I was told that they intended to circulate the parallel edition as a daily. However, a year later after I returned I learned that the Ol-Chiki version had been discontinued. The project nevertheless revealed two developments of the Jharkhand imagination in the region. On the one hand, the fact that an established Bengali-language daily considered publishing a Santali/Ol-Chiki version of their paper, despite the fact that all their Santali readers read Bengali as well, illustrates that by this time language activism and graphic politics has been successful in crafting a multilingual and multiscriptal vision of the Jharkhand polity. On the other, it also shows that unlike in the literary and cultural sphere, in the realm of news, the preferred format is still bilingual and digraphic; regional news is best consumed when aligned with a political project in which readers are aware of "others" and difference, rather than unity, is the basis for an imagined consociality.

Graphic Innovation: The Case of *Bhabna*

On a visit to Jhilimili in 2014, I received a copy of an interesting new magazine called *Bhabna* (Thought/Feeling). The editor was a younger generation Santali-language author who was raised in southern Purulia district and was thoroughly enmeshed in the literary networks of the region. He was also one of the main editors of the Santali-language magazine *Saonta Ạrsi* (Society's

Mirror), one of the first and longest running Ol-Chiki script Santali-language magazines in the area, and which had recently been discontinued. He had embarked on a novel new project, a literary magazine that included works in Bengali (Eastern Brahmi) and Santali (Ol-Chiki), challenging the monolingual ideology that is the basis of the literary and cultural genre. In an interview, he said that "90 percent of the Santali writers are *culture* based," meaning that they are writing literature or articles for exclusively Santal audiences, whereas his belief is that "literature . . . [and] the Santal language should be for everyone." As a result of this belief, and an increasing interest on the part of especially non-Santals to interact more with Santali writing and literature, he started *Bhabna*.

While he challenged the *monolingual* ideology characteristic of this genre, he still ultimately decided to use Ol-Chiki script for the writing of Santali, reinforcing the *monographic* ideology. On the one hand, he wanted to present Santali and Bengali as equal, and interactive, languages that marked out a regional literary domain "for everyone." Yet at the same time, the use of Ol-Chiki continued to signify an important difference. The political ideologies that underlie this difference was cultivated through the editor's earlier years as a publisher as he realized that publishing in Ol-Chiki was essential for writers of his generation. He recalled how when he started his first magazine, only one page was in Ol-Chiki, but after receiving substantial opposition from his peers and other writers, he and his associates decided to change the whole magazine to Ol-Chiki. In addition to his magazine, all his subsequent books and literary works were in Ol-Chiki. So within his generation of writers, publishing magazines in Ol-Chiki had become the status quo. However, he also said that "non-Santals" found Ol-Chiki "attractive" and many Bengali speakers had approached him, telling him that "there are some good things written in there, I should learn [Santali]." The use of Ol-Chiki therefore visibly marks the Santali language as distinct and equal to Bengali in ways not possible with spoken language, creating possibilities for trans-ethnic platforms of interaction that respect difference rather than subordinating it. Thus, while Bengali speakers might still not understand Santali, they are beginning to recognize it as an independent language worth engaging with as part of a regional project of autonomy.

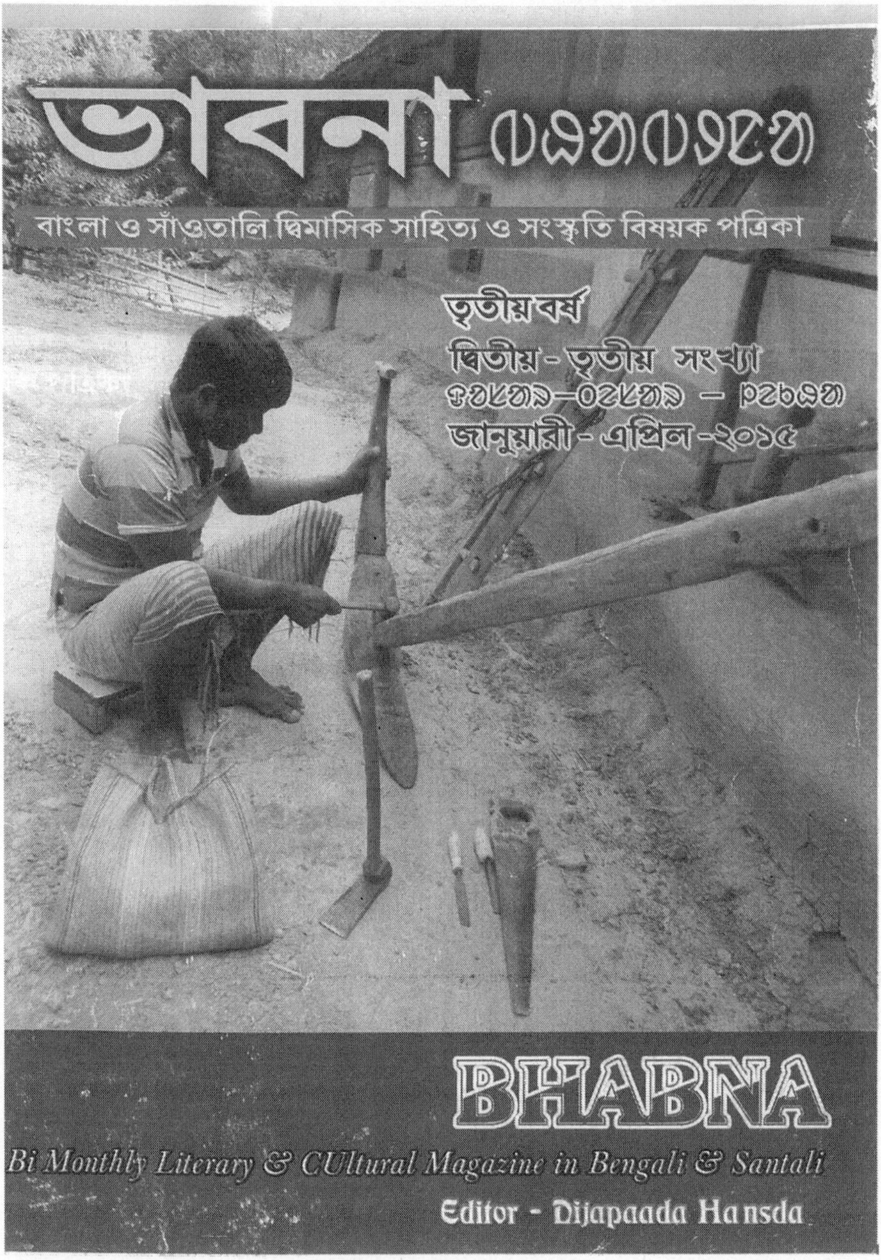

Figure 5.8 Cover page of *Bhabna*, a bilingual, digraphic bimonthly magazine in Bengali/Eastern Brahmi and Santali/Ol-Chiki with Roman also on cover (edited by Dijapada Hansda, Chilikigarh, Jhargram, West Bengal).

The cover page of the first quarter, 2015 issue (Figure 5.8) is similar to magazines such as *Sili* or the newspapers discussed above, relating the title (*Bhabna*) in Eastern Brahmi, Ol-Chiki, and Roman scripts. The subheading reads in Bengali and English, "Bi-monthly literary and cultural magazine in Bengali and Santali," whereas most of the Santali-language magazines would have this strictly in English. The bilingual subheading and the Eastern Brahmi script title is slightly larger than the Ol-Chiki, departing from the typical format. Inside the magazine, the table of contents is entirely in Eastern Brahmi (though using Santali and Bengali) while the articles are either in Ol-Chiki/Santali or Eastern Brahmi/Bengali. As the editor had mentioned, most of the Bengali articles are related to either "tribal culture" such as an article about the *Baha* (spring harvest) festival performed by Adivasis and other castes in the region, and an article about the Jharkhand movement itself. Hence, though they are written by non-Santals, the Bengali-language articles very much have a Jharkhand orientation. The Santali-language material is mostly literature in Ol-Chiki script, including poetry and one short story.

The magazine was published continuously from 2013 to 2017 and resumed again in 2018. The editor said that surprisingly he received a lot of initial opposition from Santali-language writers, who were upset at the bilingual format of the magazine, questioning why they should write for audiences that cannot understand. Such a monolingual bias is present in the literary and cultural genre, but as the existence of the newspapers shows, examples of multilingual, multigraphic publications already circulate within this sphere. The editor, however, was adamant in articulating another form of autonomy, asserting that the Santali language was not just "for Santals" (*aboak' do bang kana*), but for "everyone." "Now that Santali is taught in schools," he said, "everyone should learn it, not only the 7% of Santals, or people looking for jobs."

Graphic Interfaces: Print and Digital Media

This chapter has primarily discussed print media, but I would be remiss in not discussing the increasing importance of electronic media in the development of Santali language and the advancement of a Jharkhand-oriented politics of autonomy in West Bengal. When I started fieldwork in 2010, I was only one of two people who had an Internet connection (at that time through a USB port that linked up with a mobile network). My research assistant, at that time in class 11 in high school, had never heard of the Internet, or email, much less social media. Within a span of four years, with the availability of cheap smartphone technology and mobile data, the landscape has completely changed. Facebook and WhatsApp have become very important in the transmission of media, and many Santali-language print magazines and newspapers now have websites and Facebook pages.

While magazines such as *Sarjom Umul* are monolingual and monographic, their Facebook page shows posts in multiple scripts, including Ol-Chiki, Roman, Eastern Brahmi, and Devanagari, as well as posts in Hindi, Bengali, Santali, and English. These pages and groups, and the ease with which people may freely interact without editorial control or any monetary expense, transforms the conception of media and the accompanying political ideologies that accompany it. For example, while the *Sarjom Umul* magazine has most of its identifying information in Ol-Chiki script on the inside pages, the Facebook page has an English-language introduction in which the editors write:

> *Sarjom Umul* is a Santali magazine published from Purulia dist, WB . . . *Sarjom Umul,* the shadow of the holy tree (shorea robusta), invites all santal students, teachers engineers, doctors, writers, social workers, majhi parganas, artists, all types of employees et al. to make their society glorious. *Sarjom Umul* is to raise extreme faith among all Santals in Santali language, culture, and religion and to bring real loyalty among Santals to literature and Santali script [Ol-Chiki].[16]

According to the identifier, the Facebook page is not a replacement for the magazine, instead it serves as a digital supplement where various elements of the Santali-speaking society can express themselves in relation to the "Santali language, culture, and religion," which the magazine promotes through its printed circulation and content. However unlike the magazine, which is a final product where the vision of a monolingual, monographic society is presented in one packaged commodity, the Facebook page points to a project in the making, where people come together with an end goal of *bringing* "loyalty" to Santali literature and the Ol-Chiki script.

Previously, as Ol-Chiki script was not formatted for online communication, it prevented Ol-Chiki from being used on online platforms, resulting in a non-standard Romanized "trans-script" that proliferated in online spaces. However, the recent addition of Ol-Chiki to the Google G-Board input tools on Android devices has resulted in increasing use of Ol-Chiki on digital media (Choksi 2020). Yet the availability of Ol-Chiki inputs have not led to a monographic or monolingual hegemony. Ol-Chiki inputs have instead added one more graphic layer to the what Androutsopoulous has called the "networked multilingualism" (Androutsopoulos 2015) characteristic of social media platforms, which encompasses the variety of ways digital platform users deploy technologically mediated linguistic, graphic, and visual resources, orient themselves to networked audiences, and embed themselves in the "global digital mediascapes of the web" (188).

The "digital mediascape" both draws from the legacy of print media but also challenges it through new kinds of technology and graphic interaction, expanding the imagination of Jharkhand and the accompanying politics of

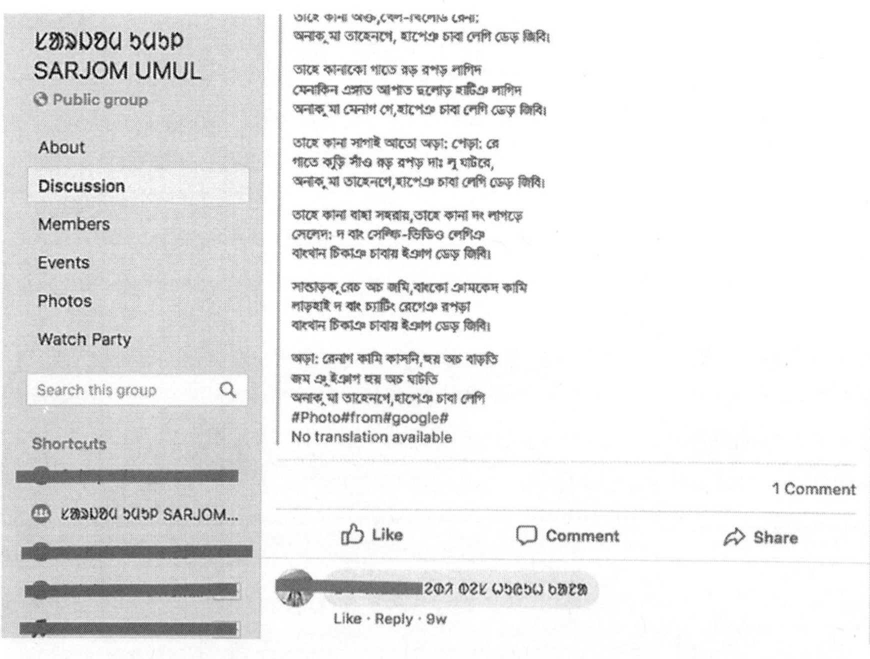

Figure 5.9 Facebook screenshot from *Sarjom Umul* group. The post is in Eastern Brahmi/Santali and comment is in Santali-Ol-Chiki.

autonomy beyond what was cultivated through print. For instance, in this one screenshot from the Facebook page (Figure 5.9), someone is reposting a Santali song in Eastern Brahmi script, something that appeared not too infrequently on the site. In this way "culture," which was promoted in Ol-Chiki script in print media such as magazines or newspapers like *Lahanti Patrika*, is here posted in the Eastern Brahmi, while if one looks at the comments below the repost, it is done using Ol-Chiki. Posts such as this reverse the binary between Eastern Brahmi and Ol-Chiki, where Ol-Chiki is increasingly becoming an everyday script of interaction on the online space, while Eastern Brahmi becomes a way posters can assert local cultural knowledge anchored in their region.

The other way the online space creates political subjectivities through politics is to link non-Santali language posts concerning various other social movements into fora such as *Sarjom Umul*. In another post (Figure 5.10), the poster exhorts in Ol-Chiki that Santals should not readily accept religious books that promote casteism and reposts a Hindi-language graphic that says "Look at the dirtiness of the Hindu holy books, how is it possible for everyone's development?" that was circulated by an Ambedkarite Dalit (Scheduled Caste) organization. This connection between a Jharkhand politics of autonomy and Ambedkarite politics was generally missing from the print media surveyed in the chapter before. However, the use of Ol-Chiki in combination with Hindi (in this case read as "national" and not "regional") brings a new kind of networked multilingualism that refigures both the meaning of graphic combination and creates new linkages within the Jharkhand imagination. This is possible through the graphic and linguistic flexibility now allowed for on such platforms.

Contrary to the prevailing common sense, which asserts that the arrival of digital media will replace print media, the situation of Santali-language media in southwest West Bengal shows a symbiotic relationship between the two. Digital offset presses have allowed for the greater use of Ol-Chiki in magazines and newspapers, and print magazines such as *Sarjom Umul* have created social media platforms to supplement and create new communities around the printed artifact. These media platforms, however, though organized around the promotion of monolingual, monographic ideologies, display a wide range of multilingual and multigraphic practices that create new forms of scalar politics that inform the

Figure 5.10 Facebook screenshot from *Sarjom Umul*, post is in Ol-Chiki/Santali on a repost picture in Hindi/Devanagari.

evolving Jharkhand imagination. Assemblages of script and language in media or on signboards are reversed or creatively reassembled to create new "networked" linkages within the digital space, integrating the politics of autonomy in West Bengal with the rapid technological innovations revolutionizing media production and conception in South Asia and the world more broadly.

Conclusion

As I have tried to suggest here, the recognition of the "other" in nonhierarchical ways has always been an historical aim of the Jharkhand movement, though as many commentators have noted, this aim was overshadowed in the development-driven, state-centered politics of later years. In the current situation in southwest West Bengal, an independent state is not possible, and there is no organized Jharkhand movement per se in southwest apart from a few scattered political parties. As a result, the movement's aims are constantly being developed and transformed through innovations in locally produced media. Magazines continue to articulate a Santali-specific reading domain in the absence of widespread recognition of the language by state institutions or mass media, while newspapers present how graphic and linguistics resources may be creatively deployed to autonomously scale regional events through the lens of a trans-ethnic political platform. Experiments like *Bhabna* attempt to challenge the boundaries between these genres, recognizing that Santali and the Ol-Chiki script have become institutionally recognized to a significant extent that it can be creatively put it in conversation with Bengali literature and develop the "Jharkhand imagination" in new and productive ways.

Digital platforms are also complementing the print media by providing forums for users to "network" different ideas and expand the Jharkhand imagination beyond the graphic politics of newspapers or magazines. The Facebook page of *Sarjom Umul*, whose print edition is monolingual and monographic, shows posts in multiple scripts, including Ol-Chiki, Roman, Eastern Brahmi, and Devanagari, and languages such as Hindi, Bengali, Santali, and English. These pages and groups, and the ease with which people may freely interact transform the conception of media and the accompanying political ideologies that accompany it. In this way, the politics of autonomy in this region of West Bengal, far from being marginal, has become even more integrated into the rapid technological innovations revolutionizing media production and conception in South Asia and the world more broadly.

6

Conclusion: Autonomy and the Global Field of Graphic Politics

As the insurgency and counterinsurgency continued to rage on in Jhilimili and the greater Jungle Mahals during the time of my fieldwork, the role of language and script—once thought to be peripheral to class struggle and radical leftist politics—began to be acknowledged in the discussions among regional leftist intellectuals. For instance, Amit Bhattacharya, a professor of history at Jadavpur University in Kolkata, published an account of the "alternative development programme" that Maoist-allied factions were implementing in the areas of southwest West Bengal under their control. The account, published in the *Economic and Political Weekly*, a well-known Indian academic journal with global circulation, documented the progress of the people's struggle in addressing traditional "development" issues such as agriculture and infrastructure, but it also adds that the movement has made notable strides in the "promotion and spread of the Santali and Kurmali languages and alchiki [sic] script." Bhattacharaya further elaborates: "as a result of globalization and domination of one language or another, thousands of indigenous languages had already gone into oblivion all over the world," but "in areas where the people's struggle is very strong, the possibility of the regeneration of local languages is a reality" (Bhattacharya 2010: 21). Graphic politics were central, as Bhattacharya suggests, to fulfill the Maoist goals of "creating a new society fit for the living" (19).

At the same time as this manifesto appeared on the pages of an English-language academic journal, the ruling Communist Party of India (Marxist), the target of Maoist ire in West Bengal, was responding to the barrage of negative media surrounding the insurgency in the Jungle Mahals, by issuing advertisements in the Kolkata editions of the Bengali dailies, in which they touted the "unprecedented importance" they have given in recent years to "Adivasi development." The advertisement listed the numbers—of new teachers hired, health centers built, and so on—but also broadcast as one of its key accomplishments, giving the Adivasis "the 'gift' (*dan*) of recognition of the Ol-Chiki language [sic]."[1] Not to be left out, the then opposition leader and national minister of railways, Mamata Banerjee of the Trinamool Congress, announced with great fanfare the renaming of the Kharagpur–Purulia Intercity Express train, which cut right through southwest West Bengal, as the "Ol-Chiki Express." She said in her speech, "I believe this much needs to be done for people who have been neglected for years."[2] This is the only train in India to be named after a script.

These pronouncements concerning Ol-Chiki by the Maoists, the government, and the opposition were not meant solely for the people of southwest West Bengal. Instead, they show how the struggles for autonomy in the Jangal Mahals region through the medium of graphic politic traveled across ethnic, caste, and regional lines, entering into the imagination of upper-caste, metropolitan Bengali-speaking audiences as a signifier for insurgency, development, and progress, among other markers. Whether employed in pursuit of social justice and class revolution (by the Maoists), or as part of an electoral strategy designed to nip the insurgency in the bud (government, opposition), the messages demonstrate a wider engagement with the historical processes of autonomy through the interface of Ol-Chiki as a result of the ongoing violence.

The alignment of insurgency, both in its negative and positive senses, with graphic politics draws on the long-standing relation between writing and the politics of autonomy that operate within the region. As this book has argued, script has been a critical semiotic modality through which Santali speakers assert temporal and spatial autonomy from hegemonic historical narratives, administrative territories, and dominant class and caste-based social orders. The graphic politics through which Santals and other Adivasis articulate notions of autonomy have evolved through their deep historical interaction with different forms of writing. The word for writing (*ol*) has traditionally signified among Austro-Asiatic speaking groups the practice of ritual diagramming that mediated interactions between spirits, humans, and shared histories of migration and dispersal. Distinct from spoken language (*roṛ*), writing (*ol*) transforms space and time, drawing the spirits (*bonga*) into the world in order to accomplish ritual action. It is no surprise then that in Santali retellings of the *Hul*, the fraternal heroes of the rebellion Sidhu and Kanhu had knowledge of writing, contrary to colonial accounts that described them as non-literates with a supernatural fascination for the white man's letters.

As Christian missionaries arrived in the wake of the large-scale devastation in the region following the *Hul*, they devised an independent writing system for Santali, providing a Roman alphabet complete with diacritic marks that delineated phonetic and grammatical aspects for the Santali language. They also recorded for the first time narratives, songs, and other oral performance traditions into script. In doing so they promoted another vision of autonomy in which Santals were ethno-linguistically distinguished from neighboring groups, caste Hindu and otherwise. While the missionaries linked this form of autonomy to Christian missionization, subsequent social movements among the Santals, such as the Kherwar, elaborated these notions of autonomy to articulate a non-Christian, Santal-specific religious and cultural ideology. Those active or supportive of the movement continued the missionary project by relating ritual, narrative, and performance material in graphic form, often utilizing the dominant Indic script of the region, Eastern Brahmi.

At the turn of Independence, a demand for an independent state of Jharkhand had taken root across much of the Adivasi areas of eastern India. However, statehood was only one aspect of the vision of Jharkhand. It also involved a demand for greater autonomy in the wake of the formation of a putatively democratic India. While the demand for an independent state never fully took hold among Santal communities, and the resulting state only encompassed the districts of southern Bihar, leaving out districts in Odisha and West Bengal, the politics of autonomy articulated by the movement began to inform everyday practices and conceptions of community and territory. In addition, there was a proliferation of independently created scripts that arose around this time, which carried forward not only the grammatical and phonetic system initially delineated by the missionaries but also created novel graphic outlays that articulated with natural landscapes, ritual practices, and histories of loss, recovery, and dispersal. As a politics of autonomy associated with the Jharkhand movement took hold among Santali-speaking communities, these scripts' popularity spread. The most successful example of this kind of graphic politics was the Ol-Chiki script, which circulated widely through nonformal education, oral performance genres such as song and drama, and, later, through the increasing availability of digital technology.

The book documents how the presence of written Santali—in Ol-Chiki but also in Roman and Eastern Brahmi, and the use of Santali in combination with English and Bengali—has served to perpetuate a politics of autonomy associated with the Jharkhand movement, even after the areas of southwest West Bengal were left out of the Jharkhand state. Because there is no possibility for a state, the politics of autonomy in areas such as Jhilimili focus more on transforming the relations between Adivasis and caste Hindus in spaces such as the market or in institutions such as the school. These spaces have historically been marked by Bengali-language and caste Hindu hegemony, initiated through the alienation of land stemming from colonial-era laws and extended through the twentieth century with the spread of Communism and the accompanying valorization of metropolitan Bengali culture.[3] In more recent times, the area has also witnessed an increased access and importance given to education and literacy, and the spread of Bengali-language media, further entrenching the Bengali language and caste Hindu moral values in everyday life.

Yet, despite the fact that practically all Santali speakers I met were bilingual, and the Bengali language forms an integral part of their linguistic repertoire, the popularity of the Santali language has increased in recent years, especially with younger generations. This is due to the presence of graphic politics, and specifically, the increased importance of the Ol-Chiki script as a vector for a new generational vision of autonomy. The popularity of Ol-Chiki intersects with the continued presence of Jharkhand politics, the ongoing autonomous systems of tribal governance, the burgeoning multilingual and multiscriptal media culture, and institutional equity and access. While much of the discourse around Ol-Chiki is aspirational, positing it as the only script suitable for writing Santali, the presence of scripts such as Eastern Brahmi or Roman, which are also used to write Santali, provide scalar contrasts through which Ol-Chiki gains salience. Santali in Eastern Brahmi draws on the local history of writing Santali within southwest West Bengal, while Santali in nonstandard Roman marks the language as transregional. Within this framework, Ol-Chiki generates a form of autonomy that transcends state boundaries to signify the dispersed territory of a nonstate, autonomous Jharkhand region. The persistent multiscriptality of the region, of which Ol-Chiki is a part, allows graphic politics to link diverse local communities with Adivasis in other parts of South Asia, signifying the continued presence of autonomous spaces, visually and graphically contesting the hegemony of a unified, national vision of a Bengali-language state. The scalar contrasts inherent within the deployment of several scripts serve to reconstitute the region as a node in an autonomous territory stretching beyond the present-day administrative borders of either West Bengal or Jharkhand state.

Autonomy, Indigeneity, and Development

The politics of autonomy outlined in this book, and the contributions of language and script to these politics, have been historically drawn from the Jharkhand movement. Yet early leaders of the movement also sought to embed the concept of autonomy within broader global discourses of indigeneity and development. The term Adivasi (original inhabitant) was used to unite the disparate members of Scheduled Tribe groups in the Jharkhand region, and an argument for more an equitable distribution of resources and a stake in revenues produced by natural resource extraction was used to justify the fight for a separate state of Jharkhand (Singh 2003).[4] Following the formation of the Jharkhand state, indigeneity and development have been two major discourses that Adivasis, insurgent groups, and political parties within Jharkhand and on the Jharkhand peripheries have deployed to argue for greater rights and recognition from state authorities, or leverage state authority by making their demands in transnational fora. Efforts at promoting Ol-Chiki and the Santali language are often seen by scholars[5] as part of an indigenous movement worldwide to save dying cultures and languages and stem the tide of unbridled economic development on linguistic and environmental diversity.[6] However, there is also a parallel global movement for autonomy that is less discussed, but is apparent in social revolutionary movements stretching from the Kurdish regions in the Middle East to the forests of eastern Colombia and the polar Arctic. It is in these regions where new forms of political organization, and also graphic politics, are being cultivated that are not focused on presenting demands to the state or transnational institutions. These politics of autonomy intersect with indigeneity and development, but also move beyond their limitations, offering new possibilities for understanding global political movements and the drive to create new languages, scripts, and other communicational platforms.

As a popular global discourse, the term "indigeneity" has gained greater currency in Jharkhand in light of the United Nations issuing the "Declaration on the Rights of Indigenous Peoples" in 2007. This pathbreaking declaration for the first time recognized indigenous communities as global, collective right-bearing subjects. The declaration, which articulates a set of collective rights, including rights to self-determination, autonomy, language, and writing systems[7] to a people's long-term existence on specific lands and territories, provided a framework for many in the Jharkhand movement to link their struggle with an internationally recognized transnational movement. Through the framework of indigenous rights, the existence of Jharkhand, the struggle for autonomy, and the demand for the implementation of Ol-Chiki script could become a globally legitimate demand. Civil society organizations like the Jharkhand Indigenous People's Forum, based in Ranchi, the capital of Jharkhand state, played a pivotal role in representing India's Adivasis at international fora, and integrated this transnational discourse into local activism. Members of groups like the Adivasi Socio-Educational Cultural Association (ASECA) whom I talked to in places like Kolkata also told me the fight for the recognition of Ol-Chiki script was part of the movement for indigenous "language revitalization" and to stop the global demise of "endangered languages," closely echoing the discourse of global language endangerment that complements discussions of transnational indigeneity.

Similarly, development has also been one of the overarching narratives of the Jharkhand movement since its inception. As Mullick notes in his introduction to his volume on Jharkhand, the British, in crushing the Adivasi rebellions, rendered the region an "internal colony of the neighbouring nations," a situation that was then ruthlessly exploited by the Indian nation-state and its model of "development" (Mullick 2003: iv). This narrative echoes the "world-systems" approach articulated by sociologist Immanuel Wallerstein in the 1970s, in which core capitalist countries of the West deliberately enforced the underdevelopment of the peripheral countries of Asia, Africa, and South

America (Wallerstein [1974] 2011) in order to expand their own economies, arguing that the same processes applied to unequal development *within* postcolonial regions such as India. This idea of development both as a model of exploitation and, if remedied, a model of social justice, informed the demand for the creation of the Jharkhand state and also framed electoral and insurgent politics in adjacent regions like West Bengal. In fact, as the situation in the Jungle Mahals reveals, political parties and left-wing insurgents are constantly trying to one up each other on who is providing better "development" to the region and the Adivasis. Any overture to the Ol-Chiki script by the mainstream political parties in West Bengal is framed therefore as a redressal of the concerns of what the current chief minister Mamata Banerjee, in renaming the train after the Ol-Chiki script, called the "neglected" people and their region. As Sivaramakrishnan and Aggarwal (2003) note, the word "development," though emerging from a set of global discourses about the relation between cores and peripheries, has become a master signifier for how certain regions such as Jharkhand or the Jungle Mahals are politically understood.

Yet despite the power of the discourse of development and indigeneity to link the Jharkhand movement with global discourses and social movements, analysts have pointed out how both these discourses have been utilized to extend state authority over people, perpetuate social exclusion, and entrench inequality. For instance, Van Schendel (2011) documents the new political salience of the word "indigenous" in India's northeast and the hill regions of Bangladesh, arguing that the term has been used in the service of creating ethnically exclusive homelands in the name of natural belonging. He gives several examples such as Bodo groups in Assam who control an autonomous territory, have targeted Santals, Mundas, and others who are seen as outsiders under the framework of indigenous rights. The same kind of fighting has been witnessed in Nagaland, Manipur, and Arunachal Pradesh. Similarly, Ghosh (2008) has argued, in his study of the Koel-Karo movement against dam-induced displacement in Jharkhand, that the embracing of transnational discourses of indigeneity by Adivasi elite has resulted in embracing models of development that have created the conditions for further exploitation of resources and a cementing of class and urban–rural divides.[8] The discourses of development and indigeneity have resulted in the extension of state patronage networks that, as critics of development such as Mosse (2005) or

Ferguson (1990) have noted, exclude certain communities and curtail forms of autonomous political action.

The politics of autonomy I traced in this book takes a different path. Unlike development discourses or appeals to transnational indigeneity, which seeks to convert local demands into state recognition of community rights, economic well-being, and legal privileges, autonomy seeks a different relation to the state. In a politics of autonomy, political action involves the state, but does not seek state recognition as its primary target. These politics too have a global dimension, though they are rarely discussed in relation to indigenous language politics. One of the more recent popular movements for autonomy, which has neither been framed as indigenous or understood through a model of development, has been in the Kurdish regions of southeast Turkey and northern Syria. In these geographies, Kurdish groups living in the border region are striving to build a new society that does not seek emancipation from the state but the creation of autonomous communities within existing territories. In the words of the jailed leader of the Workers Party of Kurdistan and leading theorist of the movement, Abdullah Ocalan, "neither total rejection of the state, nor complete recognition of the state is useful for the democratic efforts of a civil society" (Ocalan 2011: 32).[9] He instead proposes a flexible political arrangement inclusive of multiple communities across territorial borders and boundaries of religion, language, and ethnicity. While the Santals are not engaged in such a visible and large-scale project of autonomy, in trying to build alternative forms of community within the boundaries of the nation-state, strands of the Jharkhand movement in places like southwest West Bengal bear resemblance to the Kurdish project.

Autonomy and the Global Field of Graphic Politics

Anthropologist Arturo Escobar, drawing on the *pensiamento autonomico* (autonomous thought) of social movements in Latin America such as among the Afro-descent communities in Colombia or the indigenous communities in Chiapas, Mexico, suggests that embedded in a global politics of autonomy is an idea of a "pluriverse"—a world in which many worlds fit (Escobar 2018). To materialize these pluriverses in everyday projects of autonomy, Escobar emphasizes the role of "design," the manipulation of material and space along "multi-scalar" axes that address territory, inter-existence, and inter-being. Escobar's assessment of autonomous design involves the transformation of infrastructure to encompass communal and relational spaces, the wedding of technologies such as digital media with material life in order to facilitate collaborative codesign, and the creation of platforms for music and performance art that involve large-scale public participation and transformation (197). These interventions seek to transform relations between and among communities as well as between communities and their ecological environments by deliberately crafting autonomous modes of interaction and movement through space and time.

While Escobar sketches out broad domains of autonomous design interventions, in this book I focused on the coconstitutive relationship between autonomous politics and our most basic form of material and visual communication: writing. Promoting literacy has been one of the cornerstones of development interventions, yet the discourse around literacy, coming largely from the monoscriptal and referentially oriented graphic milieus of Europe or North America, largely ignores the basic questions of graphic design and its impact. This is perhaps why linguistic anthropologists have recently turned away from the "literacy" or "literacies" framework to describe the variety of inscriptive practices present in their ethnographic sites, such as the transformation of public space through visual displays of language, the creation of new scripts, the scalar dimensions of graphic registers, or the ways in which script interacts with oral performance. Instead, as Debenport and Webster (2019) argue, studies of graphic practice now have moved toward a framework of "graphic pluralism," in which aspects of inscription, including design, intersect with other domains of communicative practice and contribute to the circulation and durability of social ideologies around territory, community, and history.

The book has demonstrated the role graphic politics plays in autonomous design intervention in one small corner of eastern India. Yet the use of graphic politics is not limited to the Santali-speaking regions alone but can be seen throughout the world in different movements for autonomy. A striking photo, for instance, in the news coverage of the announcement by the new government of Rojava in Syria functioning under a democratically autonomous federalist system in the city of Rmeilan shows the officials sitting in front of a banner that shows Kurdish, Turkish, Arabic, and Assyrian written in the Roman and Arabic scripts.[10] In presenting official proclamations in multiple scripts and languages, the banner visually challenges the long-standing ideologies of both the Turkish and Syrian nation-states in which a homogenous language and script is seen as an integral part of national identity and territorial unity.

The multiplicity of scripts was one part of an autonomous design vision employed to transform Rojava into a dynamic and interlinked "pluriverse," which created a space of multiplicity that transversed territory and created a frame for nonhierarchichal orderings for the diverse linguistic practices of Kurdish and other ethnic groups in the region. These graphic displays of autonomy are visible in multiple forms of design intervention throughout the world, such as the way Inuit speakers in Canada alter mundane features of the everyday environment such as stop signs to assert their sovereignty vis-à-vis the state and connect with the transnational circumpolar community (Daveluy and Ferguson 2009), or the means by which graffiti writers from New York to Melbourne to Jerusalem/al-Quds craft "graffscapes" that carve out spaces of autonomy that transgress racial and class segregation and contest the denial of access to public spaces that structure the neoliberal urban landscape (Pennycook 2010, Peteet 1996).

Prevailing theories of language locate communication primarily in the mind, a product of an innate "faculty of language" (Chomsky 2002) or as driven by individual intentionality (Searle 1983). These frameworks leave limited scope for seeing the potentiality for collective political imaginations[11] in linguistic practice. A foregrounding of the graphic, however, as the case in Jhilimili highlights, provides a framework in which we may ascertain how language becomes a critical means for the transmission of political ideas such as autonomy across boundaries of time and space, ethnicity and caste, and even the linguistic code itself. Language thus becomes more than speech or reference and more than a denotational emblem of a particular ethnic group, region, or grammatical code. The graphic provides a resource for those who have either been left out, or have never been part of, or have actively rejected the boundaries and demands of the nation-state to articulate an alternative political imagination. In exposing the lacunae in our common sense understandings of the relation between language and politics, graphic politics offers those of us who strive for autonomous thought and action hitherto unexplored possibilities for unmaking and remaking our world.

Notes

1 Introduction

1 Irvine (1989), Gal (1988, 1989).

2 This script is commonly called the "Bengali" or "Assamese-Bengali" script, and also called "Eastern Nagari." It derives from the eastern variant of Brahmi script, and as such to minimize confusion with scripts such as Devanagari, I am calling it here "Eastern Brahmi" as a shorthand for Brahmi-derived.

3 Rosalind Morris, in her review of the legacies of Derrida for anthropology remarks that the concept of arche-writing inherently contains a criticism of "empiricism and phenomenology," which are the two epistemological foundations for fieldwork in contemporary anthropology. Thus, even though anthropologists have incorporated Derrida into their work, the full implications of his method have (perhaps by necessity) been ignored. (Morris 2007: 356).

4 This notion has informed linguistics from the time of Herder to Chomsky, see Irvine 2006 for a conceptual history. The idea that shared language forms the basis for community in anthropology is also equally old. See Hymes (1968) for a dated, yet underappreciated critique.

5 Silverstein (1998, 2000). For an even more forceful criticism of the concept of "languages," see Makoni and Pennycook (2005).

6 For literature on "language ideologies" see Silverstein (1979), Woolard and Schiefflin (1994).

7 On the failure of script reform in Japan, see Unger (1999). For accounts of how multiscriptality functions in the Japanese, see Robertson (2017) or Joyce et al. (2012) for recent studies.

8 For more on why the graphic becomes salient under conditions of multiscriptality, see Choksi and Meek (2016). For a recent exposition of the continued importance of graphic politics to South Asia, see Carmen and Sohoni (2018), which is the introduction to a special issue of *South Asian History and Culture* on the politics of script in South Asia.

9 See Raman (2012) for the political influence of scribal communities in both the early modern and early colonial periods.

10 For instance, Islamic reformers at institutions like Deoband, in north India, promoted the use of Urdu and used it as part of the Islamicization missions. See Metcalf (1982).

11 See Kar (2008) or Sengupta (2012) for more on debates around the Assamese language.

12 The Fifth and Sixth Schedules to the Indian Constitution provide a degree of autonomy for areas with Scheduled Tribe plurality, including a Tribal Advisory Council. Jharkhand is listed under the Fifth Schedule but not West Bengal state. The Sixth Schedule is reserved for Northeast areas and provides for even a larger degree of legal autonomy. This is outlined in Part X of the Indian Constitution. Guaranteed as part of the legal autonomy of the Fifth Schedule are the rights of local tribal councils to make decisions at the local level ordinarily made by elected village panchayats, see the Provisions of the Panchayat (Extension to Scheduled Areas) Act, 1996. For an overview, refer to Bhagat-Ganguly and Kumar (2020).

13 Parvez (2017). Parvez discusses a larger "politics of redistribution" as critical to the creation of Muslim autonomy, while in France, a "politics of recognition" results in withdrawl from the political sphere. She does not explore the role of the graphic explicitly, but it shows up in her ethnographic examples and forms a background to the politics of redistribution that she argues for.

14 For more on the way the "primitive" was employed in relation to Adivasis in India, see Banerjee (2006), Skaria (2003), or more recently, Chandra (2017). For a discussion of the notion of the primitive in relation to the larger concept of "indigenous," see Moreton-Robinson (2004) and Smith (2013).

15 The debate on whether to "assimiliate" Scheduled Tribe (Adivasi) communities such as the Santals has been present since the origins of Indian anthropology. See Sinha (2005) for the debates between two of the great scholars on opposite sides of these debates, G. S. Ghurye and Verrier Elwin.

16 "Continuity" is in fact central to indigenous politics even in settler-colonial societies. For instance see Audra Simpson's (2011) work on the politics of "refusal" among members of the Mohawk nation on the US–Canada borderlands, which as Sturm (2017) notes replaces the the "logic of elimination" with the "logic of continuity."

17 The Norwegian missionary L. O. Skrefsrud and other Christian missionaries started using Roman script in nineteenth century.

18 In addition to Cherokee and Hmong and other cases from the Americas and Southeast Asia, Africa (particularly West Africa) has had several examples of revealed scripts created often by speakers with no experience of literacy. See Kelly (2017).

19 This is particularly used in the cases for newly invented scripts in Southeast Asia, such as in describing Hmong (Smalley et al. 1990), and Eskaya (Kelly 2016).

20 See Chandra (2016) for a criticism of the concept of milleniarism in the context of colonial-era Adivasi rebellions in eastern India.

21 Cf. Mukharji (2009), Banerjee (2007).

22 For more on how this occurred, see the essays in Section 1 ("Mamata or Maoists: Who Failed Peace") in Roy (2012).
23 See essays in Munda and Mullick (2003).
24 See Orans (1965) for an analysis of the Santal migrant labor in Jamshedpur and also the role of Ol-Chiki script there.
25 In another context, one can see Sivaramakrishnan's (2000) analysis of joint forest management in West Bengal in the 1990s to show how Jharkhand politics and local headmen system combined to exclude certain communities, such as the Kharia (who still are excluded and invisible in most political circumstances in places like Jhilimili).
26 In 2017, the district was bifurcated into West Midnapur and Jhargram districts. Jhargram district is the one that now borders Jhilimili.

2 *Ol* as an Autonomous Practice

1 http://sahitya-akademi.gov.in/aboutus/cotlit.jsp, accessed July 17, 2017.
2 See Note 11 for information on the Fifth and Sixth Schedules.
3 See Sundar (2009) for more on these acts and their ramifications in Jharkhand.
4 This notion of autonomy echoes the assertion made by Pickeril and Chatterton (2006) where they write "Autonomy is necessarily an emergent and in many cases residual property within and often against a dominant order, a desire rather than an existing state of being" (737).
5 This idea of historical "Santal Raj," known by many names, is outlined in numerous historical accounts of Santal revolts; for instance, see Sarkar (1985) or Bannerjee (1999).
6 Materialization is a form of what linguistic anthropologists have called *semiotic transduction*, "the act of transforming something across semiotic modalities . . . the movement from indivisible to visible, from immaterial to material, and from intelligible to sensible" Keane (2013: 10).
7 This meaning is by no means unique to Santali. *Ol* means write/draw in multiple Munda languages, and it also has cognates for diagramming in other Austro-Asiatic languages, even those that are not formally written, such as in Bit in Laos (Badenoch, personal communication). For this same observation in Bhili languages, see Devy (2009: 7), in particular his essay "Writing and Aphasia"; for Sohra, see Elwin (2009: 183). This is also true for many languages in native America (see Boone and Mignolo, 1994).
8 Saussure (1959) echoed in important works of linguistics like Bloomfield (1935) or Chomksy (1965).

9 The "autonomous" school of literacy is most famously expounded in Goody and Watt (1963), Goody (1986), and Ong 1988). For a review and critique of this school, see Street (2006).

10 See also Salomon and Nino-Murcia (2011) for a study of continuities between Quipu knot systems and written records of communication in Andean Peru.

11 This means that these diagrams form both a record of history (such as migrations) as well as an interpretative frame for understanding future events, cf. Parmentier (1985).

12 For a criticism of Guha and the religious explanations for Adivasi insurgency, see Sivaramakrishnan (1995) or Chandra (2016).

13 Andersen et al.. (2011) translate *konkaena* as "pretending to be mad" and explain this in footnote (p. 179). *Konka-ena* means to become "silent," but sometimes can be used in contexts of possession too. Anderson et al. says this is evidence of Tudu's criticism of the two brothers, and thus has a negative connotation.

14 *Murmu ṭhakur ko do baba puthi baba ko paḍhao a Badoli konyda gaḍtelikhon calak' kan* The Murmu priests, oh my father, read books, oh my father, on Badoli konyda fort, writing is occurring (Santali song, Hembrom 2007: 19).

15 Bodding (1922). Letter by Bodding to missionaries (MS Fol 1686, 9: 2 (n.d.)), Santalia Archive, National Library, Oslo.

16 For more on the effects of missions on native languages and language ideologies, see Keane (2007), Errington (2008), Irvine (2008), and Hanks (2012).

17 See Andersen (2009) for more on syncretic elements in the Kherwar movement.

18 See Jaipal Singh's presidential address to the Adivasi Mahasabha, 1948 (Munda and Mullick 2003).

19 See Das (2010) for a short discussion on the Sonaram Soren-led revolt in Mayurbhanj in 1948–1949. For more on Oriya linguistic nationalism and the marginalization of Adivasi languages and territorial claims, see Mishra (2020).

20 A script's logic is similar to that of the relation between image and language in the heterodox *tantra* traditions; see Rambelli (2013) for Japanese Shingon Buddhism or Timalsinha (2015) in Indian *tantric* tradition.

21 See Choksi (2018).

22 See Debarshi Dasgupta's article in the Indian newsmagazine *Outlook*, "Ink-tipped Arrows" (2010) for more on ongoing script-making activities among different Adivasi groups in India. https://www.outlookindia.com/magazine/story/ink-tipped-arrows/267220, accessed July 20, 2017.

23 See, for instance, Kelly (2018) on new scripts in Southeast Asia; Kelly (2017) for new scripts in Africa; or Bender (2002), Daveluy and Ferguson (2009), or Feliciano-Santos (2017) for case studies from the Americas.

3 Scaling Multiscriptality in a Village Market

1 Santalia MS 8 1448, vol. S, number XX, National Library, Oslo (translation by the author).

2 The idea of d/Deafness and sign systems in relation to caste evaluation in South Asia is explored in Hoffman-Dilloway's (2016) monograph on Deaf politics and sign languages in Nepal.

3 The representation of the Santals speaking a rustic Bengali has a long history in Bengali language media; see for instance Satyajit Ray's classic movie *Aranyer din ratri* (Days and Nights in the Forest) or more recently the popular Bengali TV drama *Ishti Kutum*.

4 For example Blommaert et al. (2005, 2014), Blommaert (2010, 2013), and Das (2016).

5 The play, written by Amineshwar Hembrom in 2010, was called *Jotke tin' mere met' dak'* (I wiped away my tears).

6 This article was actually one that I wrote in the local Santali-language magazine *Tetre*, outlining research on Santali language that has been conducted by linguists based in Europe, the United States, and Japan (Choksi 2010).

7 "Iconic" is a term taken from the semiotics of Charles Sanders Peirce (1955), which means a relation of "resemblance." In this case script is come to be seen as isomorphic with language and subject to scalar evaluation. This is different than an "indexical" relation, or one of contiguity, or a "symbolic" relation, which is one of convention.

8 Constitution of India, Article 343.1, http://rajbhasha.nic.in/en/constitutional-provisions, accessed July 20, 2017.

9 The politics surrounding the three-language formula has been discussed most commonly for education; see Aggarwal (1988), Ladousa (2005), and Khubhchandani (2008), but little has been discussed regarding its presence within the linguistic landscape of South Asia.

10 This is neither the case for Jharkhand state, where the official language is Hindi, and signboards are only in Roman and Devanagari.

11 For more on the legal structures of Jharkhand and the undermining of them through the state structure, see Sundar (2009).

12 Carr and Lempert describe "interscalability" in the way different potential scalar qualities or dimensions can be made to reinforce each other, almost as a kind of scaffolding upon which people rely but "take for granted" as "interscalar assemblages" as the result of such interscalar processes. The concept of "interscalability" derives from linguistic anthropological discussions of

"interdiscursivity" (Silverstein 2005) and intertextuality (Kristeva 1980; Briggs and Bauman 1992).

13 For a detailed discussion of Santali-language film in creating ideas of community and territory beyond region, see Schleiter (2014).

14 The use of written Santali was rare in Jharkhand Party messaging, I only saw one or two tokens in the bazaar; however, it was nonexistent in Communist Party messaging. Code-switching between spoken Santali and Bengali at political rallies was common among all parties.

15 Indeed the way Ol-Chiki or Santali was characterized in these examples is similar to the kind of recognition politics prevalent in liberal settler states such as Australia; see Povinelli (2002).

16 Samaddar (1998). See also Raheja-Goodwin (1996) for a discussion on the "entextualization" of communities as criminals in colonial India.

17 Local insurgents allied with the People's Committee Against Police Atrocities, which originated in Lalgarh (near Jhilimili), were alleged to have cut rail tracks in order to disrupt train traffic. The loco driver of the trans-subcontinental Gyaneswhari express (Calcutta to Mumbai) did not notice the damaged tracks at night and as a result some of the bogeys derailed. The train had been derailed for a while, when an oncoming freight train, unaware that derailed carriages were strung along the opposite track, proceeded full speed on the tracks, and slammed into the derailed cars, killing all those aboard the derailed carriages.

18 The police distrust of tribal populations and scouring of villages for insurgents is one major reason for the start of the current phase of the insurgency, hence the name "People's Committee Against *Police* Atrocities."

19 This is a move that many Ol-Chiki activists would deny, explicitly claiming their activities are "non-political." The relationship between Santali intellectuals and the Maoist movement is complex, although I did not hear any explicit support of the Maoists in Jhilimili; the relationship to the movement must be understood in terms of a longer-standing demand for the politics of autonomy (cf. Rana 2012).

20 "Manmohan: Naxalism the Greatest Threat," *The Hindu*, http://www.thehindu.com/news/national/Manmohan-naxalism-the-greatest-internal-threat/article16886121.ece, accessed July 16, 2017.

4 Caste, Community, and Santali-Language Education

1 Ambedkar says in his address to the All-India Scheduled Caste Federation in Bombay on May 6, 1945 that "The Aboriginal Tribes have not developed any political sense to make the best use of their opportunities and they may easily

become instrucments in the hands of either a majority or minority and therefore disturb the balance without doing any good to themselves…" (Note 69, 2014 Annotated Critical Edition of *Annihilation of Caste*).

2 While categories like Scheduled Tribe (ST) and Scheduled Caste (SC) were inserted in the Constitution as an index of backward status both economically and ritually due to the presence of a caste system, the "other backward caste" category was implemented alongside this by the Mandal Commission, which released its report in 1979, but whose contents were finally implemented in 1990. As Jaffrelot argued, the Mandal Commission report and the agitations that followed made these categories more "political" than "socioeconomic" (Jaffrelot 2006).

3 Ministry of Tribal Affairs, Government of India. http://tribal.nic.in/Content/IntroductionScheduledTribes.aspx, accessed April 7, 2015.

4 For more on how this category arose and the problems in its identification see Ramaiah (1992).

5 The most famous anthropological account of the hierarchy of caste is Dumont's (1980) formulation, which counterposes the illiberal (and ahistorical) *homo hierarchichus* of India vs. the *homo aequalis* of liberal societies.

6 Through these classifications, Dirks (1989) argues, "caste" became a way of organizing civil society in colonial and postcolonial India. For a case study of how this operates, see Middleton (2016) on the fight for ST status in Darjeeling, India, and how groups "perform" backwardness to access state benefits and privileges, or Moody (2015) for a similar complex relation to the ST status among the Dhanka in Rajasthan.

7 Constitution of India (2016) Article 29, available at https://www.constitutionofindia.net/constitution_of_india/fundamental_rights/articles/Article%2029, accessed June 25,2015, my emphasis.

8 See Irvine (2006) for difference of language and speech community. Also see Chapter 1.

9 Tanabe (2007: 569). Also see Nielson 2015 for more on community as a "moral" accomplishment in the context of social movements in West Bengal

10 The concept has been further elaborated in Gal and Irvine (2019).

11 Gal (2016: 121). Gal uses the Peirceian term "qualia" to describe how abstract qualities become embodied and experienced across different communicative modalities (Gal 2016: 15). Also see Chumley and Harkness (2013).

12 For discussion of intimacy see Webster (2015) or Herzfeld (1997).

13 This follows with De Certeau's (1984) notion of "scriptural economy" in which writing is divorced from oral performance practice in order to be viewed as transparent with a rational, modern order. Also see the introduction of Collins and Blot (2003) for further elaboration.

14 In fact, the goal of the promotion of literacy was, as government policymakers argue, inherent in the many of the Indian Constitution's provisions. See National Commission to Review the Working of the Constitution, Consultation paper on Literacy in the Context of the Constitution of India, Government of India, 2001.https://legalaffairs.gov.in/sites/default/files/(III)Literacy%20in%20the%20context%20of%20the%20Constitution%20of%20India%20.pdf, accessed October 15, 2020

15 "Literacy for All." UNESCO. http://en.unesco.org/themes/literacy-all, accessed June 26, 2016.

16 For an example, see ASECA Jharkhand syllabus http://sumihansdajamshedpur.blogspot.jp/, accessed August 6, 2017.

17 This formula has been guaranteed but often fails in practice. See Khubchandani (1981) or Mohanty (2010).

18 Ruud (2003); see also Bhattacharya (2016).

19 Though people of a variety of caste backgrounds participate in the spread of metropolitan culture, D. Sen (2016) argues that the dominance of Bengali metropolitan culture is still an intentional example of upper-caste dominance in Bengal, a form of "bhadralok casteism" (p. 103).

5 Santali-Language Print Media and the Jharkhand Imagination

1 Anderson (1983).

2 The growing stream of literate readers ensured that newspaper remained an important part of the media scene despite the presence of television and later, the Internet. See Jeffrey's (2000) important work on the growth of India's vernacular language news media.

3 The use of the term "imagination" in anthropological analysis has recently come under legitimate scrutiny by scholars, with some such as Stankiewicz (2016) suggesting that the polyvalence and lack of explanatory specificity of the term warrants its disuse altogether. However, in using the term I share Hoffman-Dilloway's sentiments in response to Stankiewicz's criticism, in which she suggests that "processes of 'shoring up what we believe but cannot prove' [Stankiewicz, 801] about broader social scales however precisely characterizes the shared interpretative work undertaken by both anthropologists and those we study . . . Further reflexively, those processes themselves are often the object of study" (Hoffman-Dilloway 2018: 283). I see the term "imagination" as a link term, however flawed, between studies of media and nationalism, the linguistic

anthropological study of processes of scaling and reflexivity, and the politico-aspirational projects of people themselves.

4 For instance, Chatterjee (2012: 48) calls for more studies of the "national-popular" through what he calls the "vernacular."

5 See Aloysius (2003) who argues that in the embrace of developmentalism and regionalism the Jharkhand movement has lost this "cultural" sense of what Alam has called the "we-together."

6 "Disjuncture" is one of the essential elements of what Appadurai (1996) calls the work of the imagination.

7 For more on this discussion of the intersections between language, materiality, and ideology in relation to media, see Gershon (2010), Agha (2011), and Shankar and Cavanaugh (2012).

8 Permanent Settlement Act of Bengal, 1793, regularized the tenure of landholders (zamindars), giving them effective property rights over their holdings. This allowed British colonial authorities to extract regular taxation from landlords without entering into negotiations. This formalized the relationship between government officials and landlords, as well as between landlords and tenants, and thus eliminated the informal negotiations between various community leaders and local officials that characterized previous tribute regimes. Because tax payment was guaranteed by law, landlords evicted tenants who could no longer generate the required revenue. Permanent Settlement was the first instance of a Western-style private property regime instituted in India. See Guha (1963).

9 See Dasgupta (1985) and Sammadar (1998) for a greater discussion of these revolts in the Jangal Mahal area and their role in forging a regional consciousness.

10 For instance, see missionary B. Borrenson (1900, August 17) [Letter to Baidyanat] Santali Mission Collected Papers (MS Fol 4190, p. 132 [p. 408]). National Library, Oslo, Norway.

11 The same processes that took place, for instance, in the Soviet Union. See Graber (2012).

12 See Nag (1997) for more on the rise of little magazines in West Bengal and the networks surrounding them.

13 Mahadev Hansda, personal communication.

14 The use of the same code does not invoke the same reporting stance or invocation of public, even in the mainstream press. For a detailed analysis of the divergent views of readership and audience along class lines in two widely circulating Tamil-language newspapers, see Cody (2009a).

15 In fact this could be seen as a related, but reverse process of what Neyazi (2010) has called "localization" in which the Hindi metropolitan media decentralized production processes and incorporated more local events into their news. Hence

in Neyazi's analysis "national" papers become local, while in this case, "local" papers become "national."

16 https://www.facebook.com/groups/665333906852163/about/, accessed January 14, 2020.

6 Conclusion: Autonomy and the Global Field of Graphic Politics

1 *Adibashi kolyane nojirobihin gurutto paschimbonge* (Unprecedented importance being given to adivasi development). Advertisement issued by West Bengal government, *Anandabazar Patrika* (Kolkata edition), February 3, 2011.

2 "Mamata to Centre: Pull out Jangalmahal Forces." *The Times of India*, October 7, 2010. http://timesofindia.indiatimes.com/india/Mamata-to-Centre-Pull-out-Jangalmahal-forces/articleshow/6703395.cms, accessed August 25, 2014.

3 The linkage between the development of the concept of culture in the history of Bengal and the spread of communism in the twentieth century related to the global circulation of cultural discourse is outlined in Sartori (2008).

4 Singh (2003).

5 For example, Amit Bhattacharya, in the quote mentioned earlier in the chapter.

6 The equation of linguistic and biological diversity has a long history and has informed the global movmenet for language revitalization. See for instance Brenzinger (2007) or Krauss (1992). This has relation has been criticized by those working on language revitalization, for a summary see Hill (2002), Meek (2010), or Perley (2012).

7 UN Declaration on the Rights of Indigenous Peoples (2008).

8 Also see Shah (2010).

9 For more on the ideological underpinnings of this project and its implementation, see Leezenberg (2016).

10 "Syrian Conflict: Kurds to Declare a Federal System," BBC News, http://www.bbc.com/news/world-middle-east-35826668, accessed April 7, 2018.

11 See Murphy (2004) on the importance of visible semiotic media in collaborative imaginative endeavors.

References

Aggarwal, Kailash S. 1988. "English and India's Three-language Formula: An Empirical Perspective." *World Englishes* 7 (3): 289–98.

Agha, Asif. 2011a. "Commodity Registers." *Journal of Linguistic Anthropology* 21 (1): 22–53.

Agha, Asif. 2011b. "Meet Mediatization." *Language & Communication* 31 (3): 163–70.

Ahmad, Rizwan. 2008. "Scripting a New Identity: The Battle for Devanagari in Nineteenth Century India." *Journal of Pragmatics* 40 (7): 1163–83.

Ahmad, Rizwan. 2011. "Urdu in Devanagari: Shifting Orthographic Practices and Muslim Identity in Delhi." *Language in Society* 40 (3): 259–84.

Alam, Javeed. 2003. "The Category of Non-Historic Nations and Tribal Identity in Jharkhand." In *The Jharkhand Movement: Indigenous Peoples' Struggle for Autonomy in India*, edited by Rāmadayāla Muṇḍā, and S. Bosu Mullick, 194–205. Copenhagen: International Work Group for Indigenous Affairs.

Aloysius, G. 2003. "Ideologies and Hegemonies in the Jharkhand Movement." In *The Jharkhand Movement: Indigenous Peoples' Struggle for Autonomy in India*, edited by Rāmadayāla Muṇḍā, and S. Bosu Mullick, 206–15. Copenhagen: International Work Group for Indigenous Affairs.

Ambedkar, B. R. 2014. *Annihilation of Caste: The Annotated Critical Edition.* New Delhi: Navayana.

Andersen, Peter B. 2008. "Literacy and the Legitimation of the Santal Hul: A Retrospective from the 1890s." In *People of the Jangal: Reformulating Identities and Adaptations in Crisis*, edited by Marine Carrin and Harald Tambs-Lyche, 173–93. New Delhi: Manohar.

Andersen, Peter B. 2009. "Revival, Syncretism, and the Anti-colonial Discourse in the Kherwar Movement 1871–1910." In *India and the Indianness of Christianity: Essays on Understanding—Historical, Theological, and Bibliographical—in Honor of Robert Eric Frykenberg*, edited by Richard Fox Young, 127–43. Cambridge: Wm. B. Eerdmans Publishing.

Andersen, Peter B., Marine Carrin, and Sagram Santosh Kumar Soren. 2011. *From Fire Rain to Rebellion: Reasserting Ethnic Identity through Narrative.* New Delhi: Manohar.

Anderson, Benedict. 1983. *Imagined Communities: Reflections on the Origin and Spread of Nationalism*. London: Verso.

Androutsopoulos, Jannis. 2015. "Networked Multilingualism: Some Language Practices on Facebook and Their Implications." *International Journal of Bilingualism* 19 (2): 185–205.

Appadurai, Arjun. 1996. *Modernity at Large: Cultural Dimensions of Globalization*. Minneapolis: University of Minnesota Press.

Banerjee, Prathama. 1999. "Historic Acts? Santal Rebellion and the Temporality of Practice." *Studies in History* 15 (2): 209–46.

Banerjee, Prathama. 2006. "Culture/Politics: The Irresoluble Double-Bind of the Indian Adivasi." *Indian Historical Review* 33 (1): 99–126.

Banerjee, Sumanta. "Moral Betrayal of a Leftist Dream." *Economic and Political Weekly* (2007): 1240–2.

Baviskar, Amita. 2007. "Indian Indigeneities: Adivasi Engagements with Hindu Nationalism in India." In *Indigenous Experience Today*, edited by Marisol de la Cadena and Orin Starn, 275–304. New York: Berg.

Bender, Margaret Clelland. 2002. Signs of Cherokee Culture: Sequoyah's Syllabary in Eastern Cherokee Life. Chapel Hill, NC: University of North Carolina Press.

Bender, Margaret Clelland. 2008. "Indexicality, Voice and Context in the Distribution of Cherokee Scripts." *International Journal of the Sociology of Language* 2008 (192): 91–103.

Berk, Christopher. 2017. "Palawa Kani and the Value of Language in Aboriginal Tasmania." *Oceania* 87 (1): 2–20.

Béteille, André. 1986. "The Concept of Tribe with Special Reference to India." *European Journal of Sociology / Archives Européennes de Sociologie* 27 (2): 296–318.

Béteille, André. 1998. "The Idea of Indigenous People." *Current Anthropology* 39 (2): 187–92.

Béteille, André. 2006. "What Should We Mean by 'Indigenous People?'" In *Indigeneity in India*, edited by Bengt G. Karlsson and Tanka B. Subba, 19–32. London: Kegan Paul.

Bhagat-Ganguly, Varsha and Sujit Kumar, eds. 2020. *India's Scheduled Areas: Untangling Governance, Law, and Politics.* New Delhi: Routledge.

Bhattacharya, Amit. 2010. "Is Lalgarh Showing the Way?" *Economic and Political Weekly* 45 (2): 17–21.

Bhattacharya, Dwaipayan. 2016. *Government as Practice: Democratic Left in a Transforming India*. New Delhi: Cambridge University Press.

Bianco, James L. 2013. "Viet Nam: Quoc Ngu, Colonialism and Language Policy." In *Language Planning and Language Policy: East Asian Perspectives*, edited by Ping Chen and Nanette Gottlieb, 159–206. London: Routledge.

Blommaert, Jan. 2010. *The Sociolinguistics of Globalization*. Cambridge: Cambridge University Press.

Blommaert, Jan. 2013. *Ethnography, Superdiversity and Linguistic Landscapes: Chronicles of Complexity*. Bristol: Multilingual Matters.

Blommaert, Jan, James Collins, and Stef Slembrouck. 2005. "Spaces of Multilingualism." *Language & Communication* 25 (3): 197–216.

Blommaert, Jan, Elina Westinen, and Sirpa Lepannen. 2014. "Further Notes on Sociolinguistic Scales." *Tilburg Papers in Culture Studies* 89: 1–11.

Bloomfield, Leonard. 1935. *Language*. London: G. Allen & Unwin.

Bodding, Paul O. 1922. *Materials for a Santali Grammar I: Mostly Phonetic*. Dumka, India: Santal Mission of the Northern Churches.

Bodding, Paul O. 1924. *A Chapter of Santal Folklore*. Kristiana: Ethnografiske Museums.

Bodding, Paul O. 1925. *Santal Folk Tales*. Cambridge, MA: H. Aschehough.

Bodding, Paul O. 1983. *Santal Medicine*. Calcutta: Janasiksha Prochar Kendra.

Boone, Elizabeth Hill. 1994. "Writing and Recorded Knowledge." In *Writing Without Words: Alternative Literacies in Mesoamerica and the Andes*, edited by Elizabeth Hill Boone and Walter Mignolo, 50–76. Durham, NC: Duke University Press.

Boone, Elizabeth Hill and Walter Mignolo, eds. 1994. *Writing Without Words: Alternative Literacies in Mesoamerica and the Andes*. Durham, NC: Duke University Press.

Brandt, Carmen, and Pushkar Sohoni. 2018. "Script and Identity—the Politics of Writing in South Asia: An Introduction." *South Asian History and Culture* 9 (1): 1–15.

Brenzinger, Matthias. 2007. *Language Diversity Endangered*. Berlin: Walter de Gruyter.

Briggs, Charles L., and Richard Bauman. 1992. "Genre, Intertextuality, and Social Power." *Journal of Linguistic Anthropology* 2 (2): 131–72.

Carr, E. Summerson, and Michael Lempert. 2016. "Introduction: Pragmatics of Scale." In *Scale: Discourse and Dimensions of Social Life*, edited by E. Summerson Carr and Michael Lempert, 1–24. Berkeley: University of California Press.

Carrin, Marine, and Harald. Tambs-Lyche. 2008. *An Encounter of Peripheries: Santals, Missionaries, and Their Changing Worlds: 1867–1900*. New Delhi: Manohar.

Carrin-Bouez, Marine. 1978. "Les Diagrammes Santal." *Communications* 29 (1): 107–18.

Carrin-Bouez, Marine. 1986. "De La Langue Au Discours : Une Dialectique Du Repli Et de La Modernisation Dans Une Minorité Tribale de l'Inde." *Langage Et Société* 35 (1): 67–91.

Certeau, Michel de. 1984. *The Practice of Everyday Life*. Berkeley: University of California Press.

Chandra, Uday. 2016. "Flaming Fields and Forest Fires: Agrarian Transformations and the Making of Birsa Munda's Rebellion." *The Indian Economic & Social History Review* 53 (1): 69–98.

Chandra, Uday. 2017. "Primitive Accumulation and 'Primitive' Subjects in Postcolonial India: Tracing the Myriad Real and Virtual Lives of Mediatized Indigeneity Activism." *Interventions* 19 (3): 322–37.

Chandra, Uday, Geir Heierstad, and Kenneth Bo Nielsen. 2016. "Introduction." In *The Politics of Caste in West Bengal*, edited by Uday Chandra, Geir Heirstad, and Kenneth B. Nielson, 1–18. New Delhi: Routledge.

Chatterjee, Partha. 1993. *The Nation and Its Fragments: Colonial and Postcolonial Histories*. Princeton, NJ.: Princeton University Press.

Chatterjee, Partha. 2012. "After Subaltern Studies." *Economic and Political Weekly* 47 (35): 44–9.

Choksi, Nishaant. 2010. "Bharot Bahre Re Hod' Rod' Reyak' Charcha [Discussion of Santali Outside India]." *Tetre* 12 (8): 5–7.

Choksi, Nishaant. 2014a. "Scripting Autonomy: Script, Code, and Performance Among Santali Speakers in Eastern India". Ann Arbor, MI: University of Michigan.

Choksi, Nishaant. 2014b. "Scripting the Border: Script Practices and Territorial Imagination Among Santali Speakers in Eastern India." *International Journal of the Sociology of Language* 2014 (227): 47–63.

Choksi, Nishaant. 2017. "From Language to Script: Graphic Practice and the Politics of Authority in Santali-language Print Media, Eastern India." *Modern Asian Studies* 51 (5): 1519–60.

Choksi, Nishaant. 2018. "Script as Constellation Among Munda Speakers: The Case of Santali." *South Asian History and Culture* 9 (1): 92–115.

Choksi, Nishaant. 2020. "From Transcript to Trans-Script: Romanized Santali across Semiotic Media." *Signs and Society* 8 (1): 62–92.

Choksi, Nishaant, and Barbra Meek. 2016. "Theorizing Salience: Orthographic Practice and the Enfigurement of Minority Languages." In *Awareness and Control in Sociolinguistic Research*, edited by Anna Babel, 228–52. Cambridge: Cambridge University Press.

Chomsky, Noam. 1965. *Aspects of the Theory of Syntax*. Cambridge, MA: MIT Press.

Chomsky, Noam. 2002. *On Nature and Language*. Cambridge: Cambridge University Press.

Chumley, Lily Hope, and Nicholas Harkness. 2013. "Introduction: Qualia." *Anthropological Theory* 13 (1–2): 3–11.

Cody, Francis. 2009a. "Daily Wires and Daily Blossoms: Cultivating Regimes of Circulation in Tamil India's Newspaper Revolution." *Journal of Linguistic Anthropology* 19 (2): 286–309.

Cody, Francis. 2009b. "Inscribing Subjects to Citizenship: Petitions, Literacy Activism, and the Performativity of Signature in Rural Tamil India." *Cultural Anthropology* 24 (3): 347–80.

Cody, Francis. 2013. *The Light of Knowledge Literacy Activism and the Politics of Writing in South India*. Ithaca, NY: Cornell University Press.

Colak, Yilmaz. 2004. "Language Policy and Official Ideology in Early Republican Turkey." *Middle Eastern Studies* 40 (6): 67–91.

Collins, James, and Richard K. Blot. 2003. *Literacy and Literacies: Texts, Power, and Identity*. New York: Cambridge University Press.

Dasgupta, Sangeeta. 2016. "Mapping Histories: Many Narratives of Tana Pasts." *The Indian Economic & Social History Review* 53 (1): 99–129.

Das, Kalpana. 2010. "Tribal Revolt in Orissa." *Orissa Review*, August, 47–9.

Das, Sonia N. 2016. *Linguistic Rivalries: Tamil Migrants and Anglo-Franco Conflicts*. New York: Oxford University Press.

Dasgupta, Swapan. 1985. "Adivasi Politics in Midnapore 1760–1924." In *Subaltern Studies IV: Writings on South Asian History and Society*, edited by Ranajit Guha, 101–35. New Delhi: Oxford University Press.

Daveluy, Michelle, and Jenanne Ferguson. 2009. "Scripted Urbanity in the Canadian North." *Journal of Linguistic Anthropology* 19 (1): 78–100.

Debenport, Erin, and Anthony K. Webster. 2019. "From Literacy/Literacies to Graphic Pluralism and Inscriptive Practices." *Annual Review of Anthropology* 48 (2019): 389–404.

Derrida, Jacques. 1976. *Of Grammatology*. Baltimore, MD: Johns Hopkins University Press.

Derrida, Jacques. 1988. *Limited Inc*. Evanston, IL: Northwestern University Press.

Derrida, Jacques. 1993. "Structure, Sign and Play in the Human Sciences." In *A Postmodern Reader*, edited by Joseph Natoli and Linda Hutcheon, 223–42. Albany, NY: SUNY Press.

Devy, G. N. 2009. *The G. N. Devy Reader*. Hyderabad: Orient Blackswan.

Diringer, David. 1962. *Writing*. London: Thames and Hudson.

Dirks, Nicholas B. 1989. "The Invention of Caste: Civil Society in Colonial India." *Social Analysis: The International Journal of Anthropology* 25 (September): 42–52.

Drèze, Jean, and Amartya Sen. 2002. *India: Development and Participation.* Oxford: Oxford University Press.

Dumont, Louis. 1980. *Homo Hierarchicus: The Caste System and Its Implications.* Chicago: University of Chicago Press.

Elwin, Verrier. 2009. *The Oxford India Elwin: Selected Writings.* New Delhi: Oxford University Press.

Errington, Joseph. 2008. *Linguistics in a Colonial World: A Story of Language, Meaning, and Power.* Malden, MA: Blackwell.

Escobar, Arturo. 2018. *Designs for the Pluriverse: Radical Interdependence, Autonomy, and the Making of Worlds.* Durham, NC: Duke University Press.

Feliciano-Santos Sherina. 2017. "How Do You Speak Taíno? Indigenous Activism and Linguistic Practices in Puerto Rico." *Journal of Linguistic Anthropology* 27 (1): 4–21.

Ferguson, James. 1990. *The Anti-politics Machine: "Development," Depoliticization, and Bureaucratic Power in Lesotho.* Cambridge: Cambridge University Press.

Gal, Susan. 1989. "Language and Political Economy." *Annual Review of Anthropology* 18 (1): 345–67.

Gal, Susan. 2016. "Sociolinguistic Differentiation." In *Sociolinguistics: Theoretical Debates*, edited by Nikolas Coupland, 113–36. Cambridge: Cambridge University Press.

Gal, Susan and Judith T. Irvine. 2019. *Signs of Difference: Language and Ideology in Social Life.* Cambridge: Cambridge University Press.

García, María Elena. 2003. "The Politics of Community: Education, Indigenous Rights, and Ethnic Mobilization in Peru." *Latin American Perspectives* 30 (1): 70–95.

Gelb, Ignace J. 1952. *A Study of Writing; the Foundations of Grammatology.* London: Routledge and Kegan Paul.

Gershon, Ilana. 2010. "Media Ideologies: An Introduction." *Journal of Linguistic Anthropology* 20 (2): 283–93.

Ghosh, Arunabha. 1993. "Jharkhand Movement in West Bengal." *Economic and Political Weekly* 28 (3/4): 121–7.

Ghosh, Kaushik. 2008. "Between Global Flows and Local Dams: Indigenousness, Locality, and the Transnational Sphere in Jharkhand, India." *Cultural Anthropology* 21 (4): 501–34.

Goffman, Erving. 1981. *Forms of Talk.* Philadelphia: University of Pennsylvania Press.

Goody, Jack, and Ian Watt. 1963. "The Consequences of Literacy." *Comparative Studies in Society and History* 5 (3): 304–45.

Goody, Jack. 1986. *The Logic of Writing and the Organization of Society*. Cambridge: Cambridge University Press.

Gorter, Durk. 2006. *Linguistic Landscape: A New Approach to Multilingualism*. Bristol: Multilingual Matters.

Graber, Kathryn. 2012. "Public Information: The Shifting Roles of Minority Language News Media in the Buryat Territories of Russia." *Language & Communication* 32 (2): 124–36.

Guha, Ranajit. 1963. *A Rule of Property for Bengal; an Essay on the Idea of Permanent Settlement*. Paris: Mouton.

Guha, Ranajit. 1988. "The Prose of Counter-insurgency." In *Selected Subaltern Studies*, edited by Ranajit Guha and Gayatri Chakravorty Spivak, 45–88. New York: Oxford University Press.

Guha, Sumit. 2013. *Beyond Caste: Identity and Power in South Asia, Past and Present*. Leiden: Brill.

Gumperz, John J., and Robert Wilson. 1971. "Convergence and Creolization: a Case from the Indo-Aryan/Dravidian Border in India." In *Pidginization and Creolization of Languages*, 151–67. Cambridge: Cambridge University Press.

Gumperz, John J. 1982. *Discourse Strategies*. Cambridge: Cambridge University Press.

Hanks, William F. 2010. *Converting Words: Maya in the Age of the Cross*. Berkeley: University of California Press.

Hanks, William F. 2012. "Birth of a Language: The Formation and Spread of Colonial Yucatec Maya." *Journal of Anthropological Research* 68 (4): 449–71.

Hansdak', Hanuk'. 2009. *Santali Parsi Lahanti Hor* (*Path of Progress of the Santali Language*). Dumka, India: Self-published.

Hembrom, Parimal. 2007. *Santali Sahityer Itihas (History of Santali Literature)*. Kolkata: Nirmal Publications.

Herzfeld, Michael. 1997. *Cultural Intimacy: Social Poetics in the Nation-State*. New York: Routledge.

Hill, Jane H. 2002. "'Expert Rhetorics' in Advocacy for Endangered Languages: Who Is Listening, and What Do They Hear?" *Journal of Linguistic Anthropology* 12 (2): 119–33.

Hoffmann-Dilloway, Erika. 2018. "Linguistic Anthropology in 2017: It Could Be Otherwise." *American Anthropologist* 120 (2): 278–90.

Hoffmann-Dilloway, Erika. 2016. *Signing and Belonging in Nepal*. Washington, DC: Gallaudet University Press.

Hull, Matthew S. 2012. *Government of Paper: The Materiality of Bureaucracy in Urban Pakistan*. Berkeley: University of California Press.

Hymes, Dell. 1967. "Linguistic Problems in Defining the Concept of 'Tribe.'" In *Essays on the Problem of Tribe*, edited by June Helm, 23–48. Seattle, WA: University of Washington Press.

Irvine, Judith T. 1989. "When Talk Isn't Cheap: Language and Political Economy." *American Ethnologist* 16 (2): 248–67.

Irvine, Judith T. 2006. "Speech and Language Community." In *Encyclopedia of Language and Linguistics*, 689–98. Amsterdam: Elsevier.

Irvine, Judith T. 2008. "Subjected Words: African Linguistics and the Colonial Encounter." *Language & Communication* 28 (4): 323–43.

Isaka, Riho. 2002. "Language and Dominance: The Debates over the Gujarati Language in the Late Nineteenth Century." *South Asia: Journal of South Asian Studies* 25 (1): 1–19.

Jaffrelot, Christophe. 2006. "The Impact of Affirmative Action in India: More Political than Socioeconomic." *India Review* 5(2): 173–89.

Jaworski, Adam, and Crispin Thurlow, eds. 2010. *Semiotic Landscapes: Language, Image, Space*. New York: Continuum.

Jeffrey, Robin. 2000. *India's Newspaper Revolution: Capitalism, Politics, and the Indian-language Press, 1977–99*. London: Hurst & Company.

Joyce, Terry, Bor Hodoščék, and Kikuko Nishina. 2012. "Orthographic Representation and Variation Within the Japanese Writing System: Some Corpus-based Observations." *Written Language & Literacy* 15 (2): 254–78.

Kar, Bodhisattva. 2008. " 'Tongue Has No Bone': Fixing the Assamese Language, C. 1800–c. 1930." *Studies in History* 24 (1): 27–76.

Kaviraj, Sudipta. 1992. "Writing, Speaking, Being: Language and the Historical Formation of Identities in India." *Nationalstaat Und Sprachkonflikte in Süd-und Südostasien*, edited by Hrsg. von Dagmar Hellmann-Rajanayagam and Dietmar Rothermund, 25–68. Stuttgart: Franz Steiner Verlag.

Keane, Webb. 2007. *Christian Moderns: Freedom and Fetish in the Mission Encounter*. Berkeley: University of California Press.

Keane, Webb. 2013. "On Spirit Writing: Materialities of Language and the Religious Work of Transduction." *Journal of the Royal Anthropological Institute* 19 (1): 1–17.

Kelly, John. 2006. "Writing and the State: China, India, and General Definitions." In *Margins of Writing, Origins of Cultures*, edited by Seth L. Sanders, 15–32. Chicago: Oriental Institute of the University of Chicago.

Kelly, Piers. 2016. "Introducing the Eskaya Writing System: A Complex Messianic Script from the Southern Philippines." *Australian Journal of Linguistics* 36 (1): 131–63.

Kelly, Piers. 2017. "The Invention, Transmission and Evolution of Writing: Insights from the New Scripts of West Africa." *SocArXiv*, March.

Kelly, Piers. 2018. "The Art of Not Being Legible. Invented Writing Systems as Technologies of Resistance in Mainland Southeast Asia." *Terrain. Anthropologie & Sciences Humaines*, no. 70 (October) 38–48.

Khubchandani, Lachman. 1981. *Language, Education, Social Justice*. Pune: Centre for Communication Studies.

Khubchandani, Lachman. 2008. "Language Policy and Education in the Indian Subcontinent." In *Encyclopedia of Language and Education*, edited by Nancy H. Hornberger and S. May, 369–81. New York: Springer.

King, Christopher Rolland. 1994. *One Language, Two Scripts: The Hindi Movement in the Nineteenth Century North India*. New Delhi: Oxford University Press.

King, Robert D. 1997. *Nehru and the Language Politics of India*. New Delhi: Oxford University Press.

Kisku, Motilal. 2011. "Shubhecha Barta [Congratulation Note]." *Lahanti Patrika Sammelan Souvenir Edition*, March 12, 2011.

Krauss, Michael. 1992. "The World's Languages in Crisis." *Language* 68 (1): 4–10.

Kristeva, Julia. 1980. *Desire in Language: A Semiotic Approach to Literature and Art*. New York: Columbia University Press.

Krylova, Anastasia. 2016. "Письменности Языков Мунда [Original Scripts of Munda Languages]." *Zograph Papers* 38: 7–8.

Ladousa, Chaise. 2002. "Advertising in the Periphery: Languages and Schools in a North Indian City." *Language in Society* 31(2): 213–42.

Ladousa, Chaise. 2005. "Disparate Markets: Language, Nation, and Education in North India." *American Ethnologist* 32 (3): 460–78.

Leezenberg, Michiel. 2016. "The Ambiguities of Democratic Autonomy: The Kurdish Movement in Turkey and Rojava." *Southeast European and Black Sea Studies* 16 (4): 671–90.

Lepsius, Karl. 2014. *Standard Alphabet for Reducing Unwritten Languages and Foreign Graphic Systems to a Uniform Orthography in European Letters*. Amsterdam: John Benjamins.

Lotz, Barbara. 2007. "Casting a Glorious Past: Loss and Recovery of the Ol Script." In *Time in India: Concepts and Practices*, edited by Angelika Malinar. New Delhi: Manohar.

Mahapatra, Sitakant. 1986. *Modernization and Ritual: Identity and Change in Santal Society*. New Delhi: Oxford University Press.

Makoni, Sinfree, and Alastair Pennycook. 2005. "Disinventing and (Re)Constituting Languages." *Critical Inquiry in Language Studies* 2 (3): 137–56.

Marcucci, Matthew. 2009. "Sinographic Languages: The Past, Present, and Future of Script Reform." *Sino-Platonic Papers* 189: 81–101.

McCarthy James. 2005. "Scale, Sovereignty, and Strategy in Environmental Governance." *Antipode* 37 (4): 731–53.

Meek, Barbra A. 2010. *We Are Our Language: An Ethnography of Language Revitalization in a Northern Athabascan Community*. Tucson, AZ: University of Arizona Press.

Meek, Barbra A. 2014. "'She Can Do It in English Too': Acts of Intimacy and Boundary-making in Language Revitalization." *Language & Communication*, 38 (September): 73–82.

Meek, Barbra A. 2016. "Shrinking Indigenous Languages in the Yukon." In *Scale: Discourse and Dimensions of Social Life* , edited by E. Summerson Carr and Michael Lempert, 70–90. Berkeley: University of California Press.

Metcalf, Barbara D. 1982. *Islamic Revival in British India: Deoband, 1860–1900*. Princeton, NJ: Princeton University Press.

Middleton, Townsend. 2016. *The Demands of Recognition: State Anthropology and Ethnopolitics in Darjeeling*. Stanford, CA: Stanford University Press.

Mignolo, Walter. 1994. "Afterword: Writing and Recorded Knowledge in Colonial and Postcolonial Situations." In *Writing without Words: Alternative Literacies in Mesoamerica and the Andes*, edited by Elizabeth Hill Boone and Walter Mignolo, 292–312. Durham, NC: Duke University Press.

Mir, Farina. 2010. *The Social Space of Language: Vernacular Culture in British Colonial Punjab*. Berkeley: University of California Press.

Mishra, Pritipuspa. 2020. *Language and the Making of Modern India:Nationalism and the Vernacular in Colonial Odisha, 1803–1956*. New Delhi: Cambridge University Press.

Mohanty, Ajit K. 2010. "Languages, Inequality and Marginalization: Implications of the Double Divide in Indian Multilingualism." *International Journal of the Sociology of Language*, 205 (2010): 131–54.

Moodie, Megan. 2015. *We Were Adivasis: Aspiration in an Indian Scheduled Tribe*. Chicago, IL: University of Chicago Press.

Moreton-Robinson, Aileen. 2004. "Whiteness, Epistemology, and Indigenous Representation." In *Whitening Race: Essays in Social and Cultural Criticism*, 75–88. Canberra: Aboriginal Studies Press.

Morris, Rosalind C. 2007. "Legacies of Derrida: Anthropology." *Annual Review of Anthropology* 36: 355–89.

Mosse, David. 2005. *Cultivating Development: An Ethnography of Aid Policy and Practice*. London: Pluto Press.

Mullick, S. Bosu. 2003. "Introduction." *The Jharkhand Movement: Indigenous Peoples' Struggle for Autonomy in India*, edited by Rāmadayāla Muṇḍā and S. Bosu Mullick, iv–xvii. Copenhagen: International Work Group for Indigenous Affairs.

Mukharji, Projit Bihari. 2009. 'Communist' dispossession meets 'reactionary' resistance: The ironies of the parliamentary Left in West Bengal." *Focaal*, 54 (2009): 89–96.

Murmu, Raghunath. n.d. *Lakchar Seren'* [Culture Songs]. Jhargram, West Bengal: Marsal Bamber.

Murmu, Raghunath. n.d. *Ronod'* [Grammar]. Jhargram, West Bengal: Marsal Bamber.

Murmu, Ramchand. 1997. *Ishrod* [God-sound]. Jhargram, West Bengal: Sadhu Ramchand Murmu Memorial Trust.

Murmu, Ramchand. 2011. *Sadhu Ramchand Anadmala [Poetry Collection].* Kolkata: West Bengal Santali Academy.

Murphy, Anne. 2018. "Writing Punjabi across Borders." *South Asian History and Culture* 9 (1): 68–91.

Murphy, Keith M. 2004. "Imagination as Joint Activity: The Case of Architectural Interaction." *Mind, Culture, and Activity* 11 (4): 267–78.

Nag, Dulali. 1997. "Little Magazines in Calcutta and a Postsociology of India." *Contributions to Indian Sociology* 31 (1): 109–33.

Neyazi, Taberez Ahmed. 2010. "Cultural Imperialism or Vernacular Modernity? Hindi Newspapers in a Globalizing India." *Media, Culture & Society* 32 (6): 907–24.

Nielson, Kenneth B. 2015. "Community and the Politics of Caste, Class, and Representation in the Singur Movement, West Bengal." In *New Subaltern Politics: Reconceptualising Hegemony and Resistance in Contemporary India*, edited by Arif G. Nilson and Srila Roy, 202–24. New Delhi: Oxford University Press.

Niezen, Ronald. 2003. *The Origins of Indigenism: Human Rights and the Politics of Identity.* Berkeley: University of California Press.

Ocalan, Abdullah. 2011. *Democratic Confederalism*. London: Transmedia.

Ong, Walter J. 1988. *Orality and Literacy: The Technologizing of the Word.* London: Routledge.

Orans, Martin. 1965. *The Santal: a Tribe in Search of a Great Tradition*. Detroit, MI: Wayne State University Press.

Parmentier, Richard J. 1985. "Diagrammatic Icons and Historical Processes in Belau." *American Anthropologist* 87 (4): 840–52.

Parvez, Z. Fareen. 2017. *Politicizing Islam: The Islamic Revival in France and India*. Oxford: Oxford University Press.

Peirce, Charles Sanders. 1955. "Logic as Semiotic: The Theory of Signs." In *Philosophical Writings*, edited by J. Buchler. Mineola, NY: Dover.

Pennycook, Alistair. 2010. "Spatial Narrations: Graffscapes and City Souls." In *Semiotic Landscapes: Language, Image, Space*, edited by Adam Jaworski and Crispin. Thurlow, 137–50. New York: Continuum.

Perley, Bernard C. 2012. "Zombie Linguistics: Experts, Endangered Languages and the Curse of Undead Voices." *Anthropological Forum* 22 (2): 133–49.

Peteet, Julie. 1996. "The Writing on the Walls: The Graffiti of the Intifada." *Cultural Anthropology* 11 (2): 139–59.

Pickerill, Jenny, and Paul Chatterton. 2006. "Notes Towards Autonomous Geographies: Creation, Resistance and Self-management as Survival Tactics." *Progress in Human Geography* 30 (6): 730–46.

Pollock, Sheldon I. 2006. *The Language of the Gods in the World of Men: Sanskrit, Culture, and Power in Premodern India*. Berkeley: University of California Press.

Povinelli, Elizabeth A. 2002. *The Cunning of Recognition: Indigenous Alterities and the Making of Australian Multiculturalism*. Durham, NC: Duke University Press.

Povinelli, Elizabeth A. 2011. "The Governance of the Prior." *Interventions: International Journal of Postcolonial Studies*. 13(1), 13–30.

Raheja, Gloria Goodwin. 1996. "Caste, Colonialism, and the Speech of the Colonized: Entextualization and Disciplinary Control in India." *American Ethnologist* 23 (3): 494–513.

Rai, Amrit. 1984. *A House Divided: The Origin and Development of Hindi/Hindavi*. New Delhi: Oxford University Press.

Rajagopal, Arvind. 2001. *Politics after Television: Hindu Nationalism and the Reshaping of the Indian Public*. Cambridge: Cambridge University Press.

Ramaiah, A. 1992. "Identifying Other Backward Classes." *Economic and Political Weekly* 27 (23): 1203–7.

Raman, Bhavani. 2012. *Document Raj: Writing and Scribes in Early Colonial South India*. Chicago: University of Chicago Press.

Rambelli, Fabio, 2013. *A Buddhist Theory of Semiotics: Signs, Ontology, and Salvation in Japanese Esoteric Buddhism*. London: Bloomsbury.

Rana, Santosh. 2012. "Mamata or Maoists: None Cared for Democracy." In *War and Peace in Junglemahal People, State and Maoists*, edited by Biswajit Roy, 107–12. Kolkata: Setu Prakashani.

Robertson Wesley C. 2017. "He's More Katakana Than Kanji: Indexing Identity and Self-presentation Through Script Selection in Japanese Manga (comics)." *Journal of Sociolinguistics* 21 (4): 497–520.

Roy, Biswajit, ed. 2012. *War and Peace in Junglemahal People, State and Maoists*. Kolkata: Setu Prakashani.

Ruud, Arild Engelsen. 2003. *Poetics of Village Politics: The Making of West Bengal's Rural Communism*. New Delhi: Oxford University Press.

Salomon, Frank and Mercedes Niño-Murcia. 2011. *The Lettered Mountain: A Peruvian Village's Way with Writing*. Durham, NC: Duke University Press.

Salomon, Richard. 1998. *Indian Epigraphy: A Guide to the Study of Inscriptions in Sanskrit, Prakrit, and the Other Indo-Aryan Languages*. Oxford: Oxford University Press.

Samaddar, Ranabir. 1998. *Memory, Identity, Power: Politics in the Jungle Mahals (West Bengal), 1890–1950*. Hyderabad: Orient Longman.

Samaddar, Ranabir. 2007. *The Materiality of Politics: Volume 2: Subject Positions in Politics*. New Delhi: Anthem Press.

Sapir, Edward. 1921. *Language, an Introduction to the Study of Speech*. Oxford: Oxford University Press.

Sarkar, Tanika. 1985. "Jitu Santal's Movement in Malda, 1924–1932: A Study in Tribal Protest." In *Subaltern Studies IV: Writings on South Asian History and Society*, edited by Ranajit Guha, 136–64. New Delhi: Oxford University Press.

Sartori, Andrew. 2008. *Bengal in Global Concept History: Culturalism in the Age of Capital*. Chicago: University of Chicago Press.

Saussure, Ferdinand de. 1959. *Course in General Linguistics*. New York: Philosophical Library.

Schleiter, Markus. 2014. "VCD Crossovers: Cultural Practice, Ideas of Belonging, and Santali Popular Movies." *Asian Ethnology* 73 (1/2): 181–200.

Searle, John R. 1983. *Intentionality: An Essay in the Philosophy of Mind*. Cambridge: Cambridge University Press.

Sen, Dwaipayan. 2016. "An Absent-minded Casteism?" In *The Politics of Caste in West Bengal*, edited by Uday Chandra, Geir Heirstad, and Kenneth B. Nielson, 103–24. New Delhi: Routledge.

Sengupta, Madhumita. 2012. "War of Words: Language and Policies in Nineteenth-century Assam." *Indian Historical Review* 39 (2): 293–315.

Shah, Alpa. 2010. *In the Shadows of the State: Indigenous Politics, Environmentalism, and Insurgency in Jharkhand, India*. Durham, NC: Duke University Press.

Shah, Alpa. 2011. "Who Cares for a New State: The Imaginary Institution of Jharkhand." In *The Politics of Belonging in India: Becoming Adivasi*, edited by Daniel J. Rycroft and Sangeeta Dasgupta, 217–30. London: Routledge.

Shankar, Shalini, and Jillian R. Cavanaugh. 2012. "Language and Materiality in Global Capitalism." *Annual Review of Anthropology* 41 (1): 355–69.

Shohamy, Elana, and Durk Gorter, eds. 2008. *Linguistic Landscape: Expanding the Scenery*. London: Routledge.

Shulman, David. 2016. *Tamil: A Biography*. Cambridge, MA: Harvard University Press.

Silverstein, Michael. 1979. "Language Structure and Linguistic Ideology." *The Elements: A Parasession on Linguistic Units and Levels*, edited by P. R. Clyne, W. E. Hanks, and C. L. Hofbauer, 193–247. Chicago: Chicago Linguistic Society.

Silverstein, Michael. 1998. "Contemporary Transformations of Local Linguistic Communities." *Annual Review of Anthropology* 27: 401–26.

Silverstein, Michael. 2000. "Whorfianism and the Linguistic Imagination of Nationality." In *Regimes of Language: Ideologies, Polities, and Identities*, edited by Paul Kroskity, 85–138. Santa Fe, NM: School of American Research Press.

Silverstein, Michael. 2005. "Axes of Evals." *Journal of Linguistic Anthropology* 15 (1): 6–22.

Simpson, Audra. 2014. *Mohawk Interruptus: Political Life across the Borders of Settler States*. Durham, NC: Duke University Press.

Singh, K. S. 2003. "Tribal Autonomy Movements in Chota Nagpur." In *The Jharkhand Movement: Indigenous Peoples' Struggle for Autonomy in India*, edited by Rāmadayāla Muṇḍā and S. Bosu Mullick, 88–109. Copenhagen: International Work Group for Indigenous Affairs.

Singh, Jaipal. 2003. "Jai Jharkhand, Jai Adivasi, Jai Hind!" In *The Jharkhand Movement: Indigenous Peoples' Struggle for Autonomy in India*, edited by Rāmadayāla Muṇḍā and S. Bosu Mullick, 2–14. Copenhagen: International Work Group for Indigenous Affairs.

Singh, Udaya Narayana. 2001. "Multiscriptality in South Asia and Language Development." *International Journal of the Sociology of Language* (150).

Sinha, A. C. 2005. "Colonial Anthropology Vs. Indological Sociology: Elwin and Ghurye on Tribal Policy in India." In *Between Ethnography and Fiction: Verrier Elwin and the Tribal Question in India*, edited by Tanka Bahadur Subba and Sujit Som, 71–85. Hyderabad: Orient Blackswan.

Sivaramakrishnan, K. 2000. "Crafting the Public Sphere in the Forests of West Bengal: Democracy, Development, and Political Action." *American Ethnologist* 27 (2): 431–61.

Sivaramakrishnan, K. 2006. "Situating the Subaltern: History and Anthropology in the Subaltern Studies Project." *Journal of Historical Sociology* 8 (4): 395–429.

Sivaramakrishnan, K., and Arun Agrawal. 2003. "Regional Modernities in Stories and Practices of Development." In *Regional Modernities: The Cultural Politics of Development in India*, edited by K. Sivaramakrishnan and Arun Agrawal, 1–45. Stanford, CA: Stanford University Press.

Schendel, Willem Van. 2011. "The Dangers of Belonging: Tribes, Indigenous Peoples, and Homelands in South Asia." In *The Politics of Belonging in India: Becoming*

Adivasi, edited by Daniel J. Rycroft and Sangeeta Dasgupta, 19–43. London: Routledge.

Skaria, Ajay. 1997. "Shades of Wildness Tribe, Caste, and Gender in Western India." *The Journal of Asian Studies* 56 (3): 726–45.

Skaria, Ajay. 2003. "Development, Nationalism, and the Time of the Primitive: The Dangs Darbar." In *Regional Modernities: The Cultural Politics of Development in India*, edited by K. Sivaramakrishnan and Arun Agrawal, 215–36. Stanford, CA: Stanford University Press.

Skrefsrud, L. O. 1887. *Hodkoren Mare Hapdam Ko Reyak' Katha [Stories of the Santal Ancestors]*. Benagaria, India: Benagaria Mission Press.

Smalley, William A., C. K. Vang, and G. Y. Yang. 1990. *Mother of Writing: The Origin and Development of a Hmong Messianic Script*. Chicago: University of Chicago Press.

Smith, Linda Tuhiwai. 2013. *Decolonizing Methodologies: Research and Indigenous Peoples*. New York: Zed Books.

Sohoni, Pushkar. 2018. "Colonial and Postcolonial Debates about Polygraphia in Marathi." *South Asian History and Culture* 9 (1): 38–46.

Stankiewicz, Damien. 2016. "Against Imagination: On the Ambiguities of a Composite Concept." *American Anthropologist* 118 (4): 796–810.

Street, Brian V, ed. 1993. *Cross-cultural Approaches to Literacy*. Cambridge: Cambridge University Press.

Sturm, Circe. 2017. "Reflections on the Anthropology of Sovereignty and Settler Colonialism: Lessons from Native North America." *Cultural Anthropology*, 32 (3): 340–8.

Sundar, Nandini, ed. 2009. *Legal Grounds: Natural Resources, Identity, and the Law in Jharkhand*. New Delhi: Oxford University Press.

Tanabe Akio. 2007. "Toward Vernacular Democracy: Moral Society and Post-postcolonial Transformation in Rural Orissa, India." *American Ethnologist* 34 (3): 558–74.

Tapp, Nicholas. 2015. "Of Grasshoppers, Caterpillars, and Beans: A Historical Perspective on Hmong Messianism." *TRaNS: Trans-Regional and -National Studies of Southeast Asia* 3 (2): 289–318.

Timalsina, Sthaneshwar. 2015. *Language of Images: Visualization and Meaning in Tantras*. New York: Peter Lang.

Trix, Frances. 1999. "The Stamboul Alphabet Of Shemseddin Sami Bey: Precursor to Turkish Script Reform." *International Journal of Middle East Studies* 31 (2): 255–72.

Truschke, Audrey. 2016. *Culture of Encounters: Sanskrit at the Mughal Court*. New York: Columbia University Press.

Tschacher, Torsten. 2018. "From Script to Language: The Three Identities of 'Arabic-Tamil.'" *South Asian History and Culture* 9 (1): 16–37.

Tudu, Mahatman. 2011. *Paschimbongo shorkar olchiki-ke aini svikriti deyni [West Bengal Government Did Not Give Ol-Chiki Legal Recognition]*. Banipur, West Bengal, India: Santal Employees Social Organisation.

Unger, J. Marshall. 1996. *Literacy and Script Reform in Occupation Japan: Reading between the Lines*. New York: Oxford University Press.

Schendel, Willem Van. 2011. "The Dangers of Belonging: Tribes, Indigenous Peoples, and Homelands in South Asia." In *The Politics of Belonging in India: Becoming Adivasi*, edited by Daniel J. Rycroft and Sangeeta Dasgupta, 19–43. London: Routledge.

Wallerstein, Immanuel. 2011. *The Modern World-System I: Capitalist Agriculture and the Origins of the European World-Economy in the Sixteenth Century*. Berkeley: University of California Press.

Weaver, Jace. 2000. "Indigenousness and Indigeneity." In *A Companion to Postcolonial Studies*, edited by Henry Schwarz and Sangeeta Ray, 221–35. Malden, MA: Wiley-Blackwell.

Webster, Anthony. 2015. *Intimate Grammars: An Ethnography of Navajo Poetry*. Tucson, AZ: University of Arizona Press.

Woolard, Kathryn A., and Bambi B. Schieffelin. 1994. "Language Ideology." *Annual Review of Anthropology* 23 (January): 55–82.

Yang, Anand A. 1998. *Bazaar India: Markets, Society, and the Colonial State in Gangetic Bihar*. Berkeley: University of California Press.

Zide, Norman. 1999. "Three Munda Scripts." *Linguistics of the Tibeto-Burman Area* 22 (2): 199–232.

Index